$17.00

Issues and Prospects for the New
International Economic Order

Issues and Prospects for the New International Economic Order

Edited by
William G. Tyler
University of Florida

Lexington Books
D.C. Heath and Company
Lexington, Massachusetts
Toronto

Library of Congress Cataloging in Publication Data

Main entry under title:
   Issues and prospects for the new international economic order.

   1. International economic relations—Addresses, essays, lectures.   2. Un-
derdeveloped areas—Foreign economic relations—Addresses, essays, lec-
tures.
I. Tyler, William G.
HF1411.I85   382.1   77-78367
ISBN 0-669-01445-1

International Standard Book Number: 0-669-01445-1

Library of Congress Catalog Card Number: 77-78367

Contents

Preface

This book is about the problems of the Third World in the international economic order. In recent years the difference in economic interests between the developed and developing countries has become more apparent. Moreover, the developing countries are becoming more adroit both in articulating their interests and in exercising their limited power to obtain their objectives. The developing countries' call for a "new international economic order" symbolizes their dissatisfaction and frustration with the existing international economic system. Economic and political relations between the industrialized Northern countries and the less developed Southern nations are undergoing important changes, and the North-South dimension of international relations will certainly be vital in the future. This book examines some of the questions involved in the calls for a new international economic order.

This volume grew out of a conference organized under the auspices of the International Studies Association/South and held at the University of Virginia in late October 1976. Many pertinent papers were presented at the conference, but space limitations have precluded the inclusion of all of them in the volume. For the same reason, it has also been impossible to include discussants' comments.

Efforts have been made in the volume to represent different viewpoints on what is certainly a controversial topic. These efforts have not been entirely successful. The general tone of the collection is skeptical about the economic and political viability of the new international economic order and what it can do to eliminate poverty and promote development in the Third World.

The contributors to the volume are economists and political scientists of divergent opinions and professional backgrounds. While most of the contributors are currently based in American academic institutions, a number of national backgrounds is evident, including individuals originally from Egypt, Guyana, Czechoslovakia, Germany, and India, as well as the United States.

A number of debts are incurred in a project such as this. Robert S. Wood and Ole R. Holsti were very helpful in organizing the conference. Thanks also go to Anne Morrall, who helped with the editing. Perhaps my greatest debt in this project is to Susan Phillips, who, in addition to competently handling the administrative details, cheerfully handled both the typing chores and my sour disposition. Finally, thanks go to my wife Maria Etelvina for being herself and putting up with all of this business.

1

Introduction
William G. Tyler

The 1970s have witnessed a watershed in economic relations between the industrial countries and the Third World. Serious shocks to the international economic order have resulted in a reappraisal of its nature and characteristics by both the rich (North) and poor (South) countries. The crumbling of postwar international monetary arrangements, culminating in the initial devaluation of the US dollar in 1971 and the subsequent floating of exchange rates, has exacerbated worldwide inflation and increased the developing countries' awareness of the importance of the international monetary system.

International trading arrangements have also undergone important changes. The system exemplified by GATT, with its emphasis on most-favored-nation treatment, reciprocity, and tariff restrictions as opposed to nontariff barriers to trade, has largely been eclipsed, if not bypassed completely. Most dramatically, the actions of the OPEC oil-producing countries have jarred the very foundations of the international economic order. While creating enormous difficulties for non-oil-producing developing countries, OPEC's collective action has held out some promise of the sweet fruits of successful primary product producers' alliances. Finally, the world recession of 1974-1976—the most significant economic downturn since the Great Depression—has emphasized the general interdependence of countries in the international economic order and the particular dependence of many developing countries on that order.

The Third World countries—that is, those developing countries generally not considered part of the socialist bloc—have experienced increasing economic difficulty. Population pressures coupled with adverse harvest and weather conditions have resulted in famine in several of the poorest countries. In addition, the massive international income transfer to the oil-producing nations has occurred in some part at the cost of the developing countries. Although estimates of the costs vary, Girgis conservatively estimates (in chapter 5) that increases in petroleum prices cost the non-oil-producing developing countries around $13 billion in 1974. This amount alone was greater than the total official development assistance extended to the developing countries in that year. Reflecting the increased prices for petroleum product inputs, prices of food and fertilizer imports for Third World countries have also risen considerably. Correspondingly, the overall barter terms of trade for the non-oil-producing developing countries have deteriorated in recent years. By 1975 they had declined 14 percent from the base period 1967-1969.[1]

1

These events have resulted in unprecedented balance-of-payments difficulties for the developing countries. By 1975 the aggregate current balance-of-payments deficit for non-oil-producing developing countries had risen to $37 billion—up from $10 billion in 1973.[2] To finance such large deficits the more creditworthy countries have borrowed extensively in the Eurocurrency and private capital markets. As a result, external indebtedness for these countries has increased substantially, so that some rescheduling of debt repayments is necessary to avoid possible default. In any case, further borrowing on commercial, nonconcessionary terms offers very little promise for financing developing country deficits. More fundamental adjustments in their economies dramatically increased concessionary financing from the developed and oil-producing countries or both are necessary. The non-oil-producing developing countries have been pushed to the brink of international bankruptcy by the international economic events they face. Further disruptions in international monetary arrangements for these countries seem inevitable, and these may adversely affect the future creditworthiness of the Third World.

Prospects for the non-oil-producing developing countries over the next 5 to 10 years are rather bleak. External financing of payments deficits cannot be expected to continue to defer the implicit transfer of real resources from the Third World. To grow at the relatively modest rates established for the Second Development Decade, the developing countries must obtain additional sources of foreign exchange. The necessary expansion of export earnings will probably not occur. Commodity prices for exports from the less developed countries are not expected to increase substantially over the next few years. Moreover, the developing countries have problems gaining access to export markets with non-traditional export products—especially manufactures. At the same time, inappropriate economic policies in the developing countries themselves frequently preclude the reallocation of domestic economic resources into promising export lines.

The prospects for greater real aid flows to the Third World are even less encouraging. Faced with serious economic problems themselves, the industrial countries are not likely to expand their development assistance programs substantially. Even during the prosperous period between 1962 and 1973, there was no observable increase in real (that is, inflation-adjusted) official development assistance from the industrial countries comprising the OECD.[3] While the OPEC countries have recently increased their aid, the total is not expected to increase enough to enable a significant increase in projected developing country growth rates. Conseqeuently, the non-oil-producing developing countries are expected to grow at lower rates than the OECD countries during the next 5 to 10 years. Thus the gap between rich and poor in the international economy will widen still further.

Referring to the Third World in the aggregate does not mean that the economic prospects of all non-oil-producing developing countries are alike or in fact that their problems and circumstances are similar. The countries of the Third World are remarkably dissimilar, encompassing wide ranges of per capita income, natural resource endowments, and population densities. The economic prospects for countries that have recently enjoyed high growth rates, such as Brazil, South Korea, and Taiwan, are relatively encouraging, while the prospects and problems of such slow growers as India, Bangladesh, Mali, and Sudan are rather alarming. The least developed non-oil-producing countries—sometimes collectively referred to as the Fourth World—generally confront the most pressing difficulties.

Despite its diversity, the Third World has displayed remarkable solidarity on an increasing number of issues. During the first United Nations Conference on Trade and Development (UNCTAD) in Geneva in 1964 a commonality of interests and identity began to emerge among the developing countries.[4] At that meeting lines of conflict and interest between the participating nations developed along a North–South division. This was the first major international conference to witness such an alignment of interests; such conferences had normally consisted of a North–North conflict, with any participating developing countries supporting their Northern patrons for the most part. UNCTAD provided a continuing forum and focal point for the developing countries to articulate their collective interests.[5] UNCTAD's permanent staff has researched questions of Third World concern and has organized numerous consultative meetings among developing countries to collectivize interests, diminish potential conflict, and forge a common position on relations with the industrialized North.

The increased organizational capability to articulate Southern interests coincided with the growing frustration over the economic conditions and prospects of the Third World. OPEC's success with the Arab oil boycott and subsequent oil price increases provided a catalyst for an increased expression of developing countries' frustration and interests. The Third World's perceptions of its global bargaining power were radically revised. One result of greater expression and changing perceptions was the declaration of the New International Economic Order in 1974.

The entity which is formally termed the "New International Economic Order" owes its existence in name to a United Nations resolution passed at the sixth Special Session of the UN General Assembly in April and May 1974. Although the United States and other industrial countries clearly articulated their objections, the Declaration of the Establishment of a New International Economic Order was passed. It contained a number of general proposals for international economic reform which UNCTAD and other institutions oriented toward the less developed countries had been pressing for several years. Since the resolution contained only suggestions for Northern action, its passage over the objections of the North achieved only a rhetorical victory and an expression of Southern solidarity.

What the New International Economic Order actually constitutes is another matter. A United Nations declaration cannot overnight, as though by waving a magic wand, transform the structure of the international economy or even, for that matter, those institutions which represent it. Rather the New International Economic Order should be recognized for what it is—the Third World's commitment to international economic reform. Such reform aspires both to reduce poverty in developing countries and to increase the South's economic and political power within the international order.

In the aftermath of the Declaration of the New International Economic Order at the sixth Special Session, a number of similar events dramatized the divergent views and interests of North and South and increased suspicion and hostility between both groups of countries. In late 1974 the UN General Assembly passed the Charter of Economic Rights and Duties of States. The Charter, which incorporated a number of Southern claims and demands, was hotly contested by the United States and several other industrial countries. In early 1975 developing countries formulated proposals at a number of conferences to reform the international economic system along lines more advantageous to the Third World. Growing out of these discussions, the Lima Programme for Mutual Assistance and Solidarity represented the unilateral efforts of the Third World to establish a new world economic order.

All of these Southern-inspired declarations, charters, and proposals—whatever their merits—were formulated and enacted without the consent of the North. Since compliance of the North is essential to any major restructuring of international economic arrangements, many of the Third World victories over the North in international forums were without real meaning. Moreover, the radical tone of much of the Third World rhetoric, involving the "struggle against imperialism," threatens to erode the tacit Northern acceptance of the responsibility for alleviating Southern poverty.

When the seventh Special Session of the UN General Assembly was convened in September 1975 the political atmosphere was charged with suspicion and hostility. However, moderation of the US position and the emergence of a more moderate, pragmatic leadership among the Third World countries diffused the threat of a major North–South confrontation. The emphasis changed from confrontation to dialogue and negotiation.

Whether meaningful progress can be made through negotiation and accommodation depends upon the very nature of the North–South conflict. There are basically two pertinent viewpoints. The pessimistic view holds that the early 1970s witnessed the drawing of rigid ideological and material battle lines for the inevitable international struggle between rich and poor. No compromise is considered possible. The pessimists then view the conflict as a zero-sum game; the South can only gain at the expense of the North, and vice versa. The present economic relationship between North and South is viewed as essentially exploitative, and such interactions can only benefit the rich and prevent the poor countries from developing. Carried to its logical extreme, the pessimistic viewpoint sees military conflict between rich and poor as inevitable, and envisages massive wars of redistribution and possible nuclear blackmail carried out by desperate Third World countries.[6]

The more optimistic view of the North-South conflict, to which most of the contributors to this volume subscribe, holds that compromise is possible. While the economic interests of North and South frequently conflict, especially in the short run, interaction between them can be consensual as well. The North-South conflict, despite its important economic dimensions, is largely political and ideological in nature. Compromise is therefore possible. Over the long run, the economic relationship is a positive-sum game rather than a zero-sum game. Both rich and poor nations can benefit through their interactions and interdependence. Growth and increased welfare in either can be economically beneficial for both.

The issues confronting the New International Economic Order relate to the interactions between North and South. The agendas for discussion, negotiation, and accommodation include: (1) international trade relations, including commodity problems, possible producers' alliances, access to Northern markets, and trade preferences for products of the less developed countries; (2) international monetary relations and arrangements, including Third World participation in reform discussions, the establishment of the so-called "link" between international reserve creation and concessional aid, and access to Eurocurrency markets; (3) aid and other resource transfers; (4) external indebtedness of the less developed countries and possible debt relief; (5) multinational firm activities and technological transfer to developing countries; (6) the population explosion in the Third World; (7) the preservation of the environment; (8) seabed exploration and exploitation; and (9) international migration. While they are by no means unimportant, this volume does not address the last four issues. Instead we focus on the first five issues listed.

Underlying all of these issues is one central question—the distribution and redistribution of world income and wealth. The market economies of the North produce an overwhelming proportion—about 66 percent—of the world's total output of goods and services.[7] Nearly all of the schemes developed by or on behalf of the South effectively transfer real resources from the developed countries to the Third World. Commodity arrangements—whether bufferstock schemes or outright cartelization—imply higher prices and therefore seek to transfer resources to the developing countries producing those commodities. Similarly, debt forgiveness schemes, the "link" proposal, codes of conduct affecting multinational firms, poverty "reparations" suggestions, and proposals to increase the flow of concessionary financing involve the transfer of resources from rich to poor countries. While some responsible Third World spokesmen state that equality of opportunity rather than distribution is the real issue,[8] the frequent and sometimes shrill calls for "distribution justice" lend credence to the importance of the underlying distributive question. Curiously, however, in the context of the discussions of the New International Economic Order greater distributive justice has little to do with redistribution *within* developing countries, much less *among* developing countries. The question is invariably cast as redistribution from the rich developed nations to the poor less developed countries.[a]

The forums and arenas for discussion and negotiation of North–South relations now include a number of international institutions. Various United Nations agencies have previously participated in interactions and will continue to do so. The UN General Assembly, which abundantly represents Southern interests with its voting structure, suffers from both the encumbrances of large scale multilateral diplomacy and a general mistrust on the part of the industrial countries—reflecting the voting structure's favor toward the numerous Third World countries. Thus, the General Assembly cannot be expected to be a serious forum for specific questions between North and South. Rather it will continue to offer debate and articulation of interest, useful for mobilizing international opinion and conducting public relations campaigns. The UNCTAD, despite the technical and research skills of its permanent staff, also suffers from the pitfalls of large scale multilateral diplomacy and a lack of confidence on the part of the industrial countries. Consequently, it can be expected to continue to serve primarily as a forum for collectivizing and articulating Southern interests. Other international institutions such as the World Bank, the International Monetary Fund (IMF), and the General Agreement on Tariffs and Trade (GATT) can also be expected to contribute to the North–South dialogue.

One promising forum for conducting North–South negotiations on economic issues is the Conference on International Economic Cooperation, convened in Paris in December 1975. Intensive discussions have taken place at the Conference up to the time of this writing (March 1977). The agenda has been divided among different working groups discussing such issues as energy, commodities, general development problems, and development financing. While avoiding the disadvantages of cumbersome large-scale multilateral diplomacy, the conference includes representatives of the important OPEC countries, the major industrial powers, and significant and representative Third World nations. While politically charged, the Paris discussions have been moderately fruitful. This sort of institutionalization of economic negotiations seems desirable.

Considerable headway in discussions and understanding frequently occurs at nonofficial levels. The interchange of ideas among policymakers, businessmen, and academics from both North and South would increase understanding of the questions related to the North–South conflict. Research on many of the

---

[a] A cynic, observing the frequently regressive nature of taxation in developed countries and regressive nature of political power in developing countries, might be tempted to consider North–South concessional financing and resource flows as a redistribution from the poor in the rich countries to the rich in the poor countries.

questions themselves is sorely needed, especially in the developing countries. As such, it would be useful to have an international institution functioning as a North–South Center which would advance knowledge about international economic relations through research and enhance the understanding of policy-makers and businessmen through seminars and conferences.

From the South's standpoint, effective North–South bargaining requires a greater consolidation of Southern positions. Economic and political relations between Third World countries themselves are not intense. Moreover, the inter-actions that do occur are largely conditioned by the more pervasive North–South relationship.[9] While South–South relations are undergoing important changes, developing countries are far from agreement on such problems as trade prefer-ences and policies, customs unions, the treatment of multinational firms, the sharing of technology, seabed exploration, and commodity supply strategies. The rhetorical successes of the South in United Nations forums over the past few years have stemmed from Southern agreement on very general issues. More meaningful victories through negotiations with the North are contingent upon the South's ability to reach agreement on far more specific questions. Without such agreement in the Third World, the North's traditional de facto strategy of "divide and rule," based upon the largely vertical nature of developing country relations, is likely to prevail.

The South's primary bargaining power with the North currently stems from its potential ability to disrupt. As with petroleum, cutting off key primary com-modities would create serious economic disruption in the industrial world. The North depends heavily upon Southern-produced raw materials such as copper, tin, and bauxite. Nevertheless, apart from any kamikase urge, the South's power may have been greatly exaggerated in popular accounts. OPEC may prove to be unique. The conditions for forming and operating a successful producers' cartel are not so readily abundant for primary commodities other than petroleum. Nor are the countries involved in similar economic circumstances. In fact, the moderation of demands of the less developed countries at the seventh Special Session of the UN General Assembly reflects in part the South's realization that it had overplayed its hand by overestimating its bargaining power in the flush of OPEC successes.

While treating many of the larger issues of Third World participation in the international economy, Attiat F. Ott's chapter in this volume focuses on the question of whether developing countries can initiate OPEC-like successes for other commodities. After discussing problems in commodity trade and the conditions necessary for success of producers' associations, she undertakes some econometric estimates of price and income elasticities for a number of commodity exports important in the trade of the less developed countries. On the basis of these and other estimates, she projects total world exports of cocoa, sugar, cotton, rubber, tea, and copper. While she does admit some in-creased market power on the part of producers, her empirical analysis raises doubts about the ability of producers' associations to secure higher export earnings for Third World countries.

The contribution by Wilfred L. David addresses the economic dimensions of the North-South confrontation. He discusses the benefits both North and South would derive from an increased emphasis on Southern industrialization and technological transfer to the South. Sympathetic to the arguments for import substitution strategies and somewhat autarchistic development in the South, he goes on to argue for more liberal trade policies and even reparation type real resource flows on the part of the North. His premise is that increasing the bargaining power of the Third World is necessary to bring international economic progress, including greater distributive justice among nations.

Karel Holbik's essay provides an overview of the international monetary problems of the Third World. He argues that international economic stability and the economic stability of the developing countries require coordinating national demand management policies. He urges the developed countries to avoid cyclical instability, to liberalize their imports—especially of manufactures—and to assume greater responsibility for long-term assistance to developing countries. In presenting some estimates of net capital requirements, Holbik argues that the growth targets of the Second United Nations Development Decade will not be attained unless substantial increases of concessional financing for the South are forthcoming.

In chapter five Maurice Girgis relates the OPEC price increases to the functioning of the international economy. While there were initial fears about the ability of the West to "recycle" petrodollars, Girgis argues that the international payments system and adjustment mechanisms have functioned remarkably well, considering the nature and magnitude of the shocks imposed by OPEC. In discussing the future prospects of OPEC, Girgis points to Saudi Arabia's key role and its apparent willingness to absorb production cutbacks to support high oil prices.

In his contribution Richard F. Kosobud analyzes OPEC activities and prospects from a different perspective. He considers possible Western strategies and appropriate responses and analyzes the economies of bargaining between oil importers and exporters. In rejecting both the existing strategy of consumer passivity and the rather aggressive anti-OPEC strategy of sealed bids for petroleum import licenses in the US, Kosobud argues for a system of bilateral cartel bargaining between consumers and producers.

The chapter by Bernd Stecher analyzes commodity problems on a more general level than do Girgis or Kosobud. Like Ott, Stecher stresses the functioning of the market and market solutions in his critical analysis of international commodity agreements and the schemes to provide indexation of commodity prices. Stecher also provides an analysis of world industrial diversification based on international cross-section approach. From this analysis he concludes that the UNIDO target of having the Third World generate 25 percent of the world's total industrial output by the year 2000 is not unreasonable. He argues, however, that this target will not be attained. Like many contributors to this volume, Stecher favors compensatory financing of commodity fluctuation coupled with greater aid and the removal of import restrictions in the North.

In chapter eight Jaleel Ahmad focuses on Third World exports of manufactures. He argues that the vigorous promotion of manufactured exports by the developing countries is the best way to increase the South's share of total world industrial output. In addition to urging policy changes in both North and South, Ahmad recommends that the potential for South–South trade not be neglected. He further argues that international trading arrangements should emphasize accommodation to changing patterns of international comparative advantage. The present structure of production between North and South should not be permitted to ossify. The Ahmad argument basically stresses trade rather than aid to promote growth in the South. He contends that concessional financing only defers the problem of structurally changing the developing countries to enhance their comparative advantages.

Tracy Murray's contribution extends Ahmad's treatment of the barriers to the expansion of manufacturing exports in the less developed countries. Murray examines the importance of the existing tariff preferences to the Third World and also their special relevance to multinational firms. He argues that the adoption of the Generalized System of Preferences (GSP) by the major industrial countries has not significantly benefited the developing countries; nor is it likely to, in view of the existing exceptions, exemptions, and other limitations of the various GSP systems.

In chapter ten Neal P. Cohen examines the question of assisting Third World countries through debt relief. Many developing countries have piled up substantial external debts, and the rescheduling or forgiveness of such debts have been suggested by some as important ways to assist the developing countries. Cohen argues that the demands for debt relief for the less developed countries are misplaced. Very few Third World countries who need such relief would be affected. Furthermore, general problems with debt relief render it inappropriate for development assistance. Rather the emphasis should be on increasing the flow of new aid, Cohen argues.

Charles T. Goodsell's chapter focuses on the role of the multinational corporation in the international economic order. In analyzing Third World's resentment and opposition to such firms, he provides a pessimistic outlook for their long term survival in the developing countries. He argues that to survive they must adopt a more appropriate political strategy involving a greater public service function and resource transfers to host governments in less developed countries.

One reflection of the hostility that multinational firms frequently arouse in the Third World is the call for a code of conduct governing multinational firm behavior. In chapter twelve Werner J. Feld examines the various United Nations proposals for such a code. Feld sees these negotiations as political and concludes that any meaningful agreement on a code will depend upon the nature and future development of North-South relations.

Notes

1. World Bank estimates.

2. International Monetary Fund, *Annual Report,* 1976, p. 70.

3. Gerald K. Helleiner, ed., *A World Divided: The Less Developed Countries in the International Economy* (Cambridge: Cambridge University Press, 1976), p. 3.

4. For a discussion of the First UNCTAD see Richard N. Gardner, "The United Nations Conference on Trade and Development," in Richard N. Gardner and Max F. Millikan, eds., *The Global Partnership* (New York: Frederick A. Praeger, 1968), pp. 99-130.

5. See Joseph S. Nye, "UNCTAD: Poor Nation's Pressure Group," in Robert W. Cox and Harold K. Jacobson, eds., *The Anatomy of Influence and Decision Making in International Organization* (New Haven, Conn.: Yale University Press, 1973), pp. 334-370.

6. See Robert Heilbroner, *An Inquiry into the Human Prospect* (New York: W.W. Norton, 1974).

7. International Bank for Reconstruction and Development, *World Bank Atlas, 1975* (Washington: World Bank Group, 1975).

8. See, for example, Third World Forum, *Proposals for a New International Economic Order,* report prepared by a special task force of the Third World Forum, Mexico City, August 1975.

9. See H. Jon Rosenbaum and William G. Tyler, "South-South Relations: The Economic and Political Content of Interactions among Developing Countries," *International Organization* 29, no. 1 (Winter 1975): 243-274.

2

The Impact of the New International Economic Order on the Third World

Attiat F. Ott[a]

By quadrupling the price of oil, the Organization of Petroleum Exporting Countries (OPEC) dramatized the conflict between resource-producing and resource-consuming nations, or between the developing and the developed countries of the world. OPEC's actions between 1973 and 1974 clearly mark the beginning of a new economic order. Especially noteworthy in OPEC's success in unilaterally fixing the price of oil exports was the fact that the price fixing did not generate dissension among Third World countries, many of which were adversely affected, but was applauded by them and considered a model to be imitated. OPEC's action and the growing number of its would-be imitators constitute the framework for the new economic order formally born in 1974.

At its sixth Special Session in May 1974, the General Assembly of the United Nations declared the establishment of the New International Economic Order (NIEO). The new order would be based on (1) full permanent sovereignty over natural resources and their exploitation, including the host country's right to nationalization or forced transfer of ownership to its nationals; (2) the use of commodity power (through the establishment of producers' associations) to improve the terms of trade for developing nations; (3) just and equitable relations between the prices of raw materials and the prices of manufactured goods; (4) a call for global solutions to economic problems; and (5) collective self-reliance on the part of the Third World.

The second of these is clearly the most controversial and is the subject of my inquiry. This chapter focuses on some of the conditions necessary for the success of producers' associations and thus for the success of the new economic order. The first section of the chapter defines the Third World, the "old" economic order, and some of the prerequisites for the formation of a viable cartel. The second section presents price and income elasticities for some Third World raw material exports. On the basis of those price-income elasticities, I try to project the growth rate of developing world exports (world imports) in these commodities, given an assumed growth path of GNP for the developed world. The final section of the chapter offers some speculations on the future of the new economic order, in the light of our findings.

---

[a]The author wishes to thank Hak Pyo of Clark University for his work in estimating the regression equations and for his valuable comments on the paper.

The Third World and The New Order

The Third World

The formation of the Club of Seventy-seven and the United Nations Conference on Trade and Development (UNCTAD) in 1964 brought to the economic world a new dimension—the Third World. The Third World label replaced old labels commonly used to refer to the developing world.[1]

Although they perceive themselves as a bloc, Third World countries differ among themselves politically and economically. Thus, Third World countries have customarily been divided into the following subcategories:[2]

1. Oil- and other mineral-exporting countries.
2. Fast-growing exporters of manufactures.
3. All other developing countries, a subcategory divided into (a) countries whose per capita income is above $250, and (b) countries whose per capita income is at or below $250.

To gain insights into the economics and perhaps the politics of the Third World, it is useful to look at some economic indicators during the development decades of the 1960s and early 1970s. Table 2-1 shows population growth rates, gross national product (GNP), exports and imports, and the terms of trade for developing countries by subgroups. These data suggest a continued improvement in the economic position of the Third World. During the period 1960 to 1973, real GNP rose at about 6 percent, the growth rate of the purchasing power of exports more than doubled, and the terms of trade improved significantly, reaching an index level of 175 in 1974 from a level of 96 in 1960.

Despite these improvements, the Third World countries today voice disenchantment with their progress more loudly than ever before, and this disenchantment is clearly justifiable once we leave the aggregated and look at the disaggregated data. When we examine the progress of individual countries or subgroups of countries in light of development elsewhere, we can see clearly that advances of the 1960s and early 1970s did little to change the disparity in the distribution of income between the developed and developing world or among the developing countries themselves. The Gini coefficient for the developing countries, when weighted by population, rose from .35 to .41 between 1958 and 1968 while for developed countries it fell from .37 to .28 during the same period.[3] Furthermore, the gap in per capita income between the developed and developing countries seems to be widening and a new and substantial gap has begun to emerge among the developing countries themselves. Average per capita income in 1973 for developing countries was $247 (at 1972 prices) compared to $3,841 in the developed world. In 1955 it was $100 for the former and $800

Table 2-1
Key Economic Indicators for Third World Countries, by Country Groups[a]

	All Developing Countries	Major Oil Exporters	Fast Growing Manufacturers	All Other Per Capita GNP > $250	All Other Per Capita GNP < $250
Population as Percent of Total (1973)	100	15	5.5	16.6	62.8
Per Capita GNP (1973 at 1972 prices)	247	312	713	527	115
Growth Rates (average annual percentage change)					
GNP: 1960–1970	5.2	5.9	7.9	4.9	4.2
1970–1973	5.7	7.8	7.3	6.5	3.0
Per capita: 1960–1970	2.6	3.1	5.0	2.2	1.7
GNP: 1970–1973	3.1	4.9	4.4	3.8	0.5
Export Purchasing Power: 1960–1970	5.2	6.0	9.9	5.1	3.2
1970–1973	9.6	17.2	19.6	5.8	1.8
Exports Index (1970 = 100)					
Volume 1960	61	55	52	64	74
1973	118	123	171	107	103
1974	118	123	171	107	103
Unit Value 1960	81	82	77	80	84
1973	158	184	131	153	142
1974	359	644	162	241	221
Imports Index (1970 = 100)					
Volume 1960	63	65	46	63	78
1973	123	143	138	117	97
1974	123	143	138	117	97
Unit Value 1960	84	84	86	84	85
1973	139	137	141	138	141
1974	205	184	203	215	231

Table 2-1 Continued

Terms of Trade[b] (1970 = 100)					
1960	96	98	90	95	99
1973	114	134	93	111	102
1974	175	350	80	112	103

Source: UNCTAD, *Trends and Policies in the First Four Years of the Second Development Decade*, Report by the UNCTAD Secretariat (February 3, 1975).

[a]The sample contains eighty-four countries.
[b]Unit value of exports/unit value of imports.

for the latter. Among developing countries themselves, per capita income in 1973 was about \$70 for the poorer members of the Third World and \$5,000 for the oil-rich countries.

If we treat Third World countries as a bloc then we can estimate the overall gains or losses of the 1970s by using a weighted sum of the growth of income of the subgroups:

$$G = a_1 g_1 + a_2 g_2 + a_3 g_3 + \ldots + a_n g_n \qquad (2.1)$$

where G is an index of the growth of welfare for the group as a whole and a_i is the weight assigned to each subgroup:

$$i \left(\sum_{i=1}^{n} a_i = 1 \right)$$

and g_i is the rate of growth of GNP for each subgroup i. Following the methodology of Ahluwalia and Chenery, the weights for each subcategory of countries may also be set according to the degree toward which distributional aims are paramount.[4] As the weight on a particular group is raised, the index G reflects to a greater extent the growth of income in that group. Thus, for example, if we judged the success or failure of development in the 1960s according to the growth in income for the poorest members of the Third World (per capita income below \$250), we would set $a_5 = 1$, and all other $a_i = 0$, so that the growth in welfare of the Third World would be measured by g_5.

Weighting g by population, we find that the advance in GNP scored by the developing countries over the period 1970 to 1973 (shown in table 2-1) is reduced from 5.7 percent to 4.8 percent. Assuming a weight of 1 for the poorer members of the group (which constitutes 63 percent of total population), we find that the gain in welfare during 1970 to 1973 is reduced from 5.7 percent to only 3.0 percent, which is 1.2 percentage points lower than the gain in welfare achieved during the 1960s.

The New International Economic Order

The "newness" of the new economic order can best be described by reference to the old order. In the old international economic order, market forces, at least on the supply side, dominated the determination of raw materials prices in world trade. By contrast, in the new order a different system is exercised over supply. Whether this form of control will materialize through producer's associations, through income or price stabilization schemes, or through the indexation of exports, the essential ingredient in the new order is the producers' increased market power. Should raw material producers be able to exercise sufficient market power, then clearly new solutions, different from the old solutions, will be reached. If we describe the situation in terms of the familiar Mill-Marshall offer curves, then a move from point A or S to point Z in figure 2-1 would describe the solution sought under the new economic order.

Let D and D^1 represent the offer curves of the developed world and T and T^1 those of the Third World. Point A is the free competitive solution where none of the participants exercises market power. Suppose the developed countries, through multinational corporations or other forms of market power, were able to force trade to position S rather than A, where the terms of trade would be more favorable (this indeed is the claim of the Third World). Now suppose the Third World countries form producers' associations and cut back their supply and offer of raw materials from OR to OP. In this case, like the case of bilateral monopoly, the outcome is theoretically indeterminate. The new terms of trade and the trade solution may lie at Z, at Z^1 or any other point in between. If the offer curve of the developed world (given its shape) remains at

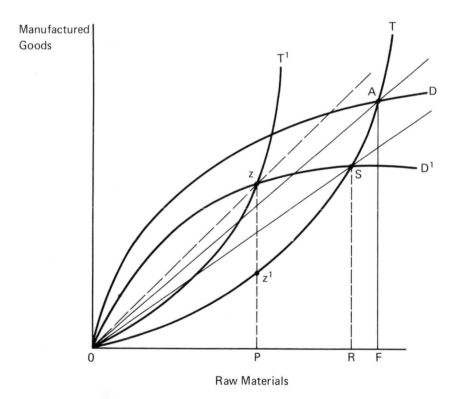

Figure 2-1. Alternative Trading Solutions Between the Developing and Developed Worlds

D^1, and the developing countries' curve shifts to T^1, the result would be improved terms of trade in the Third World. On the other hand, if the developed world offer curve shifted downward and the developing countries' curve were T, then point Z^1 might be the outcome. When the shape (elasticity of demand and supply) of the offer curves is also considered, then even with the unchanging position of the D^1 curve, point Z may not (as we will see later) result in an increase in Third World income or welfare. Export earnings may fall if the rise in prices is more than offset by the fall in the volume of raw material exports.

Prerequisite for the Success of Producers' Cartels

The success of OPEC's action (quadrupling the price of oil and simultaneously increasing earnings for its members), is an example of an effective exercise of market power. Others wanting to imitate the achievement of OPEC—a goal desired by primary commodities producers other than oil producers—must meet several conditions. First, the commodity in question must be of strategic importance—that is, it must be a basic material in interindustrial production activity and have limited substitutes. Second, producers must effectively restrict supply and must be able to afford to do so. Third, producers themselves must have the common interest and will to organize and abide by the association's decisions (no cheating).

The conditions cited above certainly exist in the markets for petroleum, petroleum by-products, and bauxite. Beyond these "success" cases, few commodities that are mainly produced by the Third World meet the necessary criteria. Substitutes exist for many of the commodities produced by Third World countries. Moreover, Third World producers are not a homogeneous group and the developing countries lack the necessary storage facilities and the financial ability to make supply reduction feasible. More critically, most of these commodities—especially the agricultural products—exhibit an extremely low long-run income elasticity of demand.

Because aggregate data on income and price elasticities of demand are not useful in assessing the success or failure of a particular producers' association, the next section reports some crude but significant findings on the value of these elasticities for six primary commodities. These are cocoa, sugar, cotton, rubber, tea and copper.

Time Series Estimation of Import Demand

Since we are mainly interested in long-run income and price elasticities, we have assumed for the purpose of estimation that the demand function of the commodity in question is fairly stable in the long run.

The Demand Function

The basic explanatory variables, as suggested by the theory of demand, are incomes and relative prices. Thus, we specify the following import demand function:

$$IM_i = \alpha \left(\frac{PIM_i}{P} \right)^{B_1} \cdot Y^{B_2} \cdot e^{B_3 t} \cdot \epsilon \qquad (2.2)$$

where IM_i = import quantity index of the ith commodity
PIM_i = import price index of the ith commodity
P = domestic price index
Y = world real GNP
t = time trend
α = constant parameter
B_1 = price elasticity coefficient
B_2 = income elasticity coefficient
B_3 = time trend coefficient
ϵ = disturbance term

In log form, equation (2.2) can be written as:

$$\log IM_i = \alpha_0 + B_1 \log \left(\frac{PIM_i}{P} \right) + B_2 \log Y + B_3 t + \epsilon \qquad (2.3)$$

The choice of the explanatory variables and data sources are given in appendix 2A.

Regression Results

The import demand function given by equation (2.3) was estimated for both world and U.S. imports for the six primary commodities listed above, using data for the period 1956 to 1972 for the United States imports and 1956 to 1971 for world imports. The results of the estimation (with reasonably good fit) are reported in table 2-2. In table 2-3, aggregated income and price elasticities as reported in the literature are shown for comparison purposes.

The estimates in table 2-2 for world imports of five of the six primary commodities look quite plausible. The t ratio, the Durbin-Watson coefficient (d) (with the exception of cotton), and the R^2 (except for copper), are satisfactory. The regression results for United States demand for imports, except for copper, are not significantly different from the first set of results—that is,

Table 2-2
Price and Income Elasticities for Selected Primary Commodities

U.S. and World Imports	$\hat{B_1}$ Price Elasticity	$\hat{B_2}$ Income Elasticity	$\hat{B_3}$ Time Coefficient	$\hat{\alpha_0}$ Constant Terms	R^2	d
U.S. Imports:						
Coca	-0.4200 (-5.130)	0.6766 (0.8459)	-0.0074 (-0.2424)	0.1558 (0.4725)	0.82	3.03
Copper	-0.4725 (-2.2778)	5.8257 (5.1447)	-0.2271 (-5.3758)	-0.1960 (-5.3758)	0.74	2.54
Tea	0.2697 (1.3513)	0.1327 (0.2126)	0.0329 (1.2936)	3.6020 (1.4028)	0.88	2.90
Rubber	0.0188 (0.1480)	0.9990 (1.1375)	-0.0138 (-0.3443)	0.5226 (0.0443)	0.91	1.14
World Imports:						
Coca	-0.4691 (-3.0243)	10.246 (4.9660)	-0.4930 (-5.0940)	-35.012 (-0.5417)	0.77	1.75
Sugar[a]	-0.1678 (-0.2900)	0.3736 (1.3203)		3.6463 (1.784)	0.48	1.51
Cotton[a]	-0.5539 (2.0187)	0.2447 (4.007)		5.9852 (3.010)	0.73	0.72
Rubber[a]	0.0672 (0.5148)	0.7530 (5.500)		0.8879 (0.6147)	0.91	1.08
Copper	-0.4758 (1.1196)	3.3736 (0.7737)	-0.1709 (-0.8474)	-8.3062 (2.8406)	0.32	1.89

Source: Author's estimates.
[a]For these three commodities, omitting time variables improved the estimation.

Table 2-3
Price and Income Elasticities for Foodstuffs and Crude Materials

	Price Elasticity −2	−1	Income Elasticity 1	2
Crude Foodstuffs				
HM[1]		–	.61	
		−.07	.11	
BM[2]	−.61 ——		—— .87	
RB[3]	−1.32 —— −.78		.39 —— .81	
Crude Materials				
HM[1]		–	.30	
BM[2]	−.53 —		.01 —— 1.20	
RB[3]	.41 —		—— 1.02	
		−.01	.2	

HM[1] refers to Houthakker and Magee.

BM[2] refers to Ball and Marwah.

RB[3] refers to Rhomberg and Boissonneault.

The results for BM and RB are reported in confidence intervals in E. Leaner and R. Stern, *Quantitative International Economics* (Boston: Allyn and Bacon, 1970), p. 35. Original data from R.J. Ball and K.M. Marwah, "The U.S. Demand for Imports, 1948–1958," *Review of Economics and Statistics* (November 1962) and from R.R. Rhomberg and L. Boissonneault, "The Foreign Sector," in J.S.D. Duesenberry, et al., eds., *The Brookings Quarterly Econometric Model of the United States* (Chicago: Rand McNally, 1965). The results for HM are from H.S. Houthakker and Stephen P. Magee, "Income and Price Elasticities in World Trade," *Review of Economics and Statistics* (May 1969), p. 80.

they neither improve nor contradict the results obtained when world demands of these commodities are estimated.

Several general comments can be made on the results:

1. Income elasticities, although they vary greatly among commodities, are relatively greater than price elasticities for all commodities (except for world imports of cotton).

2. The price elasticity has the correct sign for four out of the six commodities examined. The positive price elasticities for tea and rubber seem to reflect the influence of substitutes (not included in the regression equations)—such as coffee and synthetic rubber—on the demand for these commodities.

3. The negative coefficient obtained for the time-trend variable support the view that the demand for primary products does not shift upward or respond positively to increases in the value of demographic variables such as population growth. It also points to the well-known fact that over the long run cheap and competing substitutes for naturally produced primary commodities are usually found, developed and marketed, thereby reducing world demand for these commodities and increasing the vulnerability of the raw materials producers.

For world imports, omitting the time variable from the demand for sugar, cotton and rubber substantially improved the fit of the regressions.

A comparison of our results with aggregated elasticities reported in the literature (table 2-3) enforces the proposition that price elasticities for primary products are not very low but generally less than one. However, income elasticities of demand obtained from disaggregated data differ from those obtained when data are aggregated. Our results show income elasticities ranging from a low of .24 for cotton, to a high of 10 for cocoa, while the income elasticities reported in table 2-3 for crude foodstuffs range from .11 to .87. Our results suggest that income elasticities are highly sensitive to the degree of aggregation.

Projections of World Demand for
Selected Primary Commodities

On the basis of the regression equations reported earlier, we have attempted to project world demand for cocoa, sugar, cotton, rubber and copper through the 1980s. The projection is based on the following assumptions:

1. an annual real growth rate of GNP for the countries of the OECD (a proxy for world income of 4.7 percent for the period 1975 to 1980.
2. an annual growth rate of GNP deflator for the countries of the OECD of 15 percent for the period 1973 to 1976, and 17 percent for 1976 to 1980.
3. for commodity import prices annual growth rates of 5 percent for cocoa, 6.6 percent for sugar, 5.6 percent for cotton, 8.0 percent for rubber and 7.8 percent for copper.

The results of the projections are given in table 2-4. The predicted values of world imports reported in the table suggest a low to moderate increase in world demand for the selected primary commodities through the 1970s. Specifically, we project world imports of these commodities to increase at an annual rate of 4.61 percent for cocoa, 0.76 percent for sugar, 4.28 percent for rubber and 1.00 percent for copper. The world demand for cotton is expected to fall during this period at an annual rate of 1.77 percent. These growth rates, together with annual rates of change projected by the World Bank, are shown in table 2-5. With the exception of cotton and copper, where our projections differ significantly from those of the World Bank, the results seem to suggest future world demand for these commodities (even with projected high growth rates of OECD GNP) does not seem promising—much lower rates than those experienced during the commodity boom years of the late 1960s and early 1970s.

Given that the price and income elasticities of primary products fall around the estimated figures, our findings clearly raise some doubts on the viability of producers' associations as a vehicle for securing higher export earnings. Increas-

Table 2-4
Predicted Values of World Imports of Selected Primary Commodities,
1976 to 1980

Year	Import Quantity Index (1963 = 100)				
	Cocoa	Sugar	Cotton	Rubber	Copper
Actual					
1971	113.5	112.4	101.0	141.7	74.1
Projected					
1976	122.8	102.1	84.0	130.3	100.0
1977	126.4	104.2	82.7	135.9	100.0
1978	144.0	104.9	80.8	143.0	103.0
1979	148.1	104.9	79.3	149.3	102.0
1980	152.2	105.8	77.9	155.7	102.0

Source: Estimates are based on price and income elasticity coefficients obtained from the regression equations.

Table 2-5
Annual Rates of Change of World Imports of Selected Primary
Commodities (percent)

Commodity	Regression Equation Estimates (1972 to 1980)	IBRD Estimates (1972/74 to 1980)
Cocoa	4.6	2.4
Sugar	0.8	1.5
Cotton	−1.77	1.5
Rubber	4.3	4.5
Copper	1.00	5.9

Source: Column (2): based on predicted values (table 2-4). Column (3): World Bank estimates reported in *Effects of Price Changes on Development Prospects* (processed).

ing the price of primary commodities along the line of the OPEC increases would not be in the best interests of most of the producing-exporting nations. This leads to a question: If the success of producers' associations (at least for the commodities studied) is uncertain and members' income is not assured, why their appeal and what are the alternatives?

Their appeal, in my view, may be found in political rather than in economic arguments. The move towards producers' associations by Third World countries may dramatize the need for new channels of communications between the developed and developing worlds. By facing the developed (consuming) nations as a bloc, the developing countries may be able to coax them to reexamine their trade and aid policies. The real message the NIEO should convey, regardless of the mechanism employed, is the message that there is urgent need for redistribution of world resources and skills. As an economist who believes in the efficiency of a "free" market system, I would rather approach the issue in a more direct way. Third World countries unquestionably need resources and skills to move up and join the First World. These resources, I believe, should be transferred within the apparatus of a market system—through grants, aid and foreign investment—rather than through the distortion of commodity prices. Whether this is feasible or whether producers' associations are the answer, the next decade will clearly judge what form the international economic order will take.

Notes

1. Not all developing countries belong to the Third World. Only non-Communist developing countries are considered members, banning occasional mavericks such as Tito's Yugoslavia. Also, some developing countries are on occasion excluded for political reasons.

2. United Nations Conference on Trade and Development, *Trends and Policies in the First Four Years of the Second Development Decade,* Report by the UNCTAD Secretariat (February 3, 1975).

3. I.M.D. Little, "Economic Relations with the Third World—Old Myths and New Prospects," *Scottish Journal of Political Economy* (November 1975): 224.

4. *Redistribution with Growth,* A study by the World Bank, Hollis Chenery, Montek S. Ahluwalia, C.L.G. Ball, John H. Duloy, and Richard Jolly (Oxford University Press, 1974), p. 39.

Appendix 2A:
Data Sources

World import quantity index (IM_Q) was used as the dependent variable in equation (2.2) in lieu of volume of imports due to the lack of price deflator to deflate nominal value of imports for the period 1956 to 1971. As a proxy for world income and domestic prices, OECD real GNP and export price deflators were used. The data used are from the following sources:

1. Import Quantity Index: Bulletin of Labor Statistics and Department of Commerce Data.
2. Import Price Index: New York Commodity Market Price from "Commodity Trade" for the U.S. Data and Lending World Export Price from "International Financial Statistics" for the OECD Data.
3. Wholesale Price Index and U.S. Real GNP Index: "Economic Report of the President" (1975).
4. Export Price Deflator and OECD Real GNP Index: Economic Indicators of OECD Countries.

3 Dimensions of the North–South Confrontation
Wilfred L. David

Setting the Scene

In an address delivered in 1959, Sir Oliver Franks remarked:

Earlier the problems of East-West Tension were dominant; now we have a North-South problem of equal importance. . . . If twelve years ago the balance of the world turned on the recovery of Western Europe, now it turns on a right relationship of the industrial North of the globe to the developing South. [Franks, 1959].

The problems surrounding East–West relationships have certainly not subsided. But from a global perspective these difficulties have been compounded by the Arab-Israeli conflict, the hardening of attitudes towards the white supremacist regimes in Southern Africa, and by the global problems of oil, energy and inflation on the economic front.

The relationships between the advanced Northern countries and the poor South have now hardened into the "North–South confrontation." Overall, the major issue shaping the confrontation is international redistributive justice, as exemplified by the subsets of issues outlined below.

First, a major issue is the sharing of international economic and political power, that is, how global income, wealth and decision-making authority should be distributed with respect to international economic power. The major problem therefore revolves around the possibility of achieving a more dynamic division of labor, through which the nations of the South participate actively in the international economy.

The second issue is the conflict between nationalism and the building of a truly international economic order. In other words, can a world order be created which will accommodate nationalism while providing a truly international but much more equitable economic and political order? The third area of concern is the revolution of rising expectations in a relatively open world. The nations of the North, which comprise less than one-third of the world population, consume the lion's share of world production. One wonders, therefore, whether the poor South will ever adjust to this fact with the sophistication of modern communications systems. The affluent North may be forced to recognize the gravity of the situation. If this leads to the buildup of moral guilt on the part of the North, on the other side of the coin we can expect the buildup of jealousies on the part of the South. The clash of these two forces can give rise to tensions and perhaps unanticipated and drastic reactions.

Fourth, the real possibility of violence must be considered. Our attention has been drawn recently to the possibility of wars of redistribution between the poor South and the rich North (Heilbroner, 1974). As more Southern nations build up nuclear capabilities, even on a limited basis, the spectre of international class and racial wars looms large. While a realistic assessment would probably suggest that a war between the white Northern rich and the nonwhite Southern poor is unlikely to materialize as a full-scale nuclear confrontation, should one rule out the possibility of a highly coordinated and sustained violent action?

The fifth issue is the possible disengagement of the North from the South, springing from the radicalization of North–South relations. This brings into focus the entire question of whether the rich North really *needs* the poor South and whether the former can exist economically or otherwise without the latter. To the extent that the South is economically weak, the issue of confrontation is economically meaningless, and likely outcomes depend on the moral commitment of the North.

This list of issues merely illustrates areas of concern related to the quest for international redistributive justice. It is by no means exhaustive. Because of their complexity and heterogeneity, these issues defy economic delimitation. However, a common economic denominator could be found in the theme shaping the North–South confrontation, that is, the quest on the part of the South for a more equitable and just world economic order. This paper discusses some important variations on that theme.

The call for a New International Economic Order by the South should therefore be seen in the above light. Historically, it is an outgrowth of concerted action for new approaches to development, in the form of several demands on the North expressed in successive meetings of the United Nations Conference on Trade and Development (UNCTAD), the strengthening of the UNCTAD–Southern coalition, special ministerial meetings of the Group of Seventy-seven (now ninety-six), and Southern bargaining coalitions in the UN, IMF, GATT, etc.

The issue of North–South economic relationships came to a head in 1975 when the General Assembly of the United Nations adopted two resolutions in a "Declaration on the Establishment of a New International Economic Order," its accompanying "Programme of Action" and a related "Charter on Economic Rights and Duties." These brought together a set of proposals which had previously been put forward in UNCTAD meetings. In essence, the proposals call for a redistribution of global financial and technological resources through the following measures:

1. Economic decolonization, including the right to diversified, complete industrialization and the effective transfer of most advanced Western technologies.

2. Stimulation of increases in raw materials prices through mechanisms such as the indexation of prices of primary products to those of commodity exports of more developed countries.
3. The expanded participation of Third World countries in the operation of the international monetary system.
4. Compensation of Third World countries for the abusive exploitation of their resources during the colonial era, and recognition of their total sovereignty over those resources.
5. Cancellation of the standing debt of Third World countries.

These and other related demands of the South were elaborated in subsequent forms. The second general conference of the United Nations Industrial Development Organization (UNIDO), held in Lima during March 1975, proposed broad objectives and specific measures to encourage the industrialization of the South. The conference put forth "The Lima Declaration" and a Plan of Action on Industrial Development, which were designed to lessen economic dependence on primary products and broaden the development base. Proposals for changing the international economic order were also made in the Declaration and Action Programme on Raw Materials adopted at Dakar in February 1975, and at the 20th Conference of Commonwealth Heads of State and Governments held at Kingston, Jamaica, in April 1975.

Although the Northern nations did not always fully approve the proposals, there are signs that new attitudes of global cooperation are beginning to emerge. For example, the Declaration of Relations with Developing Countries adopted by the foreign ministers of the Organization for Economic Cooperation and Development (OECD) in May 1975 clearly expressed their intent to begin meaningful dialogue with Southern countries about establishing more balanced and equitable international economic relations.

The fourth session of the UNCTAD at Nairobi, Kenya, in May 1976, further considered the resolutions passed at the seventh Special Session of the United Nations in September 1975. The task of the conference was to translate those objectives within its province which might provide practical solutions to fundamental issues, recognizing, of course, many of the problems are concurrently being examined in other forums, such as the GATT multilateral trade negotiations and the Conference on International Economic Cooperation—the "North-South Dialogue."

An interesting feature of the fourth UNCTAD session was the demonstration of Southern unity, which contrasted remarkably with the divergence of certain developing regions or countries in earlier forums. The change of attitudes among countries is also significant, such as the United States abandoning the idea of confrontation between the South and the North in favor of a "dialogue."

In summary, the call for establishment of a more just and equitable economic order was a means of providing the less developed countries with more of the fruits of world development and with a greater say in international decision-making mechanisms. Increased Southern bargaining power is needed to attain economic progress which includes greater international redistributive justice.

Inequality and Equity

The call for a new international economic order by the South is based on two major considerations, which are by no means mutually exclusive. The first relates to the South's perception of the concrete conditions governing its under-development. One of these is the structure of international economic relationships, especially between the industrial North and the underdeveloped South. A key element in such a structure is the substantial and growing amount of world inequality.

The second major consideration concerns new ideas about progress and development now being embraced by leaders of less developed countries and economists. While interest in material growth persists, emphasis has shifted to other societal changes which bring about systematic movement toward achieving a complex set of developmental or "welfare" goals. Predominant among these is the need to reduce international and intranational inequalities.

In other words, greater equity in the international distribution of income, wealth, resources, and power has now become a major goal of policy. Programs and policies designed to reduce international inequality provide one means of achieving this objective. Inequality in the distribution of income, wealth, and economic power must be considered a fact, or an objective condition of international economic existence. That this inequality is inequitable and should be changed is an ethical judgment on the part of Southern leaders and some economists, and is therefore subjective (Bronfenbrenner, 1973).

While the underdevelopment of the South is closely correlated with the nature of political, social and economic parameters and their internal operations, the problems of underdevelopment also depend significantly on the historical structural relations between nation states. The emphasis now being placed on reducing international and intranational inequality highlights the concern for changing the relative positions of persons, groups, and nations in terms of desired values. Included in this restructured value system is the need to reduce inequality of power, wealth, prestige and access to choice. This, of course, involves both material and nonmaterial changes.

Most writers on this subject stress the internal or country-specific dimensions of inequality. For example, Dudley Seers (1969) espouses the view that there is a misconception of the main challenge of the second half of the twentieth century, which is not to achieve high growth rates in per capita GNP but to directly reduce poverty, unemployment and inequality. This finds strong support in the work of Irma Adelman (1974, 1975; with Taft Morris, 1973), and of the World Bank group headed by Hollis Chenery (1974). While most of these writers are interested in distributive equity within the domestic economy, one could hazard a guess that they would also support the hypothesis that there is a causal relationship between the international and domestic dimensions of inequality, as explored by Richard Jolly (1974).

The major dimensions of international inequality may be well known to readers, and a few stylized facts are presented below. While these refer essentially to those variables which can be measured, like GNP per capita, certain qualitative factors are also important. Some familiarity with the problems involved in measuring international differences in variables, such as per capita income, is also assumed (for example, Kravis, 1973).

First, in the well-known paper by Beckerman and Bacon (1970), based on data for 1962-1963, the skewness in the international distribution of consumption patterns is highlighted. They show that the poorest 10 percent of the world's population are responsible for less than 2 percent of world consumption, whereas the top 10 percent account for 35 percent of consumption. The poorest third of the world's population is responsible for only about 10 percent of world consumption. Thus if per capita consumption is taken as an index of economic welfare, the plight of the South is evident.

Second, as Professor Kuznets (1972) demonstrates, both the absolute and relative inequalities between the North and South have been growing recently based on the gap between North and South in both per capita output and economic structure, since there is obviously some relationship between the aggregate and structural gaps. As Kuznets remarks:

This reformulation of the gap is important because it emphasizes the association between the disparity in per capita product and those in economic structures and institutions, in noneconomic structures and in social ideology (i.e. views on man and nature prevalent in various societies). This gap is not merely between rich and poor, but between the industrialized, urbanized, mechanized, modernized countries with distinctive economic institutions, demographic processes, political characteristics and ideological patterns, on the one hand; and largely rural, agricultural, traditional countries, with only small nuclei of modern industry, modern firms, modern government and modern views, on the other. [1972, p. 4]

Third, the enormous and unprecedented gaps between rich and poor countries are accompanied by widening gaps between nations in the South. To quote Kuznets once more:

The organization of mankind into nations, and the multiplicity of nations, implies emphasis on the nation's interest as the overriding priority and permits a divisive cumulation of heritage of past history among nations. The gap is thus not merely between the aggregative and structural aspects of economic and social performance of two large groups within the world population, but between the two groups, subdivided into many relatively independent and differing units [1972, p. 5].

A fourth stylized fact is that the international size distribution of income and real consumption per capita is more unequal between countries than within the majority of countries in the North and South (Jolly, 1974; Kravis, 1973).

Fifth, these differences in incomes and real consumption patterns not only reflect financial flows but are also probably related to physical dimensions such as food, clothing, health, and education. That is, they are linked to differences in human welfare and the incidence of poverty.

Sixth, international inequality is probably a major cause of intranational inequality, though it is difficult to specify the exact nature of the causal connection. Thus, specific conditions governing the structure and functioning of the international economic order prevent countries from adopting policies designed to achieve progress that includes redistributive policies.

Since the domestic impact of international inequality is particularly felt in trading, investment and monetary relationships, as well as in the areas of technology and economic power, it is understandable that countries of the South have made some of these specific areas of concern in trying to improve their leverage with the North. Further, causality helps to explain why intranational policies for equitable growth are unlikely to affect international inequality by themselves. The empirical evidence also indicates that the absolute gap between North and South is likely to continue well into the future.

The issue can be conceptualized in terms of a matrix of inequality which is explained by three basic propositions: (1) inequality in the international relationships between North and South is evident; (2) domestic or intra-national inequality is evident in the relations between individuals and groups within nations; (3) there is some relationship between these two types of inequality with a stronger tendency for international inequality to cause intranational inequality than vice versa.

Seventh, the various forms of inequality evidenced by aggregate and structural gaps are closely related to and probably caused by international differences in world resource use and political and economic power (Knorr, 1975; Best, 1976; Sunkel, 1973).

So far we have attempted to highlight the major structural dimensions of global inequality. Although the list is by no means exhaustive, it helps to explain the issues shaping the confrontation and the South's adamant demands for equity in international economic relations. The call for a new world economic order has arisen from the need to move away from unequal partnership to a more mature, interdependent relationship. Ali Mazrui (1975) characterizes this as a movement from hierarchical relationships of the old economic order to the "sophisticated symmetry of mature interdependence" which represents the new international economic order.

An essential objective is to create conditions which will permit the nations of the South to raise the standard of well-being of their peoples. This goal is not so much idealistic humanitarianism as a political interest of most countries of the South. This politicization reflects the common desire of Southern countries to bring global attention to their problems and to reinforce their common efforts by working closely together. Those who eschew politicization of development contend that it increases difficulties and alters the nature of international deliberations on development. The nations of the South, however, are more interested in pressing their interests from a position of maturity. The crux of the matter is that development is no longer the exclusive concern of economic experts, but has now become part of the subject matter of politics.

The political drive for development promises increased political action by the South to deal with internal economic and social changes which most likely contribute to economic progress. But resolution of these fundamental internal problems largely depends on the structure and functioning of the international economic order, and specifically the nature of relationships governing transfers of trade, investment, and technology. These items were listed in the 1974 UN Declaration and we now turn our attention to some of them. We concentrate our remarks on the call for industrialization, technological transfer, trade and commercial policies, and reparations. Each of these deserves independent analysis; however, we offer some brief comments on some of the more important areas of contention.

Some Specific Issues

Balanced Industrial Development

The call for diversified and complete industrialization by the nations of the South is based on their determination to broaden their development base, with a concomitant lessening of their dependence on primary products. This involves increasing the production of manufactured and semimanufactured goods. The underlying philosophy defines modernization or progress as synonymous with industrialization. Industrialization would help the process of modernization by contributing to the production and processing of primary products and by providing products necessary to meet rising consumption and investment needs.

Industrialization and attendant changes in international division of labor and specialization are likely to prove beneficial to both the less developed nations and the world community as a whole. Their increased participation in production of manufactures is likely to bring handsome dividends to these countries because of buoyant international market conditions. There is also reason to believe that as the South industrializes, the more developed North will gain more than it loses. Achieving such a non-zero-sum outcome, however, will depend on the acceptance of certain international adjustments. The speed and nature of such adjustments will in the final analysis depend on certain needed changes in Northern attitudes, beginning with a commitment to policies designed to change the structure of international production.

The call for diversified industrialization should not be interpreted to mean a deemphasis of the primary sector. The long debate on the relative merits of agriculture and industry in the development process has now subsided. For useful summaries see Flanders, 1970; Little et al., 1970; and Healey, 1972. Assuming no unfavorable resource constraints, a modernized primary sector could help to speed up industrialization and development by creating relevant linkage effects.

While consensus exists about the means of helping less developed countries industrialize, the focus on measures to effect change must be sharpened. The heightening of this focus could be considered an achievement of the UN Declaration.

Technological Transfer

There is general agreement that technology has a central role to play in the improvement of economic conditions. It helps in the attainment of more rapid economic growth and an improved standard of living, and therefore helps a country to avoid the sacrifice and time usually necessary to achieve a self-sustained rate of economic growth. Conventionally, the contention is that the South can avoid or reduce the sacrifices and the time span required to achieve a satisfactory level of development by making use of modern technology.

The idea is that there is now a larger inventory or pool of technology on which the South can draw than there was in the nineteenth century when the Northern countries began their industrialization process. The underlying argument is that if this existing body of knowledge were made available, these countries would progress much more rapidly. Further, in a world of dynamically changing technology, a less developed country which fails to import technology would probably find itself behind in the industrialization race. Transfer and use of the most modern technology is therefore necessary for rapid industrialization. However, there are serious problems surrounding the issue of technological transfer, related to technological appropriateness and technological adaptation.

While the pace of industrialization is related to the nature of investment programs and associated management and technological factors, special consideration must be given to the resource endowments of individual countries. There is a difference between North and South in the relative availability of capital, labor and other productive factors. The modern technology developed for advanced Northern countries may therefore be inappropriate to the conditions and needs of the South.

Whether or not technology is transferred, there are real problems related to its choice. Aside from time dimensions, gestation periods and durability of processes, the saving and investment potentials of alternative technologies will have to be carefully investigated within the context of national development. In this context, countries would have to pay attention to the positive or negative employment effects of a new technology, and its foreign exchange cost and scale effects.

Problems are also posed by diversity in technological typologies and transfers. In this context, the distinction between vertical and horizontal transfers (Mansfield, 1975) is apposite. The resource and other costs are much greater when both types of transfers are involved (as is likely to be the case) than if the transfer is mainly of one type. Further, a distinction must be drawn between general technology and system-specific technology. In addition, several phases of the transfer process—material, design and capacity—have to be distinguished.

The transfer process is further complicated by the need for adaptation. In Mansfield's worlds:

The technology that is transferred must often be adapted, if it is to meet the needs of the recipient. Because markets in the recipient country are smaller, because input prices are different, because the vendor infrastructure is different with regard to capability, cost and quality, because of national differences in task, climate, and so forth, the technology must be adapted. [1975, p. 373]

The transfer of technology through adaptation is by no means without costs. Besides the costs of adapting the foreign technology to local conditions, there are direct or implicit payments for patents or licensing rights, the real costs following from restrictions, licensing and other agreements and foreign exchange constraints. It is interesting to note that at the UNCTAD, two resolutions on technological transfer were adopted by consensus. These addressed the need to modify the international system of industrial property, particularly patents, and to establish an international code of conduct for technological transfer.

In any event, it is much more difficult for less developed countries to achieve technological change than it is for their more developed counterparts. Whether technological change takes the form of adaptation or the use of an indigenous process, pervasive and profound departures from previous techniques are necessary. Old techniques may be rooted in cultural traditions, and their change may call for fundamental societal adjustments. The change may also call for factor reversals, such as capital-intensive rather than labor-intensive forms of investment, especially when the technology is transferred. Finally, research to find the most appropriate techniques (middle or intermediate technology), or to refine and adapt the appropriate techniques may prove difficult and expensive. The urgency and practical importance of this issue was also recognized at UNCTAD IV, which resolved to strengthen the technological capabilities of the South.

Trade and Commercial Policy

The issues surrounding the need to rationalize trade between North and South and the integration of the South into world trading patterns have received the most extensive treatment in the literature. (See, for example, Johnson, 1967; Di Marco, 1972; Dadone and Di Marco, 1972; Pinto and Knakal, 1972; Meier, 1975; Little, Scitovsky, and Scott, 1970.) Many of the anomalies of the present system of global trading relationships spring from the successful concentration by Northern nations on carrying out a more open trading system among themselves through successive negotiations on trade liberalization. Southern countries were, for example, little involved in the six rounds of tariff cutting negotiations under the GATT since 1947. These touched their interests only marginally.

What is significant about the declaration of a new world economic order is the interest of the Southern countries in working out their aspirations for economic progress through greater and more stable access to the markets of the industrialized North. In doing so they are forcefully raising the old issue of better integration of their trade and investment into the global pattern of relationships which has evolved among industrial countries. Endemic in their determination for hard bargaining to gain trade and development advantages are certain broad philosophical issues related to development strategy as well as others of more practical significance.

A prime issue is the relative importance of "outward-looking" versus "inward-looking" strategies for development. The emphasis was formerly on import substitution rather than export promotion. Despite the theoretical merits of import substitution, empirical studies (Little, Scitovsky, and Scott, 1970), have shown the results of the inward-looking strategies to be perverse. Import substitution may have been pushed too far because it intensified foreign exchange constraints, produced a distortion of prices by varying the prices of stimulated manufactures relative to the prices of outputs from other sectors, and generally led to increased unemployment and inequality.

The deemphasis of import substitutions and the new stress of export promotion again brings to a head considerations of the relative merits of "inward-looking" versus "outward-looking" approaches. Representative arguments for each side can be found in Streeten (1975), and Ranis (1972).

Sir Arthur Lewis, for example, feels that the problem facing the South perhaps springs from the lopsided notion of interdependence, especially because of the policies of the North. As he stated in the IEA Conference:

As an advocate of the angels, [he] would suggest that underdeveloped countries had all they needed for fast growth. They had surpluses of raw materials and fuel; could produce food; could acquire manufacturing skills; and could save if they needed to. Therefore one could say that it need make no difference to them in the long run whether or not all developed countries sank under the sea. There would be immediate losses. For example, terms of trade would change. However, underdeveloped countries would then discover that they could use their own resources, save for themselves and educate themselves. They would find that they could grow just as fast as they had done *with* the developed countries. So what had been historically true need be true no longer. [Ranis, 1972, p. 50]

I cannot tell whether this reflects Sir Arthur's current views on the problem. However, his view was then that less developed countries were expending too much effort in attempting to improve trade and other relationships with Northern countries, when it might have been better for them to concentrate on vital issues of internal development. Others see the problem as related to internal problems of corruption, class division, inequality and backwash effects.

We do not necessarily disagree with Lewis and others who argue for inward-looking strategies. These authors would undoubtedly still support some combination of intranational and international structure reforms. However, the question of deciding on an optimal mix of policies and the emphases to be placed on variables which have international import remains. The answer depends on a view of the direction and strength of causation from international to intranational inequality.

Some commentators feel that there are limited possibilities for the transformation of the international economic order, and by implication, for the economic transformation of the South within the international capitalist framework (Wallerstein, 1974). Some of them advocate a strategy of disengagement, where the South breaks its traditional links with the international capitalist system.

A strategy of disengagement could take several forms, ranging from severing relationships with the international capitalist system to changing the internal system of economic relations. It is obvious, however, that while countries of the South would like to break the traditional ties of dependence and unequal partnership with the North, the guiding principle behind their action is the need to increase rather than reduce trade with capitalist countries. Domestically, while the call for the new world economic order certainly implies that Southern countries pursue whatever developmental policies they deem fit, the emphasis on rapid industrialization and the attendant technological and investment transfers seems to imply increasing reliance on the capitalist mode of production. To the extent that the call for a new international economic order implies closer ties with the capitalist world, it might be useful to ascertain the number of Third World countries who, while calling for a change in the structure of international economic relationships, are actually increasing their ties with the socialist bloc or socializing their internal production processes or both.

Insofar as some concept of disengagement is implicit in the North–South dialogue, it should not carry a connotation of total break but should be interpreted in a weaker sense. In this context it refers to the South's call for changing the structure of traditional economic relationships. In a real sense this might involve disengagement from the old order and reengagement of a new order. However, this demands from Northern countries such radical departures from their traditional position that they may prefer to disengage themselves further from the South. This possibility is explored later in the paper.

We now comment briefly on two specific trade measures—the Generalized System of Preferences (GSP) and cartelization. As is well known, the GSP grew out of an initial attempt to mitigate the imbalance in the structure of trading relationships between North and South. However, it has had limited effects to date (Meier, 1974; Bronfenbrenner, 1976). The GSP probably needs to be integrated with the broader context of world trading relationships designed to produce a more open world economy, and where trade barriers are reduced in those areas where Southern countries have a clear comparative advantage. The need to integrate the GSP into a more open world economy has been recently addressed by Bronfenbrenner (1976).

Another issue relates to the quest for commodity power and resource diplomacy through the formation of cartels and other producers' associations in the South. These are, of course, spin-offs from the OPEC oil model, and reflect the use by Southern nations of their ownership and control of primary resources as tools of foreign economic policy. This in turn reflects the economic plight these countries face. They have made very limited progress in diversifying and expanding their production base and therefore must continue to depend on exports of primary commodities for the bulk of their income. Added to this must be their frustration over the failure of efforts to work out suitable commodity agreements, to increase their effective participation in world trade, and to increase the flow of capital and technical assistance.

These factors provide grist for the mill of the politicization of development mentioned earlier. The combination of these factors, the fortuitous circumstances facing commodity markets in the early 1970s, and the successful lead provided by the OPEC situation help to explain why the nations of the South could attempt to manipulate markets on a sustained basis to obtain prices well above competitive levels.

The move to establish commodity cartels grew out of this process. Following the OPEC lead were a number of producer associations—bauxite, phosphates, copper, tin, and bananas, to mention a few. We must now examine whether the prospects for world commodity markets justify confidence in the long run survival of sellers' markets. This question has been fully discussed in a number of recent writings (Bergsten, 1973, 1974, 1975; Varon and Takeuchi, 1974; Takeuchi and Varon, 1975; Mikesell, 1974; Stern and Tims, 1975; and Fried, 1976). The comments which follow draw heavily from these sources.

Economists usually cite four preconditions for successful cartels: (1) the demand for the commodity must be relatively inelastic, that is, insensitive to price changes—price rises must not be accompanied by excessive reductions in demand, and the possibility of substituting alternative commodities, especially from noncartel sources, must remain limited; (2) supply must be relatively inelastic—this requires that (3) the supply be controlled by a small number of producers (in the limiting case by one), and (4) members of the cartel must have the capacity for concerted collusive behavior and the financial capability needed to accumulate stocks and to forego export earnings under surplus conditions.

We must then determine whether these prospective conditions exist. The arguments on both sides are equally strong, but the negative arguments seem to be gaining ground. Those who, like Bergsten, pose an optimistic outlook for seller's markets base their contention on two trends. The first is the replacement of buyers' markets by sellers' markets and its attendant causes. One explanation is provided by the alleged relationship between commodity price increases and inflation, as exemplified in the writings of some Brookings panelists (Bosworth, 1973; Cooper and Lawrence, 1975).

While the nature and direction of causation cannot be precisely established in this case, the evidence suggests that the rise in commodity prices was at least partially responsible for triggering global inflation. This in turn produced further speculation in commodities, partly because of a loss of faith in currencies as a result of the introduction of flexible exchange rates. The increasing confidence in commodities rather than paper money produced a commodity-price spiral which lent strong support to the wage-price and profit-price spirals as essential ingredients in the world inflationary spiral.

To the extent that the arguments stated above are correct, the seller's side of the market has been strengthened. Under such circumstances, producers were provided with a favorable environment for group pressure, price leadership and other conditions necessary for raising prices further. Whether these conditions will continue to exist in the long run or whether their incidence was merely transitory must remain a matter of judgment, although, as we shall see, some economists support the latter.

The second major trend concerns the success of OPEC and the possibilities it holds for the development of similar models. Those who view the potential success of OPEC-type cartels pessimistically (Mikesell, 1974; Fried, 1976), use as arguments the relative insignificance of primary commodities in world markets and the powerlessness of producers. In the case of commodities, statistics show exports of raw materials as a relatively small proportion of world commodity exports, with a predominant position for fuels (mostly oil) and foodstuffs, and a relatively unimportant position for nonfuel minerals and other raw materials. While existence of these conditions certainly points to a potential for increased trade, they reflect limited commodity power.

Further, another stylized fact is that the flow of trade in primary commodities between Northern countries (both socialist and nonsocialist) is significantly greater than that between North and South. The South predominates in few cases.

The work of Takeuchi and Varon (1974, 1975) demonstrates that the long term prospects for successful cartelization of most primary commodities other than oil are less than favorable. Favorable prospects appear to exist for a few raw materials such as bauxite, copper, rubber, tin and hard fibers. Although production and export activity is concentrated in the hands of a few producers, whether they are in sufficient control of the factors which maintain buoyant sellers' markets is questionable. These factors may be nonexistent because of the weak financial status of these countries, the possibility of competition from substitutes from noncartel sources, and the potentially large supplies from other sources. Most of these commodities, with the possible exception of bauxite, also face a slow growth in demand.

In conclusion, while the South's attempt to regulate commodity markets by price manipulation, indexation and other schemes poses the most knotty problems for development policy, it should be interpreted as a part of the overall quest of these countries for a greater symmetry in world economic relationships. Well-conceived commodity schemes could dampen the extreme price fluctuations that have characterized commodity markets. However, these countries might realize greater long-term benefits from improved schemes for compensatory and supplementary financing.

In the final analysis, one's view of the issues very much depends on the notion of progress to which one subscribes. Conservatives continue to call for a return to free trade and nonintervention in the world market mechanism. More enlightened liberals support minor adjustments at the margin of the functioning of the international markets. Both positions have received extensive treatment in the literature. See, for example, the discussions by Strassmann (1976) and Wall (1972) of the Chicago approach to economic development, and Meier (1968) and Bauer (1972).

By contrast the reform proposals emanating from the South deny the efficacy of free trade or schemes for piecemeal international economic engineering. As such, they are designed to bring about total structural transformation of global economic relationships. This clash between opposing ideologies of development defines, to some extent, the nature of the confrontation. The fact that the confrontation shows signs of softening into a dialogue reflects the emergence of some framework for accommodation.

Reparations

In this section we offer some exploratory comments on the developing nations' call for compensation on account of the allegedly abusive exploitation of their resources by the Northern nations. Because it departs radically from the norm of demands, this call has met tremendous resistance from academic and government communities. Professor Bronfenbrenner not only refers to it euphemistically as the "reparations syndrome," but further dubs a part of the call a "Nazi 'World Order.' " (1976, p. 827)

The diplomacy of research (see Myrdal, 1968, 1975) has historically situated scholars at diverse epistemological and ontological positions, and in the limiting case, at opposite ends of the spectrum. A scholar's reaction to Bronfenbrenner's harsh language depends on his position on the ontological spectrum. While one may question the economic, political, or ideological motivations of Third World protagonists, one could instead dispassionately analyze their views. Three types of questions could then be raised. The first is whether there is any sound basis, theoretical or otherwise, for speaking about the collective debts of the more developed countries to the less developed countries. If so, then a second question is whether the debt could be estimated quantitatively. The third question is the more mundane one of imputing responsibility for the debt burden. Should it be borne by citizens, corporations, governments or other collectivities of the North? In answering these questions, we draw on approaches developed by Brown (1972), America (1972), and Marketti (1972) to the issue of reparations to Black America.

From a historical perspective, the issue of reparations has received attention at least three times in the past. Reparations were involved to some extent in US payments to defeated economies in Europe after both World Wars. There were German reparations to Israel after the Second World War. Domestically, we could refer to the Federal Statute (1946) setting up the Indian Claims Commission. The Commission was empowered to adjudicate and resolve claims arising from seizure of Indian property and breaches of status by the United States (Browne, 1972, p. 40). The appeal to historical precedent is a justification of Third World claims. The issues are different, but the existence of precedents certainly does not harm their case.

In the search for a theoretical basis for reparations, the claim could be made that international economic disparity should be viewed in historical perspective, and as such could be interpreted as the result of past exploitation of one group of nations or peoples by another group. This exploitation encompassed both human and material resources, both of which caused net income and wealth transfers to the more developed nations.

Conceptually, this gave rise to two distinct elements of debt. First, there was an immeasurable social indebtedness, or moral debt, which represents potential compensation for the psychic and cultural effects of past relations.

One element in this case is the compensation for various forms of mistreatment which caused death or injury to forebears. The second element—net economic or financial debt—allegedly results from net income and wealth transfers, sanctioned by certain legal and official economic arrangements during the days of slavery and after. Thus if we ignore the problem of potential compensation for loss due to human degradation, the issue is then to establish the factual basis of the claim that income and wealth transfers did not spring from past economic arrangements.

The next question concerns reparations for the exploitation of human resources through the unpaid labor of slave ancestors. Income was diverted from the South to the North through de jure slavery before emancipation and de factor slavery through colonial relationships of the post-Emancipation period. Another element of reparations is the hypothetical share of international wealth and income which the poor countries would now have, had they been treated more justly (Browne, 1972).

With the human resources component all we can do is point to some alternative methods of computing it. For example, the method used for calculating "unpaid black equity" by Marketti (1972) is an interesting one. Using the human capital concept and historical data on slave prices and the slave population, he arrived at the unpaid equity in the slave industry by computing the present value of the income streams which owners received from slave labor, using alternative rates of interest. Using slave prices as proxies for the present value of the exploited net income stream returned on slave capital from 1790 to 1860, he derives an implicit net income flow on which he compounds interest. He estimates the current compounded value of labor exploited from slaves at between $448 billion and $995 billion.

Browne (1972, p. 42) suggests estimating the income flow due to slave labor based on wage rates paid to labor engaged in comparable work. After the necessary adjustments for maintenance costs, the present value of the unpaid wage bill could be calculated, using appropriate interest rates.

Because of my unfamiliarity with the body of knowledge and writings on slavery in the Third World, I cannot comment on the suitability of the methods proposed by Marketti and Browne for studying that situation. However, where data is available, research on these problems might provide useful results. The same kind of analysis could be extended to the study of the post-Emancipation period. In other words, it may be possible to estimate the unpaid wage bill which accrued to plantation owners as a result of the underpayment of freemen after emancipation. The continued interest in problems connected with the profitability of slavery and the upsurge of interest in cliometric research by North American scholars certainly suggest Third World emphases.

However, unlike Black America, the Third World's claim for reparations is based on the unrequited earnings springing from exploitation of material resources. The present value of such an income stream might include, among other things, the net capitalized value of agricultural land or agricultural products or both, after raw materials and minerals have been extracted.

While the reparations problem seems to present interesting theoretical and research possibilities, there are knottier problems relating to the sharing of the debt burden between governments, corporations or citizens in the industrialized countries. Only in this limited area do Professor Bronfenbrenner's comments seem to raise the correct issues.

References

Adelman, Irma (1974), "Strategies for Equitable Growth," *Challenge* (June 1974): 37–44.

_____ (1975), "Development Economics—A Re-Assessment of Goals," *American Economic Review, Papers and Proceedings* (May 1975): 302–309.

_____ and C. Taft Morris (1973), *Economic Growth and Social Equity in Developing Countries* (Stanford: Stanford University Press).

America, Richard (1972), "A New Rationale for Income Redistribution," *Review of Black Political Economy* 2(2): 3-21.

Bauer, Peter T. (1972), *Dissent on Development: Studies and Debates in Development Economics* (Cambridge, Mass.: Harvard University Press).

Beckerman, W. and Bacon, R. (1970), "The International Distribution of Incomes," in *Unfashionable Economics: Essays in Honor of Lord Balogh* (London: Weidenfeld and Nicholson), 56-74.

Bergsten, C. Fred (1973), "The Threat from the Third World," *Foreign Affairs* (Summer 1973).

_____ (1974), "The New Era in World Commodity Markets," *Challenge* 17(4): 34-42.

_____ (1975), "The U.S. Must Deal with other Cartels," *New York Times* (June 1, 1975).

_____ and Cline, W.R. (1976), "Increasing International Economic Interdependence: the implications for research," *American Economic Review, Papers and Proceedings* 66(2): 155-161.

Best, Michael (1976), "Uneven Development and Dependent Market Economies," *American Economic Review, Papers and Proceedings* 66(2): 136-141.

Bosworth, Barry (1973), "The Current Inflation: Malign or Neglect?" *Brookings Papers on Economic Activity* (1): 263-283.

Bronfenbrenner, Martin (1973), "Equality and Equity," *Annals of the American Academy of Political and Social Science* 409: 9-23.

_____ (1976), Review Article, "Predatory Poverty on the Offensive: the UNCTAD Record," *Economic Development and Cultural Change* 24(4): 825-831.

Browne, Robert (1972), "The Economic Case for Reparations to Black America," *American Economic Review, Papers and Proceedings* 62(2): 39-46.

Chenery, Hollis B. et al. (1974), *Redistribution with Growth* (New York: Oxford University Press).

Cooper, Richard C. and Lawrence, Roger Z. (1975), "The 1972-75 Commodity Boom," *Brookings Papers on Economic Activity* (3): 671-723.

Dadone, A.A. and Di Marco, L.E. (1972), "The Impact of Prebisch's Ideas on Modern Economic Analysis," in *International Economics and Development: Essays in Honor of Raul Prebisch,* ed. L.E. Di Marco (New York: Academic Press), pp. 15-34.

David, W.L. (1976), "Welfare Economics, Political Philosophy and World Economic Welfare," Fisk University (mimeo).

Di Marco, L.E. (1972), *International Economics and Development: Essays in Honor of Raul Prebisch* (New York: Academic Press).

Flanders, M.J. (1969), "Agriculture versus Industry in Development Policy: the Planner's Dilemma Re-Examined," *Journal of Development Studies* 5(3).

Franks, Oliver (1959), "The New International Balance: Challenge in the Western World," Address before the Trustees of the Committee for Economic Development," reported in *Saturday Review* (Jan. 16, 1960); cited in *Re-Assessing the North-South Economic Relations* (Washington, D.C.: The Brookings Institution, 1970).

Fried, Edward R. (1976), "International Trade in Raw Materials: Myths and Realities," *General Series Reprint* No. 314 (Washington, D.C.: The Brookings Institution.

Healey, Derek T. (1972), "Development Policy: New Thinking about an Interpretation," *Journal of Economic Literature* 10(2): 757-797.

Heilbroner, Robert L. (1974), *An Inquiry into the Human Prospect* (New York: W.W. Norton).

Howe, James W. et al. (1975), *The U.S. and World Development: Agenda for Action* (New York: Praeger Publishers).

Johnson, Harry G. (1967), *Economic Policies toward Less Developed Countries* (New York: Praeger Publishers).

Jolly, Richard (1974), "International Dimensions," in *Redistribution with Growth,* ed. H.B. Chenery et al. (New York: Oxford University Press), pp. 158-180.

Knorr, Klaus (1975), *The Power of Nations: The Political Economy of International Relations* (New York: Basic Books).

Kravis, Irving B. (1973), "A World of Unequal Incomes," *Annals of the American Academy of Political and Social Science,* pp. 61-80.

Kuznets, Simon (1972), "The Gap: Concept, Measurement and Trends," in *The Gap between Rich and Poor Nations,* ed. G. Ranis (New York: St. Martin's Press), pp. 2-43.

Little, I.M.D., Scitovsky, T. and Scott, M. (1970), *Industry and Trade in Some Developing Countries* (New York: Oxford University Press).

Mansfield, Edwin (1975), "International Technology Transfer: Forms, Resource Requirements, and Policies," *American Economic Review, Papers and Proceedings* 65(2): 372-76.

Marketti, Jim (1972), "Black Equity in the Slave Industry," *Review of Black Political Economy* 2(2): 43-66.

Mazrui, Ali A. (1975), "The New Interdependence: From Hierarchy to Symmetry," in *The U.S. and World Development, Agenda for Action, 1975,* ed. James Howe (New York: Praeger Publishers), pp. 118-34.

Meier, Gerald M. (1968), "Free Trade and Development Economics," in *Value, Capital and Growth: Essays in Honor of Sir John Hicks,* ed. J.N. Wolfe (Endenburg: Endenburg University Press), pp. 385-414.

_____ (1974), *Problems of Co-operation for Development* (New York: Oxford University Press).

Mikesell, Raymond (1974), "More Third World Cartels Ahead?" *Challenge* 17(5): 24-31.

Myrdal, Gunnar (1968), *Asian Drama: An Inquiry into the Poverty of Nations,* Vol. I (New York: Twentieth Century Fund and Penguin).

_____ (1975), *Against the Stream: Critical Essays in Economics* (New York: Vintage Books).

Pinto, A. and J. Knakal (1972), "The Center-Periphery System 20 years later," in *International Economics and Development: Essays in Honor of Raul Prebisch* (New York: Academic Press), pp. 97-128.

Ranis, Gustav, ed. (1972), *The Gap Between Rich and Poor Nations* (New York: St. Martin's Press).

Seers, Dudley (1969), "The Meaning of Development," *International Development Review* 9(4): 2-6; reprinted in *The Political Economy of Development and Underdevelopment,* ed. Charles K. Wilber (New York: Random House, 1973), pp. 6-14.

Stern, E. and Tims, W. (1975), "Relative Bargaining Strengths of the Developing Countries," *American Journal of Agricultural Economics* (May 1975).

Strassmann, W.P. (1976), "Development Economics from a Chicago Perspective," *Journal of Economic Issues* 10(1): 63-80.

Streeten, P.P., ed. (1972a), *Trade Strategies for Development* (New York: Halstead Press).

_____ (1972b), *New Frontiers of Development Studies* (New York: Halstead Press).

Sunkel, Osvaldo (1973), "Transnational Capitalism and National Disintegration in Latin America," *Social and Economic Studies* 21(1), special issue on "Dependence and Underdevelopment in the New World," ed. N. Girvan.

Takeuchi, K. and Varon, B. (1975), "Commodity Shortages and Changes in World Trade," *Annals of the American Academy of Political and Social Science* 420: 46-59.

United Nations, General Assembly (1975), "Declaration on the Establishment of a New World Economic Order," Program for Action on the Establishment of a New International Economic Order," (May 9, 1974)"; Charter on Economic Rights and Duties of States," (December 12, 1974); Seventh Special Session, UN General Assembly, resolutions adopted in September 1975.

Varon, B. and Takeuchi, K. (1974), "Developing Countries and Non-Fuel Minerals," *Foreign Affairs* 52(3): 497–510.

Wall, David, ed. (1972), *Chicago Essays in Economic Development* (Chicago: University of Chicago Press, 1972).

Wallerstein, Immanuel (1974), "Dependence and an Interdependent World: The limited possibilities of transformation within the Capitalist World Economy," *African Studies Review* (April 1974).

4

The Financial Challenge of the New International Economic Order

Karel Holbik[a]

Among the forces which have shaped and changed the structure of international economic relations since 1945, those emanating from the new role of the developing countries—the Third World—have come to play an exceptionally significant role. The aspirations, complaints and programs of these countries will apparently exert substantial influence on international trade, finance and monetary systems and related policies.

The developing countries have spelled out their expectations for cooperation with the developed world in several conferences and documents which include the International Development Strategy of 1970, The Declaration and Programme of Action on the Establishment of a New International Economic Order (1974), the Charter of Economic Rights and Duties of States (1974) and the resolutions of the seventh Special Session of the UN General Assembly (1974).

The developing countries want to obtain a higher degree of control over their economic destiny by rearranging world trade, monetary and financial systems and restructuring many international institutions which have allegedly been managed and manipulated for the benefit of the rich nations and at the expense of the poor ones. The changes envisioned by the aforementioned documents include tariff reductions on developing countries' exportables, buffer stocks, price indexing, compensatory financing arrangements, producers' associations, distribution of international reserves, and the creation of additional sources of development financing, to cite the most important propositions.

While the Third World countries generally recognize that they themselves bear the primary responsibility for their economic emancipation and modernization, they also admit that the realization of their economic goals is predicated on the cooperation of the developed nations.

To economists concerned with international economic analysis and policy, the most interesting, and perhaps the most intriguing, aspect of the new evolving relationship between the developed and developing countries is the latter's view of both international financial relations and the innovations necessary in the trade and monetary systems.

---

[a]The views expressed in this chapter are the author's and are not necessarily those held by the United Nations.

The developing countries believe that the present financial and monetary organization is not equipped to deal with their economic problems; in fact, it has failed to further their development objectives. Their recent balance-of-payments deficits and deteriorating terms of trade furnish plentiful evidence of the Third World's vulnerability to economic instability (recessions), to inflationary pressures from the industrial nations, and to their own generally weak economic structures. These countries point out also—it seems, bitterly—that the existing international financial organizations and cooperations have obstructed their economic progress because the Third World has been granted neither the amount of official foreign aid it needs nor access to sufficient private foreign capital.

In addition, the present international financial and monetary arrangements (capital movements, international liquidity, exchange rate system) do not properly recognize the interdependence between the balance-of-payments finance and development finance; even more damaging to the developing countries, these arrangements deprive the Third World of a balance-of-payments adjustment process that would free it of heavy international indebtedness. The developing countries, especially the oil-importing ones, have therefore concluded that their short- as well as long-run prospects are poor, and perhaps disturbing, unless the existing international financial aid and monetary organization is reformed to become more equitable.

In the Third World there appears to be a consensus not only that international financial cooperation has reached a critical point but also that a change in international economic relations that supports the reforms the developing countries seek is a historical *sine qua non.*

The Third World's conviction that it is undeservedly and unfairly victimized by economic processes taking place in the industrialized countries finds expression, first of all, in the developing nations' assessment of inflation. They consider current inflationary pressures the result of secular inflationary tendencies which originate in and are transmitted from the developed market economies. The industrial nations are held explicitly responsible for the existing worldwide inflation.

Unquestionably, the Third World's terms of trade have been worsening historically because of inflation and the continuous rise in the prices of (imported) manufactures on the one hand, and the comparatively slow advance in the prices of most (exported) primary commodities on the other hand. While the prices of manufactures are known for their downward inflexibility—reflecting institutional organization such as industrial concentration, oligopolistic business structures, import protection, and unionization—the prices of most raw materials are highly flexible because of their sensitivity to changes in aggregate demand of the developed nations, among other things. Thus most business cycles bring about smaller gains for the producers of primary goods than for the suppliers of manufactures. (Wide fluctuations in primary goods prices do, however, influence the prices of manufactured goods.) The price disadvantage of the oil-importing developing countries has also been magnified in recent years by both the quadrupling of oil prices and substantial rises in the prices of imported cereals. Unavoidably, this price assymetry eventually results in balance-of-payments deficits of the Third World, especially when its exports decrease. Furthermore, higher long-term rates of inflation cause the export proceeds of primary goods producers to decline even more.

The present recession illustrates the tendency of the terms of trade to decline during the downswing of the cycle. This is demonstrated in table 4-1. While commodity prices (excluding petroleum) declined by 22.5 percent between their peak in April 1974 and April 1975, the prices of manufactured exports from the OECD countries rose by 23 percent in 1974. During the same period, decreases in the prices of vegetable oilseeds and oils, agricultural raw materials, and ores and metals approached 40 percent. (See table 4-2.) Only the prices of foodstuffs, particularly of cereals, remained at high levels (until the end of 1974).

As long as the existing international monetary arrangements as well as the framework for the international transmission of economic forces remain, the condition of the developing world cannot improve and the prospects for its steady economic growth will remain dim since international payments deficits generally depress the level of investment. Neither does it augur well for the Third World that established economic linkages (industrial as well as monetary) among the developed market economies have become the source and cause of built-in inflationary tendencies. Consequently, it is not possible to refute the developing countries' argument that international and their own economic stability calls for coordination of national demand management policies, or in other words, coordinated international economic stabilization.

In addition to inflation, the developing countries share the industrial world's recession. Coping with this also requires exceptional measures, especially if the developed market economies are relatively slow in recovering and restoring full

Table 4-1
Terms of Trade Index, 1972-1975
(1972 = 100)

	Actual		Projected	
	1972	*1973*	*1974*	*1975*
All developing countries				
(87 in sample)	100	108	186	176
Major petroleum exporters	100	110	311	301
Major fast-growing exporters				
of manufactures	100	106	99	92
All other developing countries	100	107	110	97

Source: United Nations Conference on Trade and Development.

Table 4–2

Prices of Primary Commodities and Manufactures: Coefficients of Variation, 1950–1974

(Percentage)

	Coefficient of Variation
Food and beverages	
Cocoa	11.1
Coffee	6.1
Sugar	43.3
Wheat	6.2
Rice	5.8
Beef	6.6
Bananas	3.7
Vegetable oilseeds and oils	
Copra	5.5
Coconut oil	4.4
Palm oil	4.7
Groundnuts	4.9
Groundnut oil	4.9
Soybeans	4.6
Soybean oil	5.8
Linseed	7.2
Agricultural raw materials	
Cotton	8.3
Jute	3.0
Sisal	8.3
Wool	6.2
Rubber	6.2
Ores and metals	
Copper	3.5
Lead	5.6
Zinc	3.8
Tin	2.6
Iron ore	5.4
Exports of manufactures from developed countries	2.3

Source: International Bank for Reconstruction and Development, United Nations Conference on Trade and Development, United Nations.

employment. The Third World countries consider some accommodating financial flows as the most promising means of countering the external developments that aggravate their balance-of-payments disequilibria. To finance these, the Third World cannot avail itself of either sufficient reserves or borrowing power (credit-worthiness) in international capital markets. The difficult question which the developing countries ask themselves may be formulated as follows: Shall we be expected to accumulate international liquidity and seek costly foreign loans simply because we cannot ward off the consequences of adverse developments in industrial countries? Aren't these latter economies responsible for correcting their internal imbalances?

The Third World's answer to such questions appears to be that the international financial and monetary systems should institute grant-like monetary flows (soft loans) to help these countries both overcome the stagnationist impact of the developed economies and maintain their own aggregate demand (for imports in particular), investment and national income. Economic stability in the developing countries would, after all, benefit the developed ones as well, by arresting the spread of contaminating deflationary pressures.

This also challenges and implicitly criticizes the existing international financial and monetary organization. The Third World calls for compensatory financial flows even if they do not reverse the payments disequilibria in the short and medium term. Like the IMF oil facility designed to finance the balance-of-payments deficits brought about by oil imports, similar facilities may be worth considering for other sources of deficits payments. It is noteworthy that the developing countries do not view exchange rate adjustments (depreciation) as a particularly useful policy for protecting either their import or export interests. These countries generally minimize the potential for corrective action of flexible exchange rates.

An important factor underlying the developing countries' criticism and the revisionist schemes for the international financial and monetary system is the declining contribution of the developed nations to development assistance, as reflected in tables 4-3 and 4-4.

Lagging official development aid (ODA) and the implied deficient cooperation between the "have" and "have-not" countries are responsible for the failure of many Third World nations to meet the economic growth targets envisioned in the Second UN Development Decade. In fact the beneficial effects of the rising nonconcessional flows (especially of the Eurocurrency credits) have been deprived of the supporting influence of the needed concessional (ODA) development assistance. Admittedly, only a relatively small number of creditworthy developing countries receive nonconcessional assistance and are not faced with the aid fatigue of most Western donors. Yet it is not necessarily the amount of aid that matters; the terms and continuity of external borrowing may be equally important to the developing countries, because these conditions determine, on the positive side, the rates of economic growth and export expansion, and on the negative side, the resulting debt burden (see table 4-5).

The unstable volume and unequal distribution of financial transfers have adversely affected both the balances of payments of Third World borrowers and their ability to meet debt-servicing obligations. Moreover, the creditor nations

Table 4–3

The Current Account Deficits of Non-Oil-Exporting Developing Countries and Their Financing: 1971, 1973 and 1974

(millions of dollars)

	1971		1973	1974	
Current account deficit	−13,157	(100%)	−11,315	−32,106	(100%)
Long-term financing, net	10,989	(85%)	21,885	28,408	(89%)
Official bilateral on ODA terms	4,056	(31%)	4,586	6,661	(21%)
DAC member countries	3,549	(27%)	3,712	4,629	(14%)
Developing countries	507	(4%)	874	2,032	(6%)
Other official bilateral	588	(5%)	1,423	2,183	(7%)
DAC member countries	574	(5%)	1,412	2,000	(6%)
Developing countries	14	(negl)	11	183	(0.6%)
Private flows from DAC member countries	4,370	(34%)	13,003	15,000	(47%)
Private overseas direct investment	1,726	(13%)	4,285	5,005	(16%)
Eurocurrency	1,000	(8%)	5,600	6,500	(20%)
Export credits	1,512	(12%)	500	1,495	(5%)
Other	132	(1%)	2,618	2,000	(6%)
Multilateral institutions	1,712	(13%)	1,807	4,011	(13%)
IMF oil facility				921	(3%)
Socialist countries	263	(2%)	1,066	553	(2%)
Changes in reserves (increased)	−835	(6%)	−7,538	1,516	(5%)
Short-term capital, unrecorded flows and errors and omissions	3,003 (23%)		−3,032	5,214	(16%)

Source: United Nations Conference on Trade and Development, and Organization for Economic Cooperation and Development.

have frequently dealt with the ensuing external imbalances and liquidity crises of the developing countries from a conventional commercial point of view and have disregarded the implications of these unfavorable situations for the borrowers' economic development. Traditionally, international debtors have been expected to deflate their economies, without being provided—as they should be—with financing which would enable them to overcome the balance-of-payments deficits. In terms of traditional economic analysis, countries with balance-of-payments deficits should seek correction at the expense of domestic production, consumption as well as imports, and therefore at the expense of economic growth.

This traditional approach to external balances of deficit countries does not differentiate between developed and developing economies. The Third World countries and the New International Economic Order find this explicitly objec-

Table 4-4

The Flows of Development Assistance

(millions of dollars)

Year	ODA		Nonconcessional Flows			Total Flows	
	Valued at Current Prices and Exchange Rates	*Valued at 1970 Prices and Exchange Rates*	*Bilateral Official (OOF)*	*Private Bilateral*	*Via Multilateral Institutions*	*Valued at Current Prices and Exchange Rates*	*Valued at 1970 Prices and Exchange Rates*
1961	5,151	6,190	719	3,016	320	9,205	11,131
1962	5,402	6,385	527	2,214	254	8,396	10,008
1963	5,728	6,676	240	2,590	−36	8,521	10,108
1971	7,691	7,174	989	7,308	1,042	17,030	15,991
1972	8,538	7,248	1,155	7,951	1,053	18,697	16,132
1973	9,376	6,259	2,073	10,849	619	22,917	16,116
Average annual rate of growth (percentage) 1961–1973	4.4	0.4	16.8	13.1	13.0	8.7	4.8

Source: United Nations.

Table 4-5
The Burden of Debt Servicing for 1973 (selected countries)

	Percent of GNP	*Percent of Exports*
Bolivia	3.9	18.1
Burma	0.9	16.3
Colombia	1.7	12.8
Congo	1.1	8.5
Ecuador	1.6	10.6
Egypt	4.2	31.5
Guatemala	1.8	10.5
India	1.1	24.1
Indonesia	1.3	8.0
Pakistan	2.1	25.0
Philippines	1.2	6.8
Sri Lanka	3.7	14.3
Tunisia	4.4	16.2
United Republic of Tanzania	2.5	9.6
Zaire	3.2	8.0

tionable and emphasize (1) the volatile nature of the developing countries' exports and export earnings; (2) the difficulty and the relatively high opportunity cost of any import reduction (magnified by import substitution); (3) the generally minimal capital resources (credit lines) to which developing countries have access to finance external imbalances; and (4) the meager international reserves at their disposal. When developing countries find themselves under balance-of-payments pressures, their development and any development programs they may have suffer. The Third World deplores the fact that the present international monetary organization and institutions do not consider properly and adequately the problems and idiosyncracies of the new countries and that they underestimate the adjustment processes. In the case of the Third World, adjustment is, as a rule, long-term rather than short-term. As a result, the Third World advocates a change in the international financial and monetary systems, even though some measures have recently been taken to accommodate their needs, such as the IMF Compensatory Financial Facility of 1963, the Extended Facility of 1974 and the SDRs as a source of international liquidity.

The difficulties of the developing countries would be further alleviated if the industrial nations continued to eliminate restrictions on their imports from the developing areas and if they did not employ stabilization policies which have a predictably negative effect on the Third World. Although the Third World could retaliate with protectionist measures, the developing countries would prefer to avoid economic protectionism since it would not bode well for either international trade or development. The developing countries resent the old view that they could naturally bear some of the brunt of the necessary international economic adjustment resulting from the ups and downs of the developed market economies.

A principal reason for the Third World's advocacy of the New International Economic Order is the developing countries' serious concern about their continuous deficits. The preceding commentary and illustrations have borne this out. The overriding objective of these countries is, therefore, to effect a restructuring of international trade and financial relations that will enable them to mold and eventually effectively control the economic forces that determine their welfare and advancement. Specifically, the Third World seeks to revise and amplify balance-of-payments finance, and to replace the "old" IMF institutional mechanism by new balance-of-payments adjustment techniques and processes in which the interests of development finance would be sufficiently heeded. Allegedly, the IMF system is unsatisfactory because it fails to differentiate between the balance-of-payments problems of developed nations and those of the emerging new nations. The system did not create instruments suitable to cope with the structural, long-term external imbalances of the Third World.

Clearly, the developing countries find little use for the classical balance-of-payments discipline, under which deficit countries reduce their imports and embark on policies encouraging exports. The Third World, in great need of foreign technology and equipment, but with few exportables, finds this adjustment method unacceptable chiefly because it interferes with economic development and progress. Then, too, most external deficits of the developing countries are not caused by excessive domestic spending (which as a rule underlies the internal imbalances of industrial nations), but frequently result from changing economic conditions in the developed market economies. Moreover, in the face of their continuously growing deficits, the developing countries have neither the international reserves nor the borrowing capacity required to seek funds in foreign credit markets, the use of both of which is part and parcel of the IMF adjustment mechanism. The developing countries have always known that while their demand for imports is inelastic (in the short run), their export earnings are highly volatile. Without doubt, the economic problems of the Third World will decrease somewhat and will be easier to solve if the industrial nations avoid cyclical instability, thus maintaining aggregate demand; if they liberalize imports, especially of manufactured goods, from the developing areas; and if they assume responsibility for long-term assistance to the new countries.

The Third World does not seem to consider the present forms of international economic cooperation adequate and helpful because these forms do not curb *national* economic policies with potentially detrimental effects on other economies. In the view of the developing countries, contemporary conditions in the world economy necessitate a superior framework, that is, a coordination of national policies. This will exert a harmonizing effect on the disparate international economy and the centrifugal forces operating within it.

The industrialized nations (the North) have, in their turn, come to recognize the weak situation of the Third World (the South) and have seriously considered the latter's call for reforms in international trade, finance and investment—although the developed countries appear to prefer removal of existing obstacles (reviews of present rules) rather than untested innovations.

There is general agreement among the industrial market economies that they have to respond to the aspirations of the new countries and that, indeed, the concept of international interdependence is due for redefinition. (More than any other factor, the dramatic increases in petroleum prices have compelled both the developed and developing countries to reassess their international economic positions.) The industrial nations emphasize, though, that because growing world-wide interdependence is accompanied by rising national vulnerability to external forces, contemporary international economic relations have to be managed carefully and their evolution should be controlled through intergovernmental consultation and similar channels.

Significantly, the North considers dialogue with the South essential to worldwide economic cohesion and indispensible to the equalization of international opportunity—a fundamental Third World goal. Clearly, realization of the program set forth in the documents cited earlier, including the New International Economic Order, is predicated on the extent to which the developed countries are prepared to cooperate. The international trade and financial systems cannot be unilaterally changed or corrected by the developing countries. The industrialized nations oppose several provisions of the New Economic Order, such as producer cartels; tying the prices of raw materials exports to those of imported manufactured goods; and expropriating foreign-owned assets without regard for international law. While critical of what they term "block economic power," the industrial Western nations are ready to examine methods of avoiding the North–South confrontation and converting it into a productive form of accommodation.

These attitudes of the industrial nations—the traditional aid donors and centers of international capital markets—are important to bear in mind before we comment on the financial innovations proposed by the developing countries. However, this chapter will not attempt to analyze and evaluate the proposals.

If the targets of the Second UN Development Decade are to be met, the capital requirement of the oil-importing developing countries will be as much as $100 billion by 1980, at current prices. (In 1973, the net capital inflow totaled $18 billion.) Should these countries continue to have difficulties in achieving the anticipated economic growth of 6 percent per annum, the requirement will, of course, be greater—with obvious adverse macroeconomic consequences. It is in nobody's interest that this actually take place. On the other hand, the level of economic activity in most Third World countries primarily depends on the availability of official develoment assistance (ODA), and if this declines, so will economic growth in the recipient economies. As noted previously, the performance of most aid donors has not been exemplary. Some basic projections of net capital requirements for the non-oil-producing developing countries under different growth assumptions are presented in table 4–6.

Table 4-6

Non-Oil-Producing Developing Countries: Change in Net Capital Requirements for Given Changes in Assumptions

(billions of dollars)

Changes in Assumptions	1980
Alternative growth targets of developing countries	
a. Target growth rate of non-oil-producing developing countries is reduced from 6.2 percent to 5.4 percent per year	−15.4
b. Target growth rate is reduced from 6.2 percent to 4.4 percent per year	−35.8
Alternative OECD growth assumptions	
a. OECD growth rate for the remainder of the decade is increased from 5.2 percent to 6.2 percent per year.	−9.7
b. OECD growth rate for the remainder of the decade is decreased from 5.2 percent to 4.2 percent per year.	+15.3

Source: United Nations Conference on Trade and Development.

The second source from which the capital requirement can be partly covered is the surplus of the oil-exporting countries. These funds may be channelled to other developing countries directly as well as indirectly (through developed market economies in which some oil earnings are invested). Although the contribution of this source of development finance is difficult to forecast, in 1974 the bilateral ODA from the oil-exporting developing countries amounted to $2 billion compared to $680 million in 1972 to 1973). In addition, in 1974 these countries displaced the developed nations as a major source of funds for regular lending by multilateral institutions, and provided the bulk of the financing for the IMF oil facility.

Along with the awareness of their inescapable and growing need for external finance has come the developing countries' realization that only innovations introduced into the international financial mechanism (and other complementary segments of the world economy) will help solve the Third World problems. The proposals which have received worldwide attention concern basically concessional (public) development assistance and include the link between the creation of IMF Special Drawing Rights and development funds and the development tax contemplated for imposition in the developed nations and designed as a source of development finance or interest subsidies (interest equalization fund) or both.

Suggestions concerning nonconcessionary assistance are connected with the Third Word's desire that access to foreign private capital markets be made available to more developing countries. The latter's borrowings should be facilitated by the removal of restrictive lending regulations in developed nations as well as by the outcome of the Multilateral Trade Negotiations which (along with the

Tokyo Declaration) are to be instrumental in giving the new countries preferential considerations and treatment in world trade in general and in their commercial relations with industrialized economies in particular. In most of their revisionist proposals, the developing countries seek international economic arrangements that would strengthen their role in worldwide economic and financial decision making and would also minimize their vulnerability to the cyclical business fluctuations of industrial nations, especially those which depress the real value of the developing countries' export receipts. In all its efforts, generally channelled through the United Nations Organization, the Third World is concerned about the lack of an effective mechanism to correct the asymmetry between deficit and surplus countries, which causes these countries to confront the existing institutions and systems with both challenges and dilemmas.

References

Jahangir Amuzegar, "The North-South Dialogue: From Conflict to Compromise," *Foreign Affairs* 54, no. 3 (April 1976).

Edward Bernstein et al., "Reflections on Jamaica," *Essays in International Finance,* no. 115 (April 1976).

Hollis B. Chenery, "Restructuring the World Economy," *Foreign Affairs* 53, no. 2 (January 1975).

Thierry de Montbrial, "For a New World Economic Order," *Foreign Affairs* 54, no. 1 (October 1975).

Carlos F. Diaz-Alejandro, "Less Developed Countries and the Post-1971 International Financial System," *Essays in International Finance,* no. 108 (April 1975).

Guy F. Erb and Valeriana Kallab, eds., *Beyond Dependency: The Developing World Speaks Out,* Overseas Development Council, Washington, D.C., 1975.

Reginald Herbold Green and Hans W. Singer, "Toward a Rational and Equitable New International Economic Order: A Case for Negotiated Structural Changes," *World Development* 3, no. 6 (June 1975).

Constantine Michalopoulos, "Financing Needs of Developing Countries: Proposals for International Action," *Essays in International Finance,* no. 110 (June 1975).

United Nations Conference on Trade and Development, Review of International Trade and Development, 1974, United Nations, New York, 1976.

United Nations Conference on Trade and Development, Review of International Trade and Development 1975, United Nations, New York, 1976.

United Nations Department of Economic and Social Affairs, Implementation of the International Development Strategy, Volume II, United Nations, New York, 1973.

United Nations Economic and Social Council, External Finance for Development: Recent Experience and its Implications for Policies, United Nations, 1975.

United Nations, General Assembly, Resolutions Adopted by the General Assembly During its Seventh Special Session, 1–16 September 1975, United Nations, New York, 1976.

5

Petrodollars, Adjustment Requirements, and World Income Distribution

Maurice Girgis[a]

It has been three years since the Organization of Petroleum Exporting Countries (OPEC) unleashed its vast economic power against oil-consuming countries (OCCs) in what has been frequently interpreted as an obvious economic threat to their well being.[1] When OPEC unilaterally raised the posted price of oil by almost 70 percent in October 16, 1973 and then quadrupled it three months later, economists and noneconomists alike predicted grave and dramatic consequences to world economic order. Their fears revolved around two major developments: first, the absorptive capacity of OPEC members, particularly Libya, Kuwait, Saudi Arabia, Qatar, and the United Arab Emirates was smaller than their expected oil revenues, resulting in substantial oil revenue surpluses. This oil revenue surplus, they argued, would severely tax if not totally disable the world financial and monetary systems, because (1) world banking institutions are ill-equipped to handle such a sudden vast flow of financial assets, (2) OPEC's transfer of oil revenues in the form of imported goods or financial investment or both will not be proportionate to the financial drain from the OCCs, and (3) in attempting to protect their financial deposits from unexpected exchange rate losses, certain OPEC members will abruptly withdraw large funds from one currency to another, thus spreading financial panic and causing international monetary crises.

The second major development feared by economists had macroeconomic prospects—deficits in the OCCs' balance of payments would tend to shift aggregate demand downward and supply upward to the left, resulting in higher unemployment levels along with higher prices—that is, stagflation. This fear was particularly strong, since OPEC's actions coincided with declining economic activity in most of the world, deliberately designed to slow the unsustainable growth rate of 1972 and early 1973. Economists further conjectured that such a situation would lead to "beggar thy neighbor" policies among OCCs.[2]

Three years have elapsed since these Cassandra voices echoed upon the "oil crisis" and the "recycling petrodollars crisis." These years provide not only perspective on the problem, but also sufficient data to assess the empirical legitimacy of the fears of Western economists. These data also facilitate evaluating the impact of OPEC's oil price hike on the economies of the Third World.

[a]The author is grateful to Robert R. Jost for his helpful comments and editorial assistance.

The first section of this chapter addresses the question of OPEC's future as a cartel and concludes that it will not break up, ceteris paribus, as long as the government of Saudi Arabia is willing to absorb downward shifts in world demand for oil. Recycling of surplus petrodollars is explored in the second section. Here, the hypothesis that international payments and adjustment mechanisms have worked well during the last three years appears to be verified. The third section examines shifts in world income distribution from OCCs and less developed countries (LDCs) to OPEC members. The discussion in this section explores the postulate that although OCCs' oil-related deficits are larger than those of LDCs, the economies of the LDCs suffered the most.

Future Prospects of the Oil Cartel

A cartel by definition curtails the competitive forces in the market place by setting a uniform price or by allocating specific market shares to its members or both. The OPEC cartel is relatively weak in that it sets a floor price but does not fix market quotas. This is similar to the fair trade laws in the commodity market and the behavior of legal and medical professionals in the service markets in the United States where each is permitted to sell all he can of a given commodity or service at a predetermined floor price. As such, a cartel is likely to stay intact to the extent that the product is homogeneous, the number of firms is small, levels of profits are relatively high for all members, and firms are in close geographical proximity to each other.[3]

A study of the socioeconomic profile of OPEC members reveals that they have little in common other than the cartel itself. These nations exhibit divergent political systems, and their cultural and societal fabric is quite dissimilar, with the exception of the Islamic members who constitute only half of OPEC's membership. Their gross oil receipts vary drastically, from only $4 billion in Algeria to $29 billion in Saudi Arabia during 1974, and their population distribution is even more skewed, ranging between 180,000 in Qatar and 124 million in Indonesia. Per capita income distribution is likewise skewed between a low of $100 in Indonesia and a high of over $10,000 in Qatar and Abu Dhabi. Most importantly perhaps is that their economic systems, industrial structures, levels of economic maturity, development needs and strategies, and absorptive capacities are quite dissimilar.[4] Consequently, the ability of individual OPEC member nations to harness the income-generating power of the cartel to their own development needs varies considerably. The large existing inequity between the "haves" and "have-nots" among OPEC members brings into focus the divergencies in member development needs (see table 5-1). The haves, with high income and low absorptive capacity, are Saudi Arabia, Kuwait, United Arab Emirates, Libya, and Qatar, in descending order. The have-nots, on the other hand, have high absorptive capacity relative to their oil revenues, including, in descending order, Iran, Venezuela, Algeria, Iraq, Ecuador, Nigeria, and Indonesia.[5]

The have-nots tend to insist on escalating oil prices during the cartel's ministerial negotiations, whereas the haves are more prone to opt for unchanged or even lower prices. Political considerations aside, the haves generally appear to realize the importance of keeping the price of oil well below that of other alternative sources of energy. Essentially, they reason that the greater the price disparity between energy sources, the longer the OCCs will procrastinate in launching and implementing a comprehensive and costly energy policy—à la Kennedy's space program. The haves also contend that the investment of oil surplus funds during 1974 and 1975 resulted in negative real interest rate earnings on those financial assets deposited in either Eurocurrency banks, United States or United Kingdom government securities, or international organizations such as the World Bank. Indeed, they found the nominal interest rate in most instances to be lower than the rate of inflation. Concessional and interest-free loans, obviously meant an even greater net decrease in their real incomes. Given these circumstances, it is not too surprising that the haves finally opted for some restraint in price increases. Conversely, countries with greater needs for oil revenues to finance domestic development projects, especially Algeria, Iran, Indonesia, Venezuela, and Nigeria, have stronger incentives to increase oil prices or their domestic output or both, in sharp contrast to those nations whose oil revenues greatly exceed their internal development needs.

The above hypotheses can be summarized into three points: (1) OPEC members have relatively little in common except the cartel itself; (2) there is an inherent conflict on incremental price and output changes among OPEC members; and (3) there is substantial disparity among members' oil revenues relative to their internal development needs. Why then have the poorest and neediest members not "cheated" by secretly offering their oil at concessionary prices?[6]

Theoretically, a cartel member nation can augment its income significantly by selling its output at a price lower than the cartel's, provided that the other members adhere to the higher price. A slight reduction in a given OPEC member's price could be very rewarding in view of the low price elasticity of demand for oil in general, the infinite elasticity of demand facing each producer in isolation, the unsympathetic sentiment in the OCCs toward OPEC, and the sizable difference between the posted price and the cost of production of oil ($10.51 compared to $0.25 in the Middle East, as shown in table A-3 in appendix 5A).

The business debacle of 1974 and 1975 put the OPEC organization to the test. During this period world oil consumption decreased by about 1.5 percent and OPEC oil sales declined by 10 percent as a consequence of mild weather,

Table 5-1

Estimated OPEC Investible Surplus for 1975, with Summary Data for 1973 and 1974

($ Billions) 1975

	Oil Exports (Government Take)	Non-Oil Exports	Imports f.o.b.	Services and Private Transfers	Investible Surplus 1975	1974	1973
Group I (High Income/Low Absorption)							
Saudi Arabia	48.1	0.6	−14.5	0	34.3	36.3	4.4
Kuwait	26.7	–	−5.7	−0.1	21.0	20.8	3.1
U.A.E.	7.9	0.5	−2.1	0.8	7.1	7.3	1.5
Qatar	6.5	–	−2.2	−0.1	4.2	4.4	0.3
	1.8		−0.4	−0.1	1.3	1.3	0.1
Libya	5.2	0.1	−4.1	−0.5	0.7	2.5	−0.6
Group II (Middle Income/High Absorption)							
Iran	39.9	2.5	−30.3	−2.3	9.8	17.2	0.7
Venezuela	19.9	1.0	−10.6	−0.7	9.6	10.7	1.1
Iraq	8.3	0.5	−6.5	−0.5	1.8	4.0	−0.1
	7.6	0.2	−6.6	−0.7	0.5	2.0	0.5
Algeria	3.7	0.3	−5.7	−0.3	−2.0	0.4	−0.8
Equador	0.4	0.5	−0.9	−0.1	−0.1	0.1	–
Group III (Low Income/High Absorption)							
Nigeria	10.4	3.3	−9.8	−2.3	1.6	5.4	−0.1
Indonesia	6.7	0.9	−5.1	−0.6	1.9	5.2	0.3
	3.7	2.4	−4.7	−1.7	−0.3	0.2	−0.4
OPEC Total 1975	98.1	6.6	−54.5	−4.5	45.7	58.9	4.9
1974	94.9	5.7	−36.9	−4.8	58.9		
1973	25.2	4.3	−20.3	−4.3	4.9		

Source: Sperry Lea, *Higher Oil Prices: Worldwide Financial Implications*, The British-North American Committee, 1975, Exhibit 4.

– = less than $50 million.

Columns may not add due to rounding.

the economic slump that affected all OCCs, and a modest market reaction from industrial and individual consumers to the higher cost of energy. These events unpredictably lowered OPEC's oil production and expected oil revenues and forced those OPEC countries in the throes of rapid economic development to incur large deficits in their balance of payments, to borrow heavily from Euro-currency markets, and to revise their planned development expenditures down-ward. Those countries that suffered the most from the turn of events in 1974 and 1975 and who would have benefited the most from "cheating" were Indonesia and Nigeria, and to a lesser extent, Algeria and Iraq.[7] They were reluc-tant to cheat because (1) it would have been too risky, since buyers might have unwittingly revealed their sellers, (2) the events that precipitated the lower oil revenues were temporary in nature, (3) OPEC has been a successful cartel only one or two years and greater benefits may be in store, (4) except for Iraq, the OPEC members are marginal producers, (5) some cheating was done under the guise of quality differentials anyway, and (6) the greater burden of the down-trend in world oil demand was borne willingly and deliberately by the leaders of Saudi Arabia, who lowered their nation's output from a possible capacity of 11.8 million barrels per day (b/d) to about 7 million b/d (see table 5-2).

Saudi Arabia was willing to absorb the slack in the world demand for oil, and by so doing, protected the future of the OPEC cartel. Such a seemingly unselfish response was not, however, pure altruism, but can be explained in terms of economic advantages for Saudi Arabia. Saudi Arabia's absorptive capa-city is relatively low, so it has little need for additional revenues. Second, as long as OPEC is kept alive, Saudi Arabia is guaranteed the cartel's high price for every barrel of oil it produces. Third, if OPEC continues to peg its price to world infla-

Table 5-2
Crude Oil Production of OPEC Members, 1974 and 1975 (thousand barrels/day)

	1974	1975	Change	Percent Change
Saudi Arabia	8,245	7,077	−1,168	−16.5
Iran	5,944	5,350	−594	−11.1
Venezuela	2,960	2,346	−614	−26.2
Iraq	1,892	2,216	+324	+17.1
Kuwait	2,463	2,084	−379	−18.2
Nigeria	2,155	1,787	−369	−20.7
Libyan A.R.	1,616	1,510	−106	−0.7
Abu Dhabi	1,498	1,400	−98	−0.7
Indonesia	1,372	1,313	−59	−4.5
Algeria	1,007	960	−47	−4.9
Qatar	507	439	−68	−15.4
Gabon	202	202	−2	−1.0
Ecuador	175	160	−15	−9.6

Source: IMF *Survey*, July 5, 1976, p. 200.

tion, the oil in the ground will not be less valuable in real terms than that sold today. Finally, Saudi Arabia holds the largest oil reserves and is the largest producer; as such, she holds the key to OPEC's future, which in turn gives her double bargaining power (1) in negotiating taxes, royalties, and participation rates with the oil companies and (2) in negotiating price and output changes with other members of the cartel. Politically, this newly acquired economic power will enable the leaders of Saudi Arabia to play a prime role in the Arab world in addition to elevating their political power vis-à-vis the Western Allies.[8] Since both the economic and political advantages appear unlikely to diminish in the foreseeable future, Saudi Arabia will probably choose to sustain the OPEC cartel for some time to come.[9]

The Success of Recycling Surplus Petrodollars

The fact the OPEC's huge surplus of investable funds has not precipitated a major financial or monetary crisis lends credence to the hypothesis that the recycling of petrodollars has worked reasonably well. This can be attributed to three major factors. First, OPEC countries followed a responsible and constructive course in effecting the transfer, recognized the desirability of cooperative efforts with major central banks, and discreetly avoided the potential havoc that transferring a hundred million dollars each week could have on world financial markets.[10] Second, worldwide private financial institutions proved capable of performing their intermediary function, receiving OPEC surplus funds and relending them to oil deficit countries without undue risk.[11] Third, OCCs' government borrowing to finance oil-related deficits was minimized due to the prevailing "dirty" floating exchange rate system. Had the international monetary system been under the old fixed exchange rate system, the impact of the oil price increase would have been limited to higher oil prices rather than devaluing the deficit country's currency under the floating exchange system, thus raising the prices of all imports. Here, the adjustment mechanism rests upon reduced consumer demand for imports rather than upon government borrowing.[12]

There are several ways to define "recycling".[13] The definition used here differentiates between direct and indirect recycling. Direct recycling includes the amount of investable funds which OPEC countries place in the hands of those countries needing them to finance their oil-related deficits. Indirect recycling consists of placing OPEC funds with intermediaries who in turn relend them.

Direct Recycling

This form of recycling has taken the following modes[14] (see table 5-3):

Table 5-3
Recycling Modes of OPEC Investable Funds in 1974

	$ Billion U.S.	% of Total
Direct Recycling	23.7	39.5%
Purchases of Government Securities	9.6	16.0
Official Lending to Governments		
Industrial	5.5	9.2
LDCs[a]	6.9	11.5
Direct Investment		
Industrial Countries	1.7	2.8
LDCs[b]	—	
Indirect Recycling	36.3	60.5
Eurocurrency Market	22.5	37.5
Bank Deposits in U.K. and U.S.	5.7	9.5
IMF Oil Facility or Account Subsidy (3.2)		
and World Bank (1.85)	5.1	8.5
Other	3.0	5.0
Total	60	100.0%

Source: Compiled from Sperry Lea, *Higher Oil Prices*; Organization for Economic Cooperation and Development, *Development Cooperation*; OECD, *Geographical Distribution of Financial Flows to Developing Countries,* 1976; Committee for Economic Development, *International Economic Consequences of High-Priced Energy,* 1975; US Commerce Department, *Foreign Direct Investment in the U.S.*; and IMF, *Survey,* several issues.

[a]This consists of $2.2 billion in concessional loans and $4.7 billion in nonconcessional loans.

[b]Some OPEC members, notably Kuwait, invest in LDCs through triangular arrangements; the amount is less than $.50 billion.

OPEC's Purchase of OCCs' Government Securities. For example, from 1974 through the third quarter of 1976, OPEC countries invested $2.0 and $11.5 billion respectively in United Kingdom government stocks and treasury bills and United States treasury bonds, notes and bills.[15]

Official Lending by OPEC to OCC Governments. Examples are few and the sums involved are relatively small, but OPEC did provide loans to Japan, Italy, and Canadian provinces, among others.

OPEC Grants, Soft Loans, and Concessional Oil Sales to LDCs. Since this subject is treated below, suffice it is to state that in recent years, OPEC has become an important source of financial assistance to LDCs. Aid disbursement directly through multinational organizations has increased from slightly less than $1.0 billion in 1973 to $4.6 billion in 1974 and $5.6 billion in 1975. In addition, OPEC pledged $800 million to help finance balance of payments deficits of the most seriously affected nations and committed another $400 million to be channeled through the International Fund for Agricultural Development (IFAD), provided that the OCCs contribute the equivalent of $600 million. The total sum of $1.0 billion is to be allocated interest-free to LDCs to finance either balance-of-payments deficits or specific development projects or both.[16]

Direct Investment in OCCs by OPEC Governments and Individuals. This constitutes a small portion of OPEC's total investable funds, though it is much publicized. Examples include Iran's investment in Krupp and the European Uranium Consortium, Libya's in the Fiat Company, Abu Dhabi's investment in London real estate, Kuwait's purchase of British and European real estate and a resort property in South Carolina, and private investment in the United Kindgdom's Lonrho Company and Detroit's Bank of the Commonwealth.[17] A benchmark survey prepared by the United States Department of Commerce shows that, excluding Israel, the Middle East's direct United States investment in 1974 amounted to $1.6 billion, all of which was in the petroleum industry.[18]

Indirect Recycling

OPEC's Liquid Investment in the Eurocurrency Market. This was the single most important outlet for OPEC surplus revenues in 1974. The amount invested in 1974 was about $22.5 billion or about 38 percent of total OPEC surplus revenue, and $8.2 billion in the first half of 1975. These is little doubt that the Eurocurrency market fulfilled its role during 1974 and 1975 as an intermediary between OPEC and oil-related deficit countries. Publicized Eurocurrency credits by borrowing countries indicate that LDCs borrowed $9.6 billion in 1974 and $11.5 billion in 1975. As shown in table 5-4, the OCCs borrowed $16.9 billion in 1974 and $14.6 billion in 1975.[19]

Table 5-4
Publicized Eurocurrency Credits
(Million U.S. $ or Equivalent)

Country	1974	1975
Members of Fund, World Bank	28,624.0	19,530.8
Industrial	16,915.4	4,626.9
Developing	9,605.2	11,530.1
Oil Exporters	772.5	3,136.9
Higher-income	6,979.7	7,216.5
Middle-income	1,561.7	1,105.4
Lower-income	291.3	71.3
Others	2,103.4	3,373.8

Source: IMF *Survey*, February 16, 1976, p. 49.

Portfolio Investment by OPEC Governments. Sterling deposits by OPEC in 1974 amounted to $1.7 billion and dollar deposits to $4.0 billion. There is evidence that OPEC sterling deposits continued to decline in the second half of 1974 and the first half of 1976, due largely to the decline in OPEC revenues in 1975 and the sharp improvement in the outlook for the dollar vis-à-vis the sterling. As a result, dollar deposits rose by $1.7 billion and sterling deposits fell by $1.0 billion during 1975 and the first three quarters of 1976.[20]

Loans to the IMF Oil Facility and Subsidy Account. The oil facility was set up by the IMF in June 1974 to help member nations cope with the impact of recent increases in the cost of imports of petroleum and petroleum products on their balance of payments.[21]

The IMF borrowed SDR 3,047 million to finance the 1974–75 oil facility and SDR 3,856 million for 1975-76. OPEC members contributed 87 percent and 61 percent of the total 1974-75 and 1975-76 oil facility resources respectively. Other non-OPEC contributors were Austria, Belgium, Canada, West Germany, the Netherlands, Norway, Switzerland, and Trinidad. The oil facility fund is not restricted to LDCs; in fact, 63 percent of the purchases between September 1974 and May 1976 were made by ten OCCs, of which Italy alone (SDR 1,455.2 million in three transactions) accounted for 21 percent of the grand total of SDR 6,902.4 million and England (SDR 1,000 million) for 7 percent, while 45 LDCs borrowed SDR 2,538.8 million or 37 percent of the total— most notably India (SDR 401.3 million), Korea (SDR 252.7 million), Chile (SDR 243.7 million), and Pakistan (SDR 236 million). Borrowing agreements provided for a 7 percent interest rate per annum for the 1974-75 facility and 7.25 percent for the 1975-1976 facility; there is a one-half percent service charge at the time of drawing and members are required to liquidate their debt between three and seven years.

To help the poorest LDCs meet the cost of using the oil facility resources, the IMF established in August 1975 a subsidy account with contributions from OPEC members and the OCCs. Eligibility to draw upon the resources of this account is limited to the most seriously affected (MSA) countries as defined by the United Nations.[22] This subsidy account reduces the effective interest rate from 7.71 percent to 2.71 percent. The actual amounts of subsidy or refund range from SDR 10,000 to each of Mali and Western Samoa to SDR 7.23 million to India.

Total OPEC oil receipts in 1974 thus amounted to 90 billion, of which approximately $34 billion represented imports of goods and services—a real transfer of resources amounting to 38 percent of their oil revenues. Taking into account an additional revenue of $5.0 billion from nonoil exports, OPEC's oil surplus is thus about $60 billion, which represents a transfer of financial resources. Of that amount, about $24 billion was recycled directly through OPEC and another $36 billion was recycled indirectly through private and international financial intermediaries, as shown in table 5-4. Was the amount of petrodollars recycled sufficient to absorb worldwide external imbalances resulting from the increased price of oil? The answer must be affirmative, since OPEC's oil revenues increased from $23 billion in 1973 to $90 billion in 1974; that is, they increased by $67 billion, of which $60 billion flowed back into developed and developing economies. In fact, OPEC's placement of $6 billion in United Kingdom and $11.0 billion in the United States[23] in 1974 offset almost exactly the increase in the value of net oil imports by these countries.[24]

Shifts in World Income Distribution from Developed and Less Developed Countries to OPEC Nations

In its preoccupation with the oil cartel, its future, and recycling petrodollars, world opinion failed to pay sufficient attention to the fundamental consequences of the increase in the price of oil: how much does the oil price increase affect real resources which will have to be transferred to OPEC nations? When would the OCCs have to effect the transfer? Can their future productive capacity pay off these debts without appreciable reduction in domestic consumption? How much loss is there in consumer welfare? What structural changes must the OCCs' economies undergo to meet the new and rising demand of the OPEC nations?

Obviously OPEC investment constitutes a claim against the OCCs' productive capacity and recycling is itself a form of postponing the transfer of real resources from present to future generations. The magnitude of this claim at the end of 1976 is expected to be approximately $160 billion,[25] which is almost equivalent to the total increase in the GNP of all developed countries for the calendar year 1972.

An extended treatment of this subject does not lie within the province of this study. Instead, attention will be focused on a descriptive analysis of the impact of oil price increases on income, employment and the balance-of-payments adjustments in both the developed and less developed countries.

Developed Countries

The OPEC action is likely to reduce output and employment and, at the same time, increase general price levels. An increase in the price of oil has similar effects on income and employment to imposing a tax on a product whose demand is inelastic. Unless oil consumers compensate for the increase in their spending on oil by either borrowing or dipping into their previous savings, less will be spent on other products; this will eventually reduce output and employment in the rest of the economy. The reduction in income and employment will be felt most severely in firms producing petroleum-intensive products. Furthermore, the increase price of oil implies a deterioration in the OCCs' terms of trade, which results in an additional loss in real income.[26] Third, from the supply side, output may also decline as a consequence of an upward shift in the average and marginal cost functions associated with higher energy costs; this results, ceteris paribus, in a lower profit-maximizing output at higher prices. Higher prices will prevail even if OPEC's inflow of surplus capital and increased demand for imports shifts demand upward. The new output level will depend on the magnitude of the rise in demand, but the price level will always be higher. If the increase in demand is smaller than the decrease in supply due to the oil tax, output will decline and prices increase; in modern economic jargon, this is known as "stagflation."

Finally, the oil price increases will have an inflationary impact on the economies of the oil consuming countries via income redistribution effects. That is, the OPEC price increase is tantamount to substituting foreign for domestic demand in an amount equivalent to its oil revenue, and there is no reason to expect the two demand patterns to be similar. This poses some short-run adjustment problems to the domestic economy, especially in the manufacturing sector. Unless there is sufficient excess capacity in those sectors facing increased demand by OPEC members (or by borrowers), the price is bound to increase.

From a macroeconomic standpoint, OPEC actions will transfer income from oil consumers to domestic and foreign oil producers. The direction and magnitude of this transfer can be outlined as follows:

1. If the oil price increase is construed as an import tax whose revenue accrues to the OPEC members, there is a trade diversion effect whereby output of the marginal, economically inefficient producers in the OCCs will replace foreign supplies. Since the average cost of domestic producers will rise, the higher price at home implies a transfer of income in the form of an economic rent from consumers to domestic producers. The magnitude of the economic rent is measured by the trapezoid usually presented under the new price line in conventional tariff analysis.

2. The second type of income distribution is the transfer of real resources from consumers in the OCCs to the OPEC governments. This can be measured by the volume of trade in goods and services between the OPEC and the OCC nations, which amounts to an average of $30 to 35 billion each year.

3. OPEC's oil earnings in excess of their imports constituted a net accumulation of wealth transferred from the OCC consumers. The magnitude of this factor is approximately $50 to 60 billion per annum.

Less Developed Countries

The OPEC oil price increase will likewise affect the economies of LDCs. Output and employment will fall, consumer surplus will decrease, domestic producers' profits will rise, prices of both imports and domestic production will increase, and a net shift of income in real and financial resources toward the OPEC countries will take place.

Unlike industrialized countries, however, LDCs face three major additional difficulties. First, while the impact of oil price increases on macroeconomic variables is similar in both OCCs and LDCs, it is far more traumatic for the LDCs. Higher oil prices added some $12 to $13 billion to the annual import bills of LDCs in 1974. Even had these nations been refunded the equivalent amount of money from OPEC countries, their economies would have suffered from the impact of oil price increases on their imports of petroleum-intensive products, especially fertilizers from industrial countries. In addition, the general decline in economic activity in the OCCs, which is partly attributable to higher energy costs, resulted in a lower demand for LDCs' exports. The IMF reports that while the export growth rate of non-OPEC developing countries increased 14.5 percent between 1972 and 1973, it declined to 7 percent in 1974 and was negligible in 1975. Concurrently, the terms of trade deteriorated by 4.5 percent in 1974 and by as much as 10 percent in 1975.[27] Growth in real output also declined. The annual rate of growth of GDP during 1973 to 1975 was 5.4 percent compared with 6.0 percent in the previous five years. The least developed countries, those in South Asia and in Sub-Saharan Africa, registered an annual growth rate of only 2.8 percent, which was neutralized by an almost equal growth in population.

Second, in addition to the general increase in the prices of oil and other raw materials during 1974 and 1975, LDCs faced a sharp increase in the price of imported food and fertilizers. Most LDCs are net food importers, and their added financial burden has been estimated to be $5.0 billion during the 1973-74 crop year.[28] Obviously such a drain on their foreign exchange reserves exacerbates their balance-of-payments problems.

Third, since most LDCs remained on fixed exchane rate systems, the balance-of-payments adjustment was shouldered by their governments which, instead of reducing domestic consumption through higher prices or taxes or both, invariably chose to borrow abroad to finance their escalating external debts. Partly because of the different exchange rate adjustment mechanisms in OCCs and LDCs, the former realized a current account surplus of $19.4 billion in 1975 from a deficit of $9.6 billion in 1974, while the LDCs increased their deficit from $28.6 to $37.0 billion during that period.[29] In short, the immediate problem facing LDCs during 1974 and 1975 was the financing of these deficits. As shown in table 5-5, during these two years the pattern of financing diverged significantly from previous patterns in that,[30] (1) use of reserves increased, whereas capital inflows and aid had previously been used to finance current account deficits, (2) market borrowing, especially through banking channels, increased significantly, largely reflecting the recycling of petrodollars, (3) although grant aid receipts and capital inflows in the form of direct investment continued to increase, their relative share declined, and (4) the influx of devel-

Table 5-5
Non-Oil Developing Countries: Financing of Current Account Deficits, 1968 to 1975
(In billions of U.S. dollars)

	1968	1969	1970	1971	1972	1973	1974	1975
Current account deficit[a]	6.8	5.9	8.7	11.4	9.2	9.9	28.4	37.0
Financing through transactions that do not affect net debt positions	3.1	3.3	3.8	4.5	5.1	7.8	9.1	10.0
Net unrequited transfers received by governments of non-oil developing countries	1.8	1.8	1.9	2.2	2.3	4.4	4.9	6.1
Direct investment flows, net	1.3	1.5	1.2	1.7	2.2	3.4	4.2	3.9
SDR allocations and gold monetization, net	–	–	0.7	0.6	0.6	–	–	–
Net borrowing and use of reserves[b]	3.7	2.6	4.9	6.9	4.1	2.1	19.3	27.0
Reduction of reserve assets (accumulation, –)	–1.3	–1.2	–2.2	–1.3	–6.4	–8.1	–2.5	0.8
Net external borrowing[c]	5.0	3.8	7.1	8.2	10.5	10.2	21.8	26.2
Long-term loans received by governments from official sources, net	2.6	2.8	3.1	3.3	3.6	5.1	7.6	12.6
Other long-term borrowing from nonresidents, net	1.0	1.1	1.9	2.6	4.4	4.5	8.7	9.3
From private banks abroad	0.3	0.4	0.4	1.2	2.1	3.7	7.0	8.5
Through suppliers' credits	0.7	0.8	0.7	0.2	0.3	0.3	0.8	1.3
Other sources[d]	–	–0.1	0.8	1.2	2.0	0.5	0.9	–0.5
Use of reserve-related credit facilities, net[e]	0.2	–	–0.4	–	0.4	0.2	1.3	3.4
Other short-term borrowing, net	0.6	0.7	1.7	1.6	0.5	0.2	4.3	2.9
Residual errors and omissions[f]	0.6	–0.8	0.8	0.7	1.6	0.2	–0.1	–2.0

Source: IMF *Annual Report*, 1976, table 9, p. 70.

[a]Net total of balances on goods, services, and private transfers, as defined for *Balance of Payments Yearbook* purposes (with sign reversed).

[b]Financing through changes in net debt positions (net borrowing, less net accumulation–or plus net liquidation–of official reserve assets).

[c]Includes any net use of nonreserve claims on nonresidents, errors and omissions in reported balance of payments statements for individual countries, and minor deficiencies in coverage.

[d]Including errors and residuals which arise from the mismatching of data taken from creditor and debtor records.

[e]Comprises use of Fund credit and short-term borrowing by monetary authorities from other monetary authorities.

[f]Errors and omissions in reported balance of payments statements for individual countries, plus minor deficiencies in coverage.

opment loans from foreign governments and international agencies increased substantially, accounting for about 50 percent of total net borrowing in 1975. While only a few countries faced serious obstacles in securing necessary loans during this time, carrying and amortizing an outstanding aggregate public debt of $151.4 billion (as of the end of 1974) will be a heavy burden in years to come—especially when expressed in terms of future export earnings rather than rescheduled debt payments.[31] In other words short-run financing problems appear to have been resolved at the expense of long-term claims against domestic resources.

Flow of Financial Resources from OPEC to LDCs[32]

OPEC's economic assistance to LDCs increased from about $1.0 billion in 1973 to $5.7 billion in 1974. Excluding their $3.2 billion contribution to the IMF oil facility in 1974, OPEC countries committed a total of $10.5 billion in concessional and nonconcessional loans. OPEC committed $5.2 billion to nonconcessional loans, of which only $2.5 billion was disbursed. As table 5-6 shows, nonconcessional multilateral commitments amounted to $2.7 billion, of which $2.2 billion was spent on purchases of world bank bonds ($1.85 billion) carrying interest rates of 7.5 percent to 8.5 percent; the balance went mainly to Arab organizations. Bilateral loans, on the other hand, were hard to implement, since OPEC committed $2.5 billion and the amount disbursed was only $0.3 billion. The difficulty with this type of investment, which is usually utilized as a joint

Table 5-6
Nonconcessional Financial Flows from OPEC Members in 1974
($ million)

Donor	Commitments			Estimated Disbursements		
	Bilateral	Multilateral	Total	Bilateral	Multilateral	Total
Algeria	—	22	22	—	5	5
Iran	357	364	721	20	289	309
Iraq	240	34	274	—	—	—
Kuwait	411	114	525	180	66	246
Libya	425	57	482	25	7	32
Nigeria	—	239	239	—	240	240
Qatar	92	64	156	2	25	27
Saudi Arabia	405	1,011	1,416	30	963	993
UAE	328	171	499	40	129	169
Venezuela	210	655	865	—	445	445
Total	2,468	2,731	5,199	297	2,169	2,466

Source: Organization for Economic Cooperation and Development, *Development Co-Operation,* 1975 Review, November 1975, p. 185.

venture, is that OPEC members find themselves in the role of foreign industrial investors, which is totally new to them. Lack of experience leads to excessive precautions and delayed decisions. Nonetheless a few joint ventures were signed, for example: between Iran and India in an iron mining project, where India will supply Iran with 150 million tons of iron ore over twenty years, starting in 1980; between Iran and South Korea, by which an oil refinery will be located in the Ousan industrial area in Korea; and between Kuwait and Egypt for the SUMED oil pipeline project.

OPEC's concessional aid commitments in 1974, on the other hand, totaled $5.3 billion, of which $2.2 billion was disbursed. About 73 percent of the total amount committed was allocated bilaterally. The largest donors were Saudi Arabia and Iran. Concessional aid commitments are divided nearly equally between grants and loans. The latter carries a grant element of between 28 and 38 percent. The distribution of OPEC grant commitments is concentrated among Arab and Muslim nations. The largest recipients are Egypt, Pakistan, Syria, and India.[33]

Multilateral concessional aid was likewise concentrated among Arab and Muslim nations, except for Saudi Arabia's $50 million contribution to the World Food Program and Kuwait's $32 million contribution to IDA. OPEC contributed 16 percent of worldwide official development assistance in 1974.[34]

In sum, during 1974 OPEC increased its economic assistance substantially over the $922 million it contributed in 1973. Several sources indicate that OPEC's 1975 contribution will be similar to that of 1974. However, the following points should be stressed: (1) OPEC's contribution has not offset the increased cost of oil imports, which amounted to $12 to $13 billion in 1974; (2) only $5.1 billion was placed in international organizations on nonconcessional terms; and (3) 90 percent of the $2.2 billion in concessional loans was allocated to Arab and Islamic nations. The remaining LDCs, especially those with per capita income less than $200, now have fewer options than they did prior to 1974. Only more exports and concessional loans can provide them with an alternative to restricting imports and thereby lowering their future rate of economic growth.

Concluding Remarks

This analysis has attempted to assess the OPEC cartel, its future as an economic entity, its role in recycling petrodollars, its impact on economic conditions in developed and less developed countries, and its economic assistance program to the non-oil-producing developing countries. We reached four major conclusions:

1. If the Saudi Arabian government is willing to absorb any major decreases in world demand for oil, the cartel is not likely to collapse. In fact, such a policy

is in Saudi Arabia's interest, for it enhances her bargaining power with the oil companies as well as with other OPEC members.

2. Historical evidence clearly indicates that OPEC members and world financial institutions have cooperated to bring about an orderly system of making petrodollars available to those who need them to finance balance-of-payments deficits. Petrodollars were successfully recycled either directly through OPEC governments or indirectly through financial intermediaries. Only a few of the poorest developing countries resorted to drastic internal policies for lack of sufficient funds abroad.

3. The macroeconomic impact of the oil price increases in the developed countries simultaneously retarded the rate of growth and exerted an inflationary bias. Furthermore, the increases shifted income distribution from oil consumers to domestic and foreign oil producers in the magnitude of $70 to $90 billion each year.

4. General economic conditions in the LDCs have been adversely influenced directly through the OPEC price action and indirectly through the repercussions of the oil price increases on developed economies. The total net increase in the LDCs' oil import bill amounted to $12 to $13 billion in 1974, of which $10.5 billion was committed by OPEC nations in bilateral and multilateral economic assistance programs. Of that amount, only $5.5 billion was committed on concessional basis; actual disbursement during 1974 amounted to $2.2 billion. Given the challenges of economic growth, especially in the poorest LDCs, there is a strong need for more aid, and concessional loans not only from the OPEC members but also from developed countries and multinational organizations.

Notes

1. Oil-consuming countries include only industrial countries which rely heavily on OPEC oil, for example, United States, Japan, and the Western European countries.

2. See Khodadad Farmanfarmaian et al., "How Can the World Afford OPEC Oil?", *Foreign Affairs* 53, no. 2 (January 1975): 201-222.

3. C.E. Ferguson and S. Charles Maurice, *Economic Analysis* (Homewood, Illinois: Richard D. Irwin Co., 1970), pp. 233-234.

4. For a detailed profile of the economies of OPEC nations, see table 5A-1 in appendix 5A.

5. Data on oil exports, nonoil exports, and imports of OPEC countries from 1972 to 1975 are reported in table 5A-2 in appendix 5A.

6. This is in essence what M.A. Adelman was trying to achieve by advocating that the United States purchase oil from OPEC members via secret bidding. See his testimony before U.S. Senate Subcommittee on Multinational Corporation and U.S. Foreign Policy, Ninety-fourth Congress, January 29, 1975.

GPO, *Political and Financial Consequences of the OPEC Price Increase,* Part II, 1975, p. 4.

7. Publicized Eurocurrency credits extended to these four countries accounted for 48 percent of total OPEC borrowing in 1974 and 81 percent in 1975. In 1975, the major borrowers were Indonesia ($1,636.5 million), Algeria ($500 million), Iraq ($500 million), and Iran ($245 million). See *Middle East Economic Survey* 19, no. 20 (March 5, 1976), 8–9.

8. This should be relatively easy since Saudi Arabia alone accounted for an average of 30 percent of total crude oil imports in 16 industrialized countries in 1976. Her share varied from 53.4 percent in Belgium, 32 percent in Japan, 20 percent in Germany and the United Kingdom, to 23 percent in the United States. See *Middle East Economic Survey* 20, no. 13 (January 17, 1976): 3.

9. Subsequent to the writing of this paper, OPEC members failed to ratify a proposed unified price increase in December 1976. The leaders of Saudi Arabia and UAE chose to raise the price of crude 5 percent while the remaining members decided on 10 percent. This new two-tier price system reflects the oligopolistic price leader role which Saudi Arabia aspires to play in OPEC. To underscore this leadership role, Sheik Yamani followed his initial decision by announcing plans to expand existing oil production capacity from 11.8 million b/d to 14 million b/d. The short-run expected loss in revenues to the other members—estimated at 25 percent—coupled with the long-run danger of breaking up the cartel altogether will eventually force them to get in line with Saudi Arabia.

10. Richard A. Debs, "Petro-Dollars, LDC's, and International Banks," *Monthly Review,* Federal Reserve Bank of New York (January 1976): 10–17.

11. A recent IMF staff report indicates that "bankers are generally much less concerned over possible disruptive effects of large short-term shifts or over the size of oil-related balance of payments deficits. There is a broad consensus that the banking industry was on the whole well able to come through the crisis in 1974 and to play an important role in the recycling efforts." See IMF *Review* (August 16, 1976): 244. See also Organization for Economic Cooperation and Development, *Development Cooperation,* 1975, p. 160.

12. See Harry G. Johnson, "Higher Oil Prices and the International Monetary System," in T.M. Rybczynski, ed., *The Economics of the Oil Crisis,* (New York: Holmes and Meier Publishers, 1976), pp. 166–168.

13. For a set of definitions, see Sperry Lea, *Higher Oil Prices: Worldwide Financial Implications* (The British–North American Committee, 1975), pp. 6–8.

14. Estimates of OPEC countries' allocation of surplus funds vary because they are based largely on information from the receiving countries.

15. See *Bank of England Bulletin,* various issues.

16. See IMF *Survey* (August 16, 1976): 254 and Chase Manhattan Bank, *International Finance Newsletter* (June 14, 1976).

17. Sperry Lea, *Higher Oil Prices,* Exhibit 8.

18. Direct investment represents the net claims of foreign investors on their United States affiliates against capital stock and related surplus accounts, plus the foreigners' net outstanding loans to their United States affiliates. See United States Department of Commerce, *Foreign Direct Investment in the U.S.*, Vol. 2, April 1976, Table A-7.

19: IMF *Survey* (February 16, 1976): 49.

20. IMF *Survey* (January 5, 1976): 7; Federal Reserve Bank of Chicago, *International Letter* no. 292 (September 17, 1976). and *Bank of England Bulletin* (December 1976).

21. Data on the IMF oil facility and subsidy account are from IMF *Annual Report* (1976).

22. The MSA group consists of 39 IMF members who are most affected by the increased price of petroleum and petroleum products. For more details, see IMF, *Annual Report,* 1976, pp. 58-60. As of April 30, 1976, sixteen OPEC and OCC countries pledged SDR 160 million (29 percent from OPEC and the rest from OCCs). The amount of subsidy is calculated as a percentage per annum (5 percent at present) of average daily balances, during the year, of the Fund's holdings of currency in excess of quota acquired as a result of purchase under the 1975-76 oil facility.

23. Most recent estimates show that OPEC investment in the United States was $7,108 billion in 1975 and $6,833 billion in the first two quarters of 1976. See United States Department of Commerce, *Survey of Current Business,* November 1976. The substantial increase in 1976 is attributed to an expected shift in OPEC's investment from London to New York and toward longer term investment. OPEC's total investment in the United States in 1975, including military equipment, was estimated at $20.1 billion. See *Survey of Current Business,* August 1976, p. 33.

24. Sperry Lea, *Higher Oil Prices,* p. 29.

25. This figure represents $60 billion, $40 billion, and $60 billion in 1974, 1975, and 1976 respectively. It is also assumed that the rate of return on OPEC's investment during the three year period is offset by world inflation. The increase from $40 billion in 1975 to $60 billion in 1976 is based on the projected economic recovery in the OCCs, a return to the preembargo wasteful use of oil, and the possibility of increased oil stocks in OCCs in anticipation of higher prices in 1977.

26. This is akin to the hypothetical situation in which OPEC members decide to invest their entire oil revenues in OCCs. Since capital outflow equals capital inflow (as if OPEC is a domestic industry), the aggregate level of economic activity in OCCs will be unchanged, albeit some sectoral resource redistribution. However, there would be a real income loss due to the deterioration in terms of trade equal to the amount of domestic resources owed to OPEC in exchange for their investment. See Jan Tulmir, "Oil Payment and Oil Debt and the Problem of Adjustment," in T.M. Rybczynski, ed., *Economics of the Oil Crisis,* pp. 40-41.

27. IMF, *Annual Report,* (1976), Table V, p. 12.

28. Ibid., pp. 10-11, and Committee for Economic Development, *International Economic Consequences of High-Priced Energy* (New York: Committee for Economic Development, 1975), pp. 58-59.

29. IMF *Annual Survey,* Table VI, p. 13.

30. Ibid., pp. 20-23.

31. IMF *Survey* (October 4, 1976): 291-293.

32. For an account of total world flow of financial resources to LDCs, see table 5A-4 in appendix 5A.

33. By September 1975 there were 14 loans committed by the Arab Fund for Economic and Social Development, which included ten Arab nations. The average loan is $12 million with an interest rate ranging from 4 percent to 6 percent maturity between 19 and 24 years, grace period of about 4.5 years, and a grant element ranging from 25 percent to 40 percent. See Organization for Economic Cooperation and Development, *Development Co-operation,* Table IX-3, p. 173.

34. See table 5A-3 in appendix 5A.

Appendix 5A

Table 5A-1
Economic Profile: Organization of Petroleum Exporting Countries, 1974

	Algeria	Ecuador	Indonesia	Iran	Iraq
Aggregative data					
Population					
Million persons at mid-year	16.3	7.0	127.8	32.2	10.7
Percent increase from 1973	3.7	3.3	2.6	3.0	3.5
Gross national product $ Billion 1973 US	NA	3.1	16.9	30.0	10.2
Percent increase from 1973	NA	14	8.2	16	77
Per capita (1973 US $)	NA	440	130	930	950
Industry					
Crude oil (thousand b/d)	940	160	1,380	6,040	1,820
Trade and international reserves					
Exports[b] ($ million US)	4,800	850	6,890	25,408	7,552
Government oil revenues ($ million US)	4,104	492	3,369	21,080	5,879
Oil exports (thousand b/d)	900	120	1,160	5,750	1,720
Imports[c] ($ million US)	3,715	700	4,320	9,200	2,843
United States ($ million US)	315[b]	326	685	1,900	285[b]
European Community ($ million US)	2,378[b]	NA	770	2,300	844[b]
Japan ($ million US)	154[b]	114	1,270	1,100	474[b]
International reserves ($ million US)	1,689	350	1,492	8,383	3,273

Source: United States Department of State, *Handbook of Economic Statistics,* 1975, pp. 16-17.
[a]Including about one-half of neutral zone production.

Kuwait	Libya	Nigeria	Qatar	Saudi Arabia	United Arab Emirates	Venezuela
0.9	2.2	61.3	0.2	5.9	0.2	11.6
5.7	4.4	2.8	11.3	2.8	3.7	3.0
9.6	NA	17.4	1.6	12.2	NA	16.5
118	NA	45	180	39	NA	2.6
10,670	NA	280	8,000	2,070	NA	1,420
2,550[a]	1,520	2,260	520	8,480[a]	1,680	2,970
10,763	7,881	9,559	2,255	37,132	NA	10,500
8,799	6,445	8,618	1,877	30,643	6,640	8,728
2,530	1,480	2,200	515	8,400	1,675	2,760
1,569	2,892	2,734	271	3,795	1,384	4,500
208[b]	138[b]	290[b]	NA	935	158	1,757
435[b]	694[b]	1,350[b]	NA	1,325	341	NA
279[b]	234[b]	285[b]	NA	760	288	400
8,000	3,616	5,629	1,500	14,285	3,700	6,529

[b]Data are f.o.b.
[c]Data are c.i.f.

Table 5A-2
Exports and Imports of OPEC Countries, 1972–1975
($ Million)

OPEC Country	1972 Exports Oil	1972 Exports Other	1972 Imports	1973 Exports Oil	1973 Exports Other	1973 Imports	1974 Exports Oil	1974 Exports Other	1974 Imports	1975 Exports Oil	1975 Exports Other	1975 Imports
Saudi Arabia	4,496	20	1,136	7,780	70	1,944	30,930	37	4,220	27,635	38	7,199
Libya	2,339	6	1,038	3,314	2	1,734	7,527	2	2,763	6,119	2	4,400
Kuwait	2,838	145	797	3,595	231	1,052	10,024	396	1,552	8,057	587	2,392
UAE	1,156	–	482	1,992	–	821	6,481	–	1,705	6,822	–	2,669
Qatar	381	16	138	612	18	195	1,979	36	271	1,751	37	413
TOTAL	11,210	187	3,091	17,293	321	5,746	56,941	471	10,511	50,384	664	17,010
Iran	8,638	434	2,409	5,675	576	3,393	20,886	688	5,433	19,399	578	10,343
Venezuela	2,890	236	2,403	4,384	364	2,821	10,312	521	4,247	9,654	480	5,401
Algeria	1,029	276	1,493	1,570	319	2,242	4,195	404	4,058	4,058	384	5,861
Iraq	1,242	137	713	2,138	198	906	6,907	371	2,365	8,328	428	n.a.
Ecuador	60	283	319	282	266	532	615	447	948	516	396	943
TOTAL	8,859	1,366	7,337	14,049	1,723	9,894	42,915	2,431	17,051	41,955	2,266	22,548
Nigeria	1,786	360	1,505	2,770	592	1,877	8,913	280	2,771	7,387	709	6,035
Indonesia	913	865	1,562	1,609	1,602	2,729	5,211	2,215	3,842	5,282	1,821	4,709
TOTAL	2,699	1,225	3,067	4,379	2,194	4,606	14,124	2,495	6,613	12,669	2,530	10,744
TOTAL	22,768	2,778	13,495	35,718	4,238	20,246	113,980	5,397	34,175	105,008	5,400	50,302

	1972	1973	1974	1975
Nonoil/Oil Exports				
Group I	1.7%	1.9%	0.8%	1.3%
II	15.1	12.3	5.7	5.4
III	45.4	50.1	17.5	20.0
Imports/Total Exports				
Group I	27.1%	32.6%	18.3%	33.5%
II	71.8	62.7	37.6	63.6[a]
III	78.2	70.1	39.8	70.7
Total	52.8	50.6	28.6	49.5[a]

Source: Computed from IMF, *International Financial Statistics* 29, no. 9 (September 1976).
[a]Excluding Iraq.

Table 5A-3
Cost and Profitability of Middle East Oil, Selected Years

	1948	1951	1960	1970	1973[a]	1974	1975
				Year-End			
Participation, royalty, taxes (%)							
Host Government Share of Production	9	9	9	9	25	60	60
Host Government Royalty Rates	[b]	[b]	12.5	12.5	12.5	20	20
Host Government Tax Rates	0	50	50	50	55	85	85
Prices (dollars per barrel)							
Posted price (list price)	2.05	1.75	1.80	1.80	2.90	11.25	12.40
Typical sales price	2.05	1.75	1.80	1.40	2.30	10.45	11.50
Costs (dollars per barrel)							
Operating cost (exploration and production)	(.60)	(.20)	(.20)	(.10)	(.15)	(.15)	(.25)
Host government take[c]	(.25)	(.75)	(.80)	(.95)	(1.80)	(10.10)	(11.00)
Profits (dollars per barrel)							
Oil company producing profit margin	1.20	.80	.80	.35	.35	.20	.25

Source: Exxon, *Middle East Oil*, Exxon background series, November 1976.

[a]June—prior to large price increases in October.

[b]Many original concession agreements called for a fixed payment in gold for each ton of oil exported. A ton of oil contains about 7½ barrels or 315 gallons.

[c]Includes royalties, taxes and other payments, but excludes receipts from sales of government-owned oil to nonconcession holders (third parties).

Table 5A–4
Distribution of World Financial Flows to LDCs, 1974
($ billion US)

Donor	Total Official Private, Net[a]	Official Development Assistance						
		Grants		Loans		Total	
		Total	Technical Assistance	Gross	Net	Gross	Net
Bilateral flow from OECD	23.7	5.3	2.5	3.9	2.9	9.2	8.2
Total flow from multilateral agencies	5.8	1.5	0.7	1.5	1.4	2.9	2.8
Total bilateral flow from OPEC	2.4	1.3	—	0.8	0.8	2.1	2.1
Grand Total	31.9	8.1	3.2	6.2	5.1	14.2	13.1

Source: Organization for Economic Cooperation and Development, *Geographical Distribution of Financial Flows to Developing Countries,* 1976, p. 93.

[a]Includes direct investment, long-term official flows, official export credits.

6

An International Oil Agreement Through Bilateral Cartel Bargaining?

Richard F. Kosobud[a]

Introduction

The governments of oil-importing countries have not yet, singly or jointly, devised appropriate responses to decisions of the Organization of Petroleum Exporting Countries (OPEC). Attempts by single oil-importing countries to get significantly more favorable terms than other importers have not worked. The hesitancy of members of the International Energy Agency (IEA) to go much beyond defensive procedures against another oil embargo (and agreement on even that measure seems shaky) points up the problems of joint importer action. Nor does OPEC appear to be secure in its new powerful position in the market, as revealed by its apparent anxiety to avoid direct discussions with the IEA; its visible problem with agreement on price changes; and its basic internal problem with the output allocations or prorationing that are required to support a cartel price structure. Governments in both groups seem nervous about the future role and functioning of the multinational oil companies, judging from proposals within importing countries on divestiture of existing oil companies and from the lavish attention both sides of the market pay to national oil companies.

To what extent do these pervasive signs of disequilibrium in the world's crude oil market call for basically new energy policies and institutions? It may be argued that we are witnessing the outward agitation of a market returning to a more competitive form of organization; or, at the other end of the spectrum, that we are witnessing the painful consumption and production adjustments to the supply constraints imposed by a cartel that will be a fixture in the market for a long time to come. In either case, it would be defensible, but not optimal, to let the process go on with minimum intervention, that is, to let the price mechanism provide the appropriate information, except where those most hurt are least able to bear it. This study will argue, however, that without some

[a]I have discussed the ideas presented here with a number of people in both oil-producing and -consuming countries and my debts for comments and criticisms are too large and numerous to list in detail. I must acknowledge several of these, however, and not because I secured agreement during the discussion. I benefited from discussions with Dr. Ali Boudjaja, Abu Dhabi National Oil Company; Dr. Parviz Minha, National Iranian Oil Company; Dr. Usama Jamali, OAPEC; and Prime Minister M. Salem of Egypt. I benefited from discussions with Dr. Paul Frankel, consultant; Mr. U. Lantzke, International Energy Agency; M. Thierry de Montbrial, Foreign Ministry, Paris; and Professor Dieter Schmitt, Energy Research Center, University of Cologne. I retain sole responsibility for the views (and errors) contained in this study.

innovations in the world's energy markets there is reason for grave concern about the stability of output and price decisions, about the "beggar thy neighbor" responses of governments to oil payment requirements in the balance of payments, and about the departures from reasonable economic growth paths that governments may accept because of uncertainty about energy prices.

There are three reasons for concern. The first is the economic incentives for a producers' cartel: the low price and high income elasticities of demand for crude oil, the unusual distribution of oil reserves, and the difficulties of substituting for crude oil in consumption and production. These are strong incentives to set against the internal conflicts which will rend OPEC from time to time. OPEC in some form or another is here to stay.

A second reason for concern is the dominant government role in OPEC not hitherto seen in cartels. This adds foreign policy conflict to the traditional economic conflict within the cartel. The third reason is perhaps the most intricate, but may also be the most important: the internal bargaining among consumers and among producers, mostly carried out by governments, will significantly affect the external bargaining between consumers and producers. This chapter will analyze these bargaining processes and propose a structure for the bargaining that reduces the indeterminacy of outcomes.

This chapter proposes that both producers and consumers consider a negotiated commodity agreement on crude oil over the medium-term future. This would include a simplified price structure, quantity allocations among consumers and producers, and a monitoring process. Other items could well be put on the bargaining table, such as import and export financing and investment guarantees. This agreement should result from negotiations between a buyers' or consumers' cartel and OPEC. The IEA, an incipient consumers' cartel, might be strengthened to bargain more effectively for consumers' interests. But that is getting ahead of the story. An analysis of cartel behavior is needed to reveal the nature of its internal conflicts and their probable bearing on external policies. This analysis must consider two cartels, using bilateral cartel theory. There are many questions about how a market organized along bilateral cartel lines would perform. Finally, oil consumers are not at that stage of agreement among themselves where negotiations with producers would seem feasible, nor are producers yet sufficiently agreed to deal with consumers. What moves may be made toward such agreement will be the final topic of this discussion. There are options other than bilateral cartel bargaining in the world's crude oil market, of course, but very little agreement exists on these.

The Guessing Games in the World's Crude Oil Market

Oil importers can wait or hope for OPEC's internal conflicts to break it up, as has happened with many cartels in other commodities.[1] One observer claimed to have detected signs of an impending breakdown in March 1975, hastened by the sizeable slump in demand caused by the widespread recession in the industrialized countries.[2] Such a dissolution would decrease oil prices from their lofty heights of about eighty times marginal costs in Saudi Arabia to a more competitive level. Competitive pricing would permit oil-importing countries to return to a growth path of energy consumption, allowing a smoother, slower transition from oil to coal and then to nuclear resources, which are essentially inexhaustible.[3] More aggressive consumer actions—either jointly or by the largest economic member, the United States—could include secret auctions and other measures designed to play on the inherent conflicts of interest within OPEC.[4]

Consumers could put further pressure on OPEC by rapidly developing alternative energy systems based upon coal and nuclear fission. Permitting domestic prices of crude oil to reflect fully the artificial scarcity imposed by the cartel would make this substitution process even more effective. Taxes and subsidies could be introduced to allow benefits and costs of such a program to fall more evenly on the various affected groups. Essentially, this would speed up a substitution process that would have taken place over a longer period of time, perhaps thirty years. There are problems in accelerating the development of alternative energy sources. For one thing, it is not clear what OPEC's response will be. And the speed with which alternative sources can be expanded is complicated by factors other than OPEC.[5]

Yet another distinct option is for a loosely organized group of oil-importing nations to attempt to establish a forum with producers. The United States seems to have favored this approach occasionally. Problems can be discussed and proposals considered, as in the Conference on International Economic Cooperation (CIEC). It remains to be seen whether substantive agreements can be achieved in a loosely structured forum, even though a very useful exchange of views—and perhaps a moderation of extreme actions—might result. A forum, however, lacks the prior coordination of oil importers' views required for hard bargaining over explicit terms of an agreement. Most important, OPEC has little to gain from a forum on specific oil issues.

OPEC has a counterpart to each option available to oil consumers. The embryo consumers' group, the IEA, has been in disarray on numerous issues. OPEC members can exploit this disarray by tempting consumer governments into bilateral transactions without significantly altering cartel terms. Strong OPEC members with moderate revenue requirements, such as Saudi Arabia, could respond to any sealed bid strategy by temporarily reducing production as a warning to consumers, or by submitting a low bid as a warning to cartel members tempted to break the sellers' agreement. At the first sign of an effective consumers' group, OPEC could agree to arrange a loose forum discussion on energy matters, perhaps within the CIEC framework, in an effort to head off final formation of a consumers' bargaining unit. OPEC could jeopardize alternative energy resource developments by lowering prices, perhaps temporarily. And so the argument goes. The important point is that it is an idle exercise to draw up a list of options for one side without immediately discussing the counteroptions available to the other. The crude oil market is now almost instantly interdependent; planning energy policy based on some assumed fixed response of other participants in the market is a serious mistake.

The market has not become more predictable, nor is the probability distribution of outcomes more knowable than before. The market's framework, however, leads to at least two conclusions: certain outcomes seem less probable now (for example, spontaneous OPEC dissolution), and other outcomes seem less determinate (for example, the response of prices to the discovery of new reserves). This apparent paradox is worth more detailed comment.

Certain market facts widely reported and apparently widely believed set the stage for the forthcoming energy drama. The current and medium-term price elasticity of demand for crude oil is approximately $-.15$; the income elasticity of demand is around unity; the crustal distribution of recoverable reserves is favorable to cartel formation; and the elasticities of substitution in production and consumption for crude oil in the medium term are small (much less than unity).[6] Therefore, governments sitting on significant recoverable reserves can make enormous profits by accepting some form of cartel agreement. OPEC's success to date in utilizing these market facts to its advantage is now history. If basic disagreements among members caused a breaking of the existing agreement, market conditions and past successes would provide powerful incentives to put OPEC together again. Consumers would experience an unpredictable oscillation between the sellers' cartel and dubious competition; this could be unfavorable to energy consumption and production decisions outside the OPEC domain. Thus, a move to a stable framework of workable competition in the world's crude oil market is unlikely, no matter how desirable that would be for the consumer and for the optimal allocation of crude oil production over space and time.

Another market fact which increases indeterminacy is the dominant role of governments in forming and directing OPEC, and in determining consumers' responses to OPEC. The bargaining within OPEC appears to be a matter of government skills, resources, and goals. Its outcome depends upon a member's ability to inflict and suffer losses, upon the toughness of the bargaining delegation, and upon the member's goals, including (in this instance) perceived national interest. One need not talk to more than a few of the relevant government officials to be told that the dissolution of OPEC would return individual governments to bargaining with the multinational corporations; in this situation, most governments perceive their bargaining position as very inferior. Their fear of this may be a powerful factor unifying OPEC. On the other hand, the injection of government motivations into the bargaining process makes OPEC decisions less predictable.

It is useful at this point to fit both the multinational and national oil companies into our framework. The effective nationalization of oil reserves and the development of the national oil companies have markedly diminished the power of the multinationals, a trend likely to continue in the future.[7] Because OPEC member governments are more united at the moment than governments of consuming nations, multinational oil companies are more attentive to the requirements of OPEC, but not without an anxious glance at political debate within oil-consuming nations. If consuming nations united effectively, the multinationals would then become, perhaps as they prefer, truly neutral contractors implementing the provisions of an international oil agreement.

We may conclude that government policy objectives, domestic and foreign, will be embodied both in internal cartel bargaining and in external bargaining between OPEC and consuming nations. The range of outcomes now assumes the stability of dynamic political processes and economic adjustments, lagged responses, and expectational reactions, which respond to changes in technology, consumer preference, and capital and labor costs. If, then, the price and quantity transactions of the crude oil market will be shaped by a cartel in the foreseeable future, and if the cartel's internal bargaining processes now partly replace the traditional determinants of market prices, we must examine cartel behavior and the modifications that may be required in cartel theory when governments are the members.

Analyzing Cartel Behavior

A cartel is an association of potentially competitive production or consumption decision-making units, within which members retain their separate identities and control over their policies subject to the terms of the cartel agreement. The point that members remain autonomous (unlike competing units of a large corporation) is especially important in analyzing a cartel with government constituents, such as OPEC. The types of agreements members arrange among themselves determine the behavior or bargaining capacity of the cartel toward other transactors in the market, although the seeds of discord exist in every agreement.

We will distinguish three elements of the agreement necessary for the cartel to function. First is the specification of an output (or purchase quantity) for the individual member. This may be determined by a cartel allocation process which reflects an objective such as profit maximization, or by applying an agreed-upon cartel rule such as a market or profit share. Price levels—including varying prices for distinct qualities—may be stated in the agreement, but these depend upon the quantity allocation rules. This point has been obscured in the oil market because OPEC seems to set a (posted) price rather than allocate quantities to members, but in fact it is the quantities which multinational oil companies acquire from each OPEC member that "clear" the market and validate the price. The second element is the understanding about the allocation of net revenue among members. An important distinction here is whether members transfer net revenues among themselves or whether such revenues accrue from the quantity transacted by individual members. OPEC has no explicit agreement to transfer revenues (for good reason, as we shall see).

The third element in analyzing the behavioral implications of the agreement concerns the type and extent of information members provide each other, and the measures taken on the basis of this information to monitor and to enforce the agreement. The OPEC Statute provides for an Information Department (Article 37) and provides for "the collection and collation of statistical information from the Member Countries . . ." but data suitable for monitoring and enforcement have probably not yet been secured.[8] Before looking more closely at the OPEC agreement and its implications of this internal agreement, it will be useful to analyze agreement types and their probable market performance.

Types of Internal Cartel Agreements: Collusion by Pooling Production and Transferring Net Revenues

The way in which output is allocated among (producer) cartel members and the way in which they handle net revenues will influence the cartel's equilibrium and its behavior toward other transactors in the market. If the cartel's objective is to maximize its net revenue or profits, then it can achieve that objective efficiently if each member accepts a particular output, including zero output under certain circumstances. Such efficient allocations would sometimes require transfers of net revenues, or side payments, among members.

Assume a homogeneous commodity of variable quantity and no inter-member economies or diseconomies. Cartel profits are to be maximized subject to the constraints of the members' production functions. (Each member acquires inputs in competitive markets.) Like a firm with more than one plant, the cartel ought to aggregate member marginal costs so as to choose that aggregate monopoly quantity (in an otherwise competitive market) that maximizes profits. It allocates production among the members so that marginal costs are equated. We are assuming for the moment that all cartel members have agreed to these allocations.

If member production and cost functions were identical, output would be allocated equally, and a plausible (though not necessarily realistic) allocation of profits would be equal shares. It is more realistic to assume that cartel members will have varying unit costs and varying bargaining strengths and skills, so that profit allocation may be expected to be complicated. For a two-member cartel, the main issues may be brought out diagrammatically as in figure 6-1,

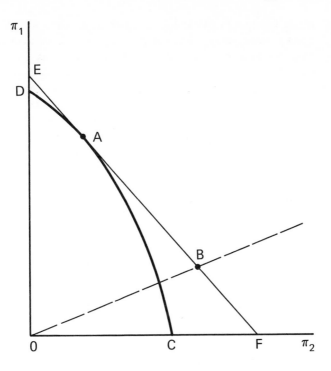

Figure 6-1. Producer Cartel Member Profit Contour and Transfer Focus

in which profits (π) for each member are plotted along the axes. Assume cost functions are such that the profit contour is DAC, which indicates profits from production to each member as its and the other member's output varies (competitive linear demand structure fixed). Competitive output yields profits at the origin. Equal cost functions would yield maximum profits where a 45 degree line through the origin was tangent to a symmetric contour. Figure 6-1 depicts a more realistic situation of different cost functions, with A being maximum profits where the line segment AB of slope −1 is tangent. Point A implies the cartel optimum quantity allocation between members but not necessarily the bargained profit allocation. Point A could be on one of the axes; if so, the idle member would have to be allocated something to keep him satisfied, because it is possible (and probable) that cartel price exceeds marginal cost of the idle member.

Any point along EF is a feasible profit allocation; depending upon the members' reserves, toughness, and ability to inflict losses, an allocation will be obtained, let us say at B. Formally this model may seem close to the two-person zero-sum game although the members have cooperated on many aspects of the situation. Changes in either supply or demand could shift the profit contour, requiring either renewed bargaining to allocate a different quantity of profits or some previously bargained rule on how to handle changes. Such shifts could be caused by consumer response to cartelization, technological change, or new reserves. For example, an isoprofit share rule, indicated by the points along line segment OB, suggests itself as one way of handling shifts in the profit contour. However, shifts are unlikely to follow any proportionate (homothetic) pattern, and a shifting, twisting contour could cause the iso-profit share allocation to deviate further from the profit shares that would be attributable to the cartel's optimum production allocation. The further profit allocation deviates from that allocation attributable to production (that is, the greater proportion transfers are of total profits), the greater the dissatisfaction at least one member feels about the rule. Even in this simplest case—a centralized producers' cartel in otherwise competitive markets—we may envision internal bargaining problems which affect the cartel's ability to choose the profit-maximizing output. For the n member cartel where n is greater than 2, coalitions and strategies among dissatisfied members could undermine the initial agreement to pool resources and make intermember transfers. This central issue can be better treated in the second type of cartel agreement, in which the assumptions of pooling and transfer are relaxed. First, however, a short digression on the long run.

Collusion by Pooling and Transfer: The Long Run

The cartel that pools resources and makes intergovernment transfers of net income has to make several adjustments in the long run that are of special interest to this inquiry. These have to do with changes in the size or number of wells, plants or installations and with the claims of new producers. We shall assume the long run is short enough not to decrease but to increase proven reserves. The main results can be obtained in a highly simplified setting; namely, that each member has only one (identical) well or plant already of long-run optimum size, that there are no intermember economies or diseconomies, that in production long-run constant returns to scale prevail, and that demand is unchanging and competitive.

New entrants in a market centralized in monopoly fashion will shift the (rising) short-run marginal cost curve to the right, expanding output and lowering price along an unchanging demand curve. This process will continue until fixed costs, which increase with each entry, have shifted the total average cost curve to a tangency position with average revenue; at this stage there is no incentive, in our model, for further entry. The industry is characterized by extra capacity, measured by the distance from the quantity produced to that quantity at the minimum point on the long-run average cost curve. This extra capacity distinguishes the long-run cartel from the monopoly solution. The cartel solution is likely to be unstable in the sense that members have a strong incentive to violate cartel rules (price exceeds marginal cost), especially if such violation could go undetected. If cartel members have difficulty agreeing on these matters, the initial agreements on the pooling of resources and transfers of net revenue will probably come unstuck; in fact, there are good reasons to believe that it will be difficult for cartel members to agree to pool resources and transfer net revenues. However, we must not lose sight of the cartel members' incentive to reunite if the cartel should fall into disarray. Competition is thus unstable in markets in which the conditions for cartelization exist.

Types of Cartel Internal Agreements: Collusions without Pooling and Transfers

No cartel on the current scene has had the type of agreement among members in which production facilities are pooled and intergovernment transfers of net revenues are made as a part of cartel decision making. This kind of internal agreement would be extremely difficult to accomplish. Where governments are involved, such agreements imply a transfer of sovereignty to the cartel that seems highly unlikely at the present stage of development of the national state. For a member to delegate to the cartel (that is, to other members) the power to set production quotas—including zero output—and to make transfer payments is to freeze that member in its present situation. If members viewed the future as uscertain, with technological and other changes certain to occur, then they will probably be reluctant to lock themselves into their present position. Bargaining positions among members are likely to be perceived as subject to more or less constant change; this is incompatible with the delegation of important economic decisions.

We should keep the analysis of the cartel that acts as a monopoly firmly in mind as we analyze the cartel that does not act as a monopoly. In the case of less explicit collusion, we assume that cartel members follow the rule Winston Churchill is supposed to have recommended to the ntional state: base behavior on permanent interests but not permanent friends. Consequently, consider members of a producers' cartel who do not divulge their production functions or costs, nor do they agree to pooling of their resources or intermember transfers of new revenue. Consider a loose agreement to share the market according to some rule. Since cartel members are assumed to comprise in the short run the total effective supply of the commodity, this agreement determines the price in a market assumed competitive on the demand side. It is possible, I shall hasten to note, to introduce noncartel producers as price takers who follow the cartel price, so that their supplies at every price may be subtracted from the total market demand curve. Countries such as the USSR, China, and perhaps Norway and the United Kingdom could be incorporated into the model in this way. The quantity (production) agreement also determines the profits each member will receive, as there is no transfer of profits among members.

These internal bargaining problems and the resultant characteristics of price and quantity agreements may be brought out conveniently by means of Stackelberg indifference maps. In figure 6-2, two members of a cartel of the type we are considering are depicted as having cost functions such that with a fixed demand structure we can trace out isoprofit curves that reveal how the profits of one member may be kept constant with varying values of the quantity vector (q_1, q_2) of outputs of the two members. The profit curves for member one are concave to that member's axis and the profit curves for two are concave to the ordinate. The profit level associated with an indifference curve is larger for the curve everywhere closer to the axis of the concerned member.[9]

Note that if the set of points depicting joint profit maximization is non-empty, it will occur at profit indifference curve tangencies such as those which fall on the line segment $E'F'$ with terminal points where a member experiences insufficient revenues to cover variable costs. The argument is that if members are aware of the consequences of varying output (sales) on profit, the bargaining

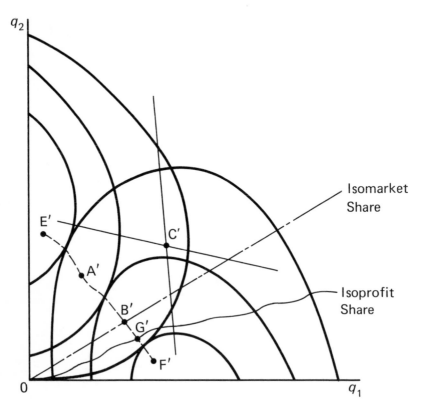

Figure 6-2. Producer Cartel Market Bargaining Locus $E'F'$

process ought to move them onto the set of quantity combinations comprising the tangency points. Quantitites at other points could be varied by bargaining so that one member could receive higher profits with no decrease for the other. Note that price varies from point to point. By contrast, if the members were noncooperative and followed Cournot-type behavior, they could achieve the Cournot solution at C' which is different from (and yields smaller profits at larger quantities than) joint profit maximization. Our very definition of cartel implies some degree of collusion, so that the Cournot (Stackelberg) methods of analysis seem inappropriate compared to the idea of joint profit maximization; however, whether the cartel will be able to reach a quantity allocation of $E'F'$ by explicit bargaining is a matter for further analysis.

The bargaining chips for cartel members are alternative quantities for each to produce. Identical production functions and input prices would yield a configuration in figure 6-2 (not shown) such that joint profit maximization and maximum profits would result from equal quantity allocations if members could agree on such a quantity allocation. There is no reason why they should. In the situation shown, where production functions differ, a cartel maximum profit position is depicted at A' (corresponding to A of figure 6-1). At A' equality of marginal costs is implied for each active member. Among the difficulties the cartel may encounter in actually reaching A' is that other points on the locus yield higher net revenues for one of the members at the expense of the other. An OPEC member such as Iran, which has stated a strong preference for increased export earnings and net revenues, may move in that direction along the locus, provided that a cartel stabilizer, such as Saudi Arabia, will accept reduced output and net revenues.

In contrast to figure 6-1, in which the isoprofit line is a straight line through the origin, figure 6-2 depicts a nonlinear function (barring identical production function). The reverse is true for isomarket shares (equating quantity allocation with production and sales). As changes occur, due, for example, to increasing demand, an isomarket share rule would typically imply varying profit shares while an isoprofit share rule would imply varying market shares. If historical market shares were accepted by cartel members as the decision rule for quantity allocation, then the intersection of that isomarket share line (arbitrarily drawn) with line segment $E'F'$, if such intersection occurred, would provide a solution to the cartel's problem. In figure 6-2 an illustrative intersection point is shown at B'. That intersection need not be the maximum profit position, although it is the position of joint profit maximization. A nonlinear isoprofit share line, one of an infinite number, has been drawn in figure 6-2, yielding yet another possible joint profit maximization solution at G'.

What can be written about the properties of any agreement reached? Any vector of quantities in the joint maximization locus yields a quantity which can be sold under cartel conditions at a price in excess of marginal costs. These quantities provide short-run profits for one or more of the cartel members, but the temptation to break cartel rules exists. A member making extra sales without being detected could consider price as equal to marginal revenue for purposes of "cheating," although significant amounts of cheating would soon become apparent. Is there a tendency to bargain to point A', maximum total profits? Movements in the locus represent gains for one member at the expense of another, so that until we have investigated bargaining strengths and skills and varying motivations, it is difficult to predict where agreement will be secured. To the extent that the bargaining locus $E'F'$ has a slope near minus unity we may infer that the two cartel members (or coalitions) have approximately equal unit cost functions; that is, their marginal costs rise at about the same rate as their production. Markedly different cost functions yield a bargaining locus approaching zero or infinite slope, and other thins being equal, would seem to create difficulty in securing agreement. Such a situation would favor the bargaining position of the low-cost producer and would make more likely a movement on the bargaining locus $E'F'$ toward larger quantities and profits for that member. It is frequently reported that Saudi Arabia is among the lowest-cost producers in OPEC; this enhances that country's bargaining power perhaps more than large reserves do.

Members with varying economic development plans may be expected to place quite different values on the price and quantity outcomes of figure 6-2. If one member now regards larger quantities of crude oil production as highly desirable because such production will build up foreign exchange reserves, that member may choose to expand production and move off the bargaining locus $E'F'$ in figure 6-2. If the ordinate measured that member's quantities, a move up and directly vertical from any point on $E'F'$ could represent increased foreign exchange reserves or market share for member two, although profits of both members would decline. Such a move could only be accomplished by selling below the cartel price.

As adjustments occur in the market over a longer period of time than the short run, it is possible to conjecture about the changing pressures that may bear on cartel agreements. As the number of members in the cartel increases, the opportunities for dissatisfaction and the costs of collusion and enforcement seem to increase, raising the possibilities of shifting coalitions, not to mention increased cheating on cartel rules. For the cartel tha manages to stay together, it would seem plausible that some simple rule has been devised by which member output decisions are made (and which leaves members better off than in the perceived competitive situation). Several simple rules for cartel decisions suggest themselves: to maintain isomarket shares or to maintain isoprofit shares. If changes in demand occur (or in technology or costs), the profit indifference curves and core of figure 6-2 would shift and likely twist so that applying either rule would mean variation in the other variable; that is, isomarket shares imply varying profit shares as the market expands or contracts, and a constant profit share rule implies varying quantities (assuming members have different production functions). Consequently, dissatisfaction with prior bargains will probably increase during a period of change in market circumstances. Iran's complaint after the December 1976 meeting of OPEC (which resulted in two levels of price increases) that its former sales volume was not being maintained suggests that a share of the market may be the rule, perhaps implicit, that OPEC members have come to accept.

We may conclude from our analysis that internal agreements do not eliminate conflicts of interest within a cartel. Particularly for the cartel whose members have widely different cost functions, reserves, and stated objectives, conflict is ever present. Devising simple rules such as isoprofit or isomarket shares may appear sensible for small changes in market circumstances, but appreciable changes are likely to move members to new positions on the producer cartel internal locus, opening up fresh bargaining problems.[10]

Internal Bargaining in a Consumers' Cartel

A consumers' cartel operating in otherwise competitive markets has problems and opportunities analogous to those of a producers' cartel. In the background the reader may imagine the discussions and bargaining of the consumers involved in the International Energy Agency. If consumer members agree to pool purchases and make intermember transfers of net revenues, the result will be an equalization of marginal revenue products at the monopsony quantity. It is that quantity which equates member aggregate marginal revenue product with aggregate marginal supply price (or marginal marginal costs), with the proviso that variable costs are covered. If marginal revenue product functions are identical, then equal quantity pruchases result in equal monopsony profit receipts by members. The consumers' cartel in turn may directly consume the commodity or sell its own commodity in a second-stage competitive market (though access of noncartel consumers to a supplier must be denied). We shall assume the cartel government members could distribute monopsony gains to their own second-stage consumers by subsidy, tax, or rationing if they desired.

If, as is likely, marginal revenue product functions are not equal among cartel members, then purchases ought to be allocated according to the rule that equates among members marginal revenue product values for the monopsony quantity. Note marginal revenue product functions are net of dometic energy supplies. The allocation of monopsony gains again may depend on bargaining, as in the comparable producers' cartel case. Any member whose marginal revenue product is too small to receive a purchase allocation will have to be paid to refrain from breaking cartel rules as long as the member's marginal revenue product is equal to or above the monopsony price. Any member recieving an allocation will find the monopsony price below its marginal revenue product and therefore, to the extent the member views the price as marginal cost (that is, additional purchase can be made without cartel retaliation), that member has an incentive to break the cartel rules.

In the more realistic case, in which cartel members do not agree to pool purchases nor to allow the cartel to make intermember transfers of profits, then cartel bargains over the quantity of purchases and associated monopsony gains. An apparatus similar to figure 6-2 could be set up and a bargaining locus displayed, being the set of outcomes representing joint maximization of monopsony profits. Will bargains tend to approach the maximum profits monopsony power could achieve? Limiting cartel member gains to those derived from purchases (rather than transfers) implies that members will tend to drive the cartel to purchase more than the pure monopsony quantity. Widely divergent marginal revenue product functions would heighten conflicts within the consumers' group. These divergencies arise in part because of varying domestic energy resources; a country such as Japan with few such resources will perceive the situation differently than the United States, which has relatively abundant resources. A joint profit maximization position may be achieved, but not necessarily the one that maximizes cartel profits.

If such an outcome is achieved initially, changing circumstances in the market will require a new agreement, and the isoprofit share rule, if applied, will require new purchase allocations (assuming varying marginal revenue product functions), or an isomarket share rule will require varying profit shares. Fresh bargaining seems to be required in each instance, and this raises the possibility that even if it is willing to bargain, the cartel will move too slowly to achieve a point in a shifting joint profit maximization set of outcomes. Can the uncertainties and fluctuations in price and quantity time paths be reduced if the market is organized along bilateral cartel lines?

Bilateral Cartel Bargaining

First consider the example of two cartels facing one another in the market. Each has agreed internally to pool resources or purchases and to make intermember transfers of net revenue. All other relevant markets are competitive. The essential difference between this model and the one discussed previously is that the demand curve can no longer be taken as given by the producers' cartel. The cartels realize that it is to their advantage to come to an agreement; given their economic aims, they will jointly maximize profits in the bilateral monopoly sense at the quantity at which marginal revenue equals marginal cost but where price must be the outcome of a bargaining process (limited at the competitive quantity between aggregate average revenue and aggregate average cost).[11] This quantity, the competitive one, is greater than any of the quantities that the producers' cartel, for example, would have sold if acting alone, and it is a larger quantity than the consumers' cartel would have bought if acting alone. The reader may persuade himself or herself of this result by first constructing in figure 6-3, panel (c) a marginal supply price in the case of a buyers' cartel which

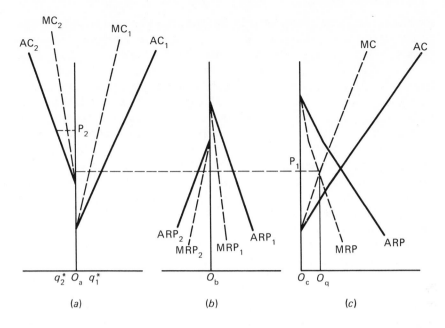

Figure 6–3. Bilateral Cartel Supply and Demand Data

would cut the marginal revenue product function to the left of the competitive output, O_cO_1. Thus, by bargaining, consumers' and producers' cartels can achieve a larger quantity, and hence increased welfare, than in the case of markets organized with only one cartel. The reason for this outcome is that for any point away from ST, the contract curve, one of the parties can offer a different price and quantity combination yielding equal profits to the other party but preferred by the first. This situation is depicted in figure 6–3, panel (c), where the line segment ST shows the range of possible prices or contract curve in this case.[12] This model is unrealistic, of course, because it assumes pooling of resources and transfer of net income, but the main proposition will continue to hold in somewhat attenuated form as we consider more realistic models.

For cartels in which members have not agreed to pool resources or purchases and make intermember transfers but recognize their interdependence by agreeing to negotiate quantities and prices, we can envision or simulate the bargaining process. The analytical apparatus of figure 6–3 will be helpful. In the first two panels, (a) and (b), the linear cost and product curves of a two-member cartel in each instance are shown, with panel (a) depicting producer member one's quantities (q_1) to the right along the abscissa from zero, and member two's quantities to the left. Panel (b) depicts quantities along the abscissa for consumer members one and two ($q_1{}'$, $q_2{}'$), while panel (c) aggregates cost and product curves. In each panel the ordinate gives price, cost, and average and marginal revenue product values on the same scale. Quantity scales are the same for (a) and (b) but not for (c). We shall examine functions of different shapes later.

Th first result to note in the case depicted is that the possible core or contract curve of price outcomes in the bilateral monopoly case is narrowed because member two on the producer's side is unwilling to accept a price below the intersection of his average cost curve with the axis. A multi-plant monopolist would have shut down this activity, but an outonomous government does not have that option as a cartel member. We are excluding side payments. Similarly, buyer two will resist any price above the intersection of his ARP_2 function with the ordinate. We conclude, therefore, that the nonpooling, nontransferring bilateral cartel contract curve will be smaller than the bilateral monopoly contract curve (in figure 6-3), and the result may be generalized to the assertion that the former will always be equal to or less than the latter.

Will there be a movement to this bilateral cartel contract curve (competitive output) from any initial point off the curve? In the bilateral cartel case, the answer is not clear. In the bilateral monopoly case such a movement could occur, increasing the net revenues of one side without reducing the other side's revenues. In the bilateral cartel this movement could worsen the position of one cartel member. (The reader may test this by choosing a price and quantity to the right of the competitive quantity and above the competitive price, and by lowering both observe the impact on seller two's profits.) However, the total gains outweigh the total losses in this case, and if side payments are introduced (by either or both of the cartels) such a movement to the competitive output may be attainable. An interesting problem emerges if we start the bargaining process at one of the extreme points, which would result from a concentration of power on one side of the market. If we start with OPEC on the sellers' side and no consumers' cartel, then the initial position has a higher price and smaller quantity than the competitive one. To bargain effectively, consumers would have to do something persuasive in the market, such as decrease their demand functions sufficiently (or threaten to decrease them) to make OPEC willing to bargain. I shall return to this point in a moment.

Our analytical model also suggests that stable market share is likely to be the rule adopted by both producers' and consumers' cartels in allocating the competitive (or agreed-upon) quantity. A stable quantity allocation need be changed only when demand or supply changes. A fixed profit share rule, however, requires for every change in price a different (probably quite different) quantity allocation. Note how extreme this would have to be to keep seller two's profit share a constant proportion of total sellers' profits. An example of a fixed market share is given in figure 6-3, panel (a), where $q_2* = \alpha q_1*$ and hence $(1 + \alpha) q_1* = O_cO_1$. Varying price results in varying profits to the sellers from stable shares. For a government with economic development or other plans requiring the satisfaction of employment and foreign exchange goals, stability of output would seem preferable to a constant proportion of a fluctuating profit volume.

Another possible rule or decision mechanism for the producers' cartel is to permit the low-cost producer to absorb certain shocks in the bilateral cartel agreement, especially demand fluctuations. Saudi Arabia, Kuwait and certain other members of OPEC appear, at times, to have played this role. If the entire adjustment process is thrown on the low-cost (member one) producer, then the changes in that member's profits may be read directly from figure 6-3. Such decreases in demand would appear to strengthen the bargaining position of a consumers' cartel, throwing the strains of an unpleasant internal bargaining process onto the producers' cartel.

The results obtained are subject to the given assumptions about the shape of demand and cost curves. Downward sloping cost curves do not materially change the argument. If crude oil is truly nearing exhaustion within thirty years or so, then the upward sloping curves of figure 6-3 may not be far from reality, and may in effect be shifting upward to the left, in which case our analysis applies, and would lead to a gradually rising negotiated price.

Toward Bilateral Cartel Bargaining?

I have already shown how the bilateral cartel model with resource pooling and net revenue transfer could lead to competitive output with price to be determined by further bargaining. This outcome is clearly superior to either a sole producers' cartel or sole consumers' cartel, in that the total gains from this outcome could more than offset any losses incurred in moving from a single to a bilateral cartel organization of the market. However, this result only holds in the rather unrealistic case of pooling and transfer. It can be argued (though in a quieter tone of voice) that a bilateral cartel market with no internal resource pooling or income transfer on either side would tend to transact a larger quantity than a single cartel market. Bilateral cartels which agree on joint profit or welfare maximization are more likely to move in this direction through negotiation. The only reason for reservation is that member conflict over internal allocation will influence and constrain the bilateral cartel bargaining. It is not possible to prove that rational behavior under conditions of joint profit or welfare maximization will lead to the contract curve or competitive quantity. However, the potential gains in trade are a real advantage of bilateral cartel organization over a single cartel.

Bilateral cartel bargaining that led to an international commodity agreement of medium-term duration, say three to five years, would offer the prospect of price stability in a market characterized by unanticipated fluctuation. Avoiding unanticipated fluctuations should facilitate investment in alternative energy resources and smooth the transition out of the age of oil. The strongest case for international commodity markets has been made on the grounds of avoiding cyclical fluctuations in price (and to some extent earnings). The unanticipated fluctuations in the crude oil market may be attributed to the erratic behavior of one cartel. Thus the case for avoidance of these fluctuations seems even stronger. Although causes for instability continue to exist (because of internal conflicts) in a bilateral cartel market, there are reasons to believe they will be less important than in other types of market organizations. Several points deserve mention in this connection.

A bilateral cartel agreement is likely to have a better chance of enforcement than a single internal cartel agreement because violation requires at least two parties, one on each side of the market, to break the agreement. Any significant violation would probably be reflected in transaction data in this highly organized market. Many consumers and producers would have an interest in maintaining adherence to the agreement. The agreement itself may cover not only the (simplified) price structure and quantity allocations for a spectrum of oil qualities, but also could cover detailed assignments to multinational oil corporations which act as technical middlemen in the process. This latter point is worth separate discussion.

The multinational oil corporations (MOCs) have not figured prominently in this discussion because they are not direct decision makers in internal or external cartel bargaining. The bilateral cartel agreement could specify their role in the market, and require of them data on stocks and flows to facilitate monitoring and enforcement of the market agreement. Such a role for the MOCs should also reduce the nervousness with which their behavior is currently regarded. Such a role for the MOCs ought also to ease the oil exporters' and importers' drive for national oil companies, which tends to destabilize the market.

The case for bilateral cartel negotiations seems strong, but can oil importers be expected to agree to a unified consumers' cartel, can OPEC be expected to accept a consumers' cartel as a bargaining force, and can such negotiations be expected to have a reasonable chance for general agreement? Labor-management collective bargaining is a possible parallel. What is different in the case of oil bargaining is the lack of supracartel government to provide ground rules.

Several moves in the direction of bilateral cartel bargaining could be made in the near future; they require, at least at the start, United States initiatives. Oil-importing countries have achieved some agreement on measures to resist another oil embargo through the International Energy Agency. That agreement provides a valuable basis for the next steps. As a very large oil importer, the United States could utilize its oil purchases to demand bargaining with OPEC on the terms of these transactions. There would be no need to intervene markedly in the market; a small government unit could coordinate the terms on which the multinational oil companies bring crude oil and refined products into the United States. Bargaining chips could include a sealed bid system or a set of policies designed to utilize alternative energy sources (for example, domestic coal) increasingly if OPEC members do not meet specified terms. OPEC will probably be unwilling to bargain immediately on these matters, so an initial period of jockeying in the market will be required. The time of initial bargaining ought to be selected with care. The terms of any agreement between the United States and OPEC could be extended to other oil-importing countries (which may elect to join the bargaining at the start), although certain reciprocal pledges ought to be made by all consumer nations.

The charge has been made that the United States has not been displeased by the formation of OPEC. As a country with vast energy resources the United States need not lose too much by artificially rigged prices, it is argued, and it stands to gain influence among countries with fewer energy resources. The argument sometimes continues by making the point that the formation of OPEC, after all, provided the basis for stability in the Middle East and elsewhere. This chapter does not support the idea that OPEC by itself is a stabilizing institution; it introduces new intracartel conflicts which bring new forces to bear on market decisions. And the idea that a country with major oil imports stands to gain by the formation of a powerful cartel is surely a strange one. As long as OPEC remains the dominant force in the crude oil markets, consumers have every incentive to try to diminish its power. The interplay of internal conflicts within OPEC and the undending attempts of consumers to diminish OPEC power by one means or another do not augur for a stable future in the market. The main idea of this study has been a proposal to structure the bargaining along more constructive lines.

Notes

1. An interesting review of previous cartel experience is available in P.L. Eckbo, "OPEC and the Experience of Previous International Commodity Cartels," MIT Energy Laboratory Working Paper no. 75-998WP (August 1975). Experience with government-dominated cartels seems too sparse to provide any guidance, however.

2. Robert Z. Aliber, "Impending Breakdown of the OPEC Cartel," *Wall Street Journal* (March 20, 1975).

3. William D. Nordhaus, "The Allocation of Energy Resources," *Brookings Papers on Economic Activity* 3 (1973): 529–570.

4. Morris Adelman, "Politics, Economics, and World Oil," *American Economic Review*, May 1974, pp. 58–67.

5. Organization for Economic Cooperation and Development, *Energy Prospects to 1985*, (February 1975), pp. 205–208, and *World Energy Outlook* (January 1977).

6. I am indebted to Mr. Edward Flom, Manager of Industry Planning, Standard Oil of Indiana, for a discussion of these facts.

7. R. Stobough, "Long Range Outlook for Multinational Enterprises in Developing Economies," Academy of International Business Conference, Cairo, December 1976.

8. *The Statute of the Organization of the Petroleum Exporting Countries,* Vienna: Erwin Metlen, 1971, pp. 20-21.

9. William Fellner, *Competition Among the Few* (New York: Augustus M. Kelley, 1960), pp. 104–115. In considering figure 6-2 one may think of a coalition of OPEC members, say Saudi Arabia and the United Arab Emirate, along the abscissa and the other members along the ordinate.

10. Compare the comments on bargaining theory in L.G. Telser, *Competition, Collusion, and Game Theory,* (Chicago: Aldine-Atherton, 1972), p. 215.

11. E. Malinvaud, *Lectures on Microeconomic Theory* (New York: American Elsevier, 1974), p. 149.

12. Loosely, the contract curve is the locus of different prices in this illustration along which any change in price benefits one and penalizes the other cartel.

7

The Prospects for a Reorganization of International Trade in Commodities

Bernd Stecher

Introduction

Less developed countries (LDCs) are much better represented in international organizations today than previously, and as such they can more effectively criticize the present imbalances and inequities in the international economic system. Statistics show where corrective action is most needed to improve the economic situation of the LDCs: Per capita income is much higher in industrial countries than in LDCs. The LDCs' share in the world's industrial production has remained more or less constant at 7 percent. More than 20 percent of the labor force in the Third World is unemployed. The foreign debt of the LDCs has grown to $150 billion (United States dollars), and some LDCs are hardly able to pay even the interest on this debt. Finally, hunger is an ever-increasing problem in the LDCs.

There are many explanations for this situation. Some claim that it is the historical outgrowth of the colonial period, while others maintain that the policies of the LDCs themselves have caused a severe misallocation of resources. Moreover, many of those people who ascribe to the former opinion also argue that the existing mechanisms for adjusting international trade relations are biased against the LDCs, because they are based on *ex post* adjustment within a market framework. Along this line, numerous recent proposals have advocated creating a "New International Economic Order" (NIEO) based on an international *ex ante* agreement on worldwide production structures. The essence of these proposals, however, contradicts basic economic theory. In reexamining the issue, there is a strong case against negotiated structural changes.

The economic content of the LDCs' challenge can be summarized in three points. They propose:

1. Establishing or improving international commodity agreements for those raw materials which are important to the exports of LDCs.
2. Inflating the prices of raw material exports from LDCs with an index of the export prices of manufactured goods from industrial countries (indexation).
3. Increasing the LDCs' share in the world's production of manufactured goods from 7 percent today to 25 percent in the year 2000.

107

The LDCs hope to improve their terms of trade vis-à-vis developed countries (DCs) through the NIEO and to secure a transfer of resources to the Third World. In view of these objectives several questions arise, two of which have special importance: (1) What are the economic costs of a NIEO based on a worldwide administration of commodity markets? and (2) is dirigism really the only solution to the development problem of the LDCs? This chapter will answer these two questions. Its conclusions rest on the following premises: (1) LDCs have to grow faster than DCs to maintain economic and political stability in the world, and (2) the process of structural changes in LDCs and DCs is necessary for a constantly growing world economy and should not be hampered.

International Commodity Agreements (ICAs) and Producers' Cartels

Many LDCs' exports are dominated by raw materials and many rely on one primary commodity export to finance their imports.[1] Clearly in such a situation the potential for instability is high, since employment and the capacity to import largely depend on the production and export of a dominating commodity. The ICAs are expected to stabilize the respective markets at higher prices. The LDCs presume that higher prices will bring them higher incomes. Stabilization aims at eliminating price fluctuations as well as fluctuations of commodities. The costs and the benefits of ICAs require examination.

Raising Prices Through ICAs

International commodity agreements are not completely analogous to the more common producers' cartel arrangements. The difference between ICAs and producers' cartels is that in the former, representatives of consuming countries are voting members who must also finance the management of the agreement. A significant criticism of cartels is that they lead to a misallocation of resources and reduce social welfare. The misallocation of resources stems from lowering production to attain higher prices. ICAs, which are directly financed by consumers, are also criticized for the misallocation of resources, but on different grounds. In this system producers absorb none or only part of the losses which occur when sales forecasts are higher than actual sales. They therefore have little or no interest in adjusting the supply of their commodity to demand. The more they produce the more they earn. While cartels tend to reduce the supply of a commodity as compared with a freely competitive situation, ICAs tend to increase availability.

The common agricultural policy (CAP) of the European Community is an outstanding example of excess supply induced by high prices. The common agricultural markets also reveal that the national and international misallocation of resources can absorb an ever-increasing share of the budgets of the member governments. In the long run this can cause severe social and political conflicts. There are, however, very important differences between organizations like the CAP and the proposed ICA; if all members of UNCTAD should join the integrated commodity program, no external market will exist through which excess supplies (and, more rarely, supply shortages) could be absorbed. If these excess' supplies could not be sold on the world market they would have to be destroyed, stored, or used for other purposes (an example is the case of milk powder in the EEC which is recycled to feed cattle, or wine which is now used to produce industrial alcohol). Obviously such developments would entail severe social welfare losses. One might argue that the negative effects of excess production do not occur if the producers are persuaded to submit to quantitative restrictions. But such quotas are only successful if investment controls are practiced simultaneously. Investment controls can be expected to work only if profits are pooled and adequately distributed among producers. This hardly seems workable, since the economic and political interests of producing countries are often very different.

The fundamental rationale of the ICA is that by raising prices of primary commodities, producing countries will achieve higher export earnings.[2] The underlying hypothesis is that the price elasticity of demand is very low, so that a price increase leads to a relatively small reduction in demand. Whether export earnings will rise in the long run, say over ten years, depends on the long-run price elasticitiy of demand. This elasticity again depends on various factors, such as: (1) the substitution between primary commodities; (2) the substitution of synthetics for raw materials; (3) the development of production techniques requiring less raw materials; and (4) the regional substitution of raw material production. The market reaction to ICAs could be the opposite of what the LDCs expect, since the long-run price elasticity of demand for many primary commodities could well be greater than unity. The reaction of industrialized countries to the OPEC increase in petroleum prices lends support to this contention.[3]

Stabilizing Prices and Export Earnings Through ICAs

A presumption of the ICA proposal assumes that revenue stability can be maintained through price stability.[4] However, the validity of this presumption depends on the related supply and demand elasticities. Price rigidity could well lead to increased instability of export earnings, if supply fluctuations had caused revenue instability. On the other hand, price rigidity could stabilize revenues if demand fluctuations had caused instabilities. The traditional methods of stabilizing raw materials prices are (1) multilateral contracts between consuming and supplying countries, (2) bufferstock schemes, and (3) quota regulations on the supply side. These schemes have been well described.[5] They all pose a major problem—correct prognosis of prices—the solution to which determines whether the chosen method will have the expected results. Especially in the case of multilateral contracts and bufferstock schemes an erroneous prognosis of prices will lead to unwarranted transfers of income, either from producing to consuming countries or vice versa. Whereas changes over time in production structure and patterns of consumption—on a relatively high level of aggregation—can be foreseen by applying rather complicated technical tools, this is not true for the future structure of prices. First, we do not know enough about the development of relative productivity or its effect on prices. Second, we must be aware that if price prediction were possible it could well be self-destructive. Third, any prognosis is based on the past. Once a system of administered prices is in operation, we no longer have a basis for prognosis, since it is unlikely that such prices reflect equilibrium. Such data cannot be used to estimate future trends. Fourth, even if it were possible to predict future prices, speculation would smooth out price trends and ICAs would no longer be necessary.[6]

These problems substantiate much of the skepticism the NIEO in general and the Integrated Commodity program in particular face. Since price stabilization will probably not succeed, and in view of the need to improve the economic position of LDCs, other schemes, which are directed at export earnings rather than prices or quantities, also merit some attention.

Compensatory financing is one way of stabilizing export earnings of developing countries. Countries dependent on raw materials exports could receive financial support when their export earnings fell below a certain level (which would be defined in advance by exporting and importing countries). It would not matter whether the decline of exports was due to decreased price or demand. LDCs would have to repay this transfer when their export earnings exceeded the target level. Compensatory financing would reduce dependency upon price and demand forecasts as long as the developed countries were willing to transfer financial resources. Moreover, this system does not hamper the market mechanism. Compensatory financing agreements only affect international monetary flows; they do not directly affect world supply and demand.

The Costs of International Commodity Agreements

In addition to the financial costs of ICAs, one might consider the welfare implications. We will estimate the welfare effects of producers' cartels and ICAs with the help of a partial analysis of producers' and consumers' surplus. The concept measures the total loss to consumers due to higher prices and decreased consumption; subtracted from this total loss are transfers from consumers to producers and government, which are not supposed to affect social welfare. The difference is called the "deadweight loss," which indicates the static costs of cartels and ICAs respectively.[7]

In the case of producers' cartels, the consumers' surplus (C^C) declines by

$$\Delta C^C = 0.5\Delta p \cdot \Delta x + p(x - \Delta x) \tag{7.1}$$

where x is the quantity demanded before formation of a cartel, and Δp and Δx are the changes in price and quantity demanded due to the cartel's policy. If marginal costs are constant (in the relevant range), the additional profits (Pr^C) of the cartel are

$$\Delta Pr^C = \Delta p(x - \Delta x) \tag{7.2}$$

Assuming that this transfer from consumers to producers does not affect social welfare, the loss to the world's welfare (W^C) is the balance from equations (7.1) and (7.2):

$$\Delta W^C = 0.5\Delta p \cdot \Delta x \tag{7.3}$$

In case of a price increase through ICA, a different misallocation of resources is to be expected; instead of the decrease in production by a cartel, the ICA leads to increased production. The cost to the world (C^{ICA}) will then be

$$\Delta C^{ICA} = \Delta p(x + z) + pz \tag{7.4}$$

where z is the additional production of the commodity and p its price before the foundation of the ICA. Assuming a linear rise in the marginal costs of production,[8] producing countries would profit (Pr^{ICA})

$$\Delta Pr^{ICA} = \Delta px + 0.5\Delta pz \tag{7.5}$$

Because the transfer of money is neutral to welfare, the net effect on the world's social welfare is thus:

$$\Delta W^{ICA} = z(0.5\Delta p + p) \tag{7.6}$$

Comparing equation (7.6) with (7.3), one can say that ICAs cause much greater welfare losses than do producers' cartels. This is always true when the ICA's production increase is greater than the cartel's production decrease.

Finally we must consider how ICAs will affect resource allocation. A logical outcome is that the primary goods sector will expand vis-à-vis competing sectors such as industry. As a result not only will the LDCs become more dependent on primary goods exports, but also other targets of the New International Economic Order, such as substantial expansion of industrial production, may be precluded.

The analysis of the costs of ICAs and producers' cartels suggests that producers' cartels harm welfare less rather than ICAs. Apart from this, another major objection to ICAs is that consuming and producing countries have diverging interests.[9] ICAs are expected to serve both consumers and producers which is of course impossible. Producers want high prices and consumers want low prices. Requiring a majority decision on every price increase in the ICA forces consumers (assuming they have the same voting weight as producers) to vote no or to vote against their own interests.[10] Moreover, differences in the economic situations of participating countries will lead to diagreement on how to manage the ICAs.

The Indexation of Prices

Indexation of export prices for primary commodities must be viewed as a target, complementary to the price-oriented cartelization goal and the income-oriented stabilization goal via International Commodity Agreements. Interest in indexation has been stimulated by the acceleration of worldwide inflation, which has caused the UN dollar price index for manufactured exports from developed countries to rise about 70 percent between 1969 and 1974. World inflation is expected to continue at annual rates slightly above those which prevailed during the postwar period until 1969.[11] This perspective has again drawn the attention of the LDCs to the development of their terms of trade which—after a short phase of "commodity price boom" (from 1973 to 1974)—have deteriorated. The developing countries fear that they face the continuing erosion of net bartering strength for several of their most important raw materials.

To stabilize the purchasing power of LDCs' export earnings, which are dominated by raw materials (approximately 80 percent), UNCTAD has issued two proposals: direct and indirect indexation. Direct indexation is aimed at setting an international agreement stabilizing the market price of a commodity on a level close to that of an indexed trend, which actually means getting a constant real price for this commodity. Indirect indexation stabilizes real income for each individual country by means of financial transfers from the importing countries. The amount of compensating transfers depends on the difference between the real export earnings of a specific developing country and a reference level, which is determined by multiplying an agreed export quantity by an indexed reference price.[12] Thus, in principle indirect indexation is a system of financial compensation, similar to the already existing schemes of the IMF and the EEC (Lome).

The chances of success for indexation as proposed by UNCTAD are questionable. There is no evidence that LDCs will be able to maintain the real price of their commodity exports by any direct indexation mechanism, because most of the raw materials are not suitable for direct indexation. Also, several industrial countries are important raw material suppliers, and would have to be integrated into an efficient system of direct indexation. Since such a system is designed primarily to smooth out price fluctuations by bufferstock operations, there is a severe prognosis problem; excess production would probably result. A misallocation of resources is to be expected in developed countries as well, because an economically rational mix of raw materials and substitutes cannot be maintained by such a system of indexation.

The indirect indexation scheme seems superior for development because it is based on maintaining import capacity. It is also easier to manage. An indirect scheme could be implemented with a high degree of selectivity and flexibility, avoiding the discrimination against raw-material-poor LDCs to the advantage of better-endowed industrial countries that would result from direct indexation. There is, of course, the same danger of resource allocation losses with the indirect scheme, as with the direct scheme; however, the danger is lessened with the indirect scheme, because production quotas—for example, as provided by UNCTAD—decrease the incentive for excess production. However, as a means of achieving a worldwide income redistribution in favor of the developing countries, the indirect indexation proposal is surely inadequate, because about 40 percent of all raw materials (excluding oil) are produced by developed countries; these countries would consequently receive the same benefits from a general direct indexation scheme as would developing countries that are well-endowed with raw materials. So far there is no evidence that industrial countries would be willing to renounce the privileges granted them in the direct scheme.

UNIDO's Projection for the Industrial Production

Among the LDCs' demands under the New International Economic Order, the demand for a redistribution of world industrial production, which envisages a 25 percent share for the developing countries in the year 2000, is quite different from their other demands. While the reorganization of commodity markets, the indexation of commodity prices and the nationalization of foreign capital are specific proposals to achieve a New International Economic Order, the 25 percent target simply describes a situation that LDCs think the new order should realize. Certainly there is no question that LDCs should be able to achieve an increased share in world industrial production because of their comparative advantage in many industrial activities. Whether or not the UNIDO proposal is a constructive target, however, is very much at issue.

An empirical attempt to assess the chances of realizing the 25 percent target meets severe methodological limitations. Given the broad range of possibilities that will influence individual investment decisions between now and 2000, projections of the LDCs' share in world industrial production are not reliable. I will nevertheless attempt such a projection, based on the results of an international cross section analysis.[13] This analysis reveals a significant relationship between the value-added share of industry in gross domestic product (GDP) and per capita income and population size. The comparison between the 25 percent target and the structural pattern for the year 2000—which has been derived from the cross section analysis—must be interpreted carefully, because it depends on the assumed growth rates for real GNP, population, and industrial production.

Using the growth rates of the UNIDO projection for purposes of illustration gives the following picture:[14] By the year 2000 the average per capita income in LDCs can be expected to be between $534 and $834 (United States dollars), depending on the assumed growth of GNP, population, and industrial production. The average income of developed countries in the year 2000 can be expected to range between $4000 and $6900 (U.S. dollars), again depending on assumptions. Given these levels of expected income, the projection of present structural patterns suggests that LDCs will achieve between 17 and 29 percent share in world industrial production by 2000. Thus on casual inspection, the 25 percent target does not seem completely unrealistic. However, this conclusion rests on the acceptance of UNIDO's projected rates of growth of GNP. Since past experience suggests that future GNP growth may not meet expectations, this conclusion may be premature. The following considerations suggest a somewhat lower rate of growth in the years to come:

1. Apart from the few oil-exporting developing countries which probably will be able to realize industrialization goals, the import capacity of most LDCs will fall sharply, thus reducing the potential for investment.

2. A reduced growth rate can also be expected in the industrialized countries. The coincidence of the oil crisis, recession and structural adjustment problems has presumably diminished production potential.

3. Additional losses in growth might occur because higher oil prices have tended to set capital-intensive substitution processes in motion in energy-intensive industries, which in the short run will reduce capital productivity.

4. Lower growth rates in the industrialized world will affect both predominantly raw-material-producing LDCs and the semi-industrialized countries. For the former group, foreign exchange earnings of primary exports will grow at a lower rate than previously, because the industrial countries will reduce their consumption of primary commodities. The semi-industrialized countries, which to a certain extent are already integrated into the international division of labor in manufactures, will also suffer, since the import demand for intermediate and final products from LDCs will expand more slowly than before.

From all these factors, I conclude that the desired 25 percent figure probably cannot be realized by the year 2000. It is more likely that the LDCs will achieve a share in world industrial production of approximately 15 percent, which in any case is a significant advance from their prevailing 7 percent share.[15]

Some Concluding Remarks

In spite of the above-mentioned objections to the main demands of the LDCs, changes in the world economic structure to bring about a more just international division of labor seem indispensable. This goal, however, cannot be achieved by merely "showing off" the advantages of the market mechanism, as industrial countries like to do. The developed countries themselves have too often distorted the market mechanism to the disadvantage of developing countries. Therefore, it is opportune to start activities in the fields of trade policy and adjustment assistance, so that all countries can begin to profit from a more equitable international division of labor which has never been based thus far on the fundamentally harmonious principle of comparative advantage. Too many governments have used their sovereignty in favor of specific pressure groups which served neither national nor international economic interests.

Of the stabilization schemes for commodity export earnings, we believe the "compensatory financing" approach is the most suitable. In case the export earnings are relatively small, it provides financial support for any country heavily dependent on the export of raw materials. When earnings are high, the money is paid back. "Compensatory financing" is a way to stabilize the total earnings of commodity exports. This approach could serve not only as a tool for stabilization but also as a tool for transferring financial resources. In the latter case it is intended to fix the "normal" export earnings, which would be the basis for transfers from developed countries with excessive earnings and to charge only low interest until the developing countries make the compensatory reimbursements (or even to dispense with the reimbursements). Both solutions would mean that commodity agreements would increasingly be organized as a kind of alimentation.

In the field of trade policy the industrialized countries should agree:

To extend the "General Scheme of Preferences" to all products including the so-called "sensitive" goods, in which the LDCs' comparative advantages are most likely to lie;

Not to fix ceilings;

To remove all nontariff barriers.

Since even a total liberalization could definitely not secure a sufficient influx of foreign exchange earnings to meet the rapidly rising import needs of the developing countries, the industrialized countries should ultimately intensify their efforts to comply with their often-reiterated promise of providing 0.7 percent of their GNP as development aid.

Notes

1. Among these countries are Ghana (cocoa), Colombia (coffee), Dominican Republic (sugar), Sri Lanka (tea), Panama (bananas), Chile (copper), Jamaica (bauxite), and Sudan (cotton).

2. Higher export earnings, of course, have no ultimate purpose themselves but are thought to raise welfare (national income).

3. Therefore, Chenery's prognosis of 1974 is increasingly refuted by actual developments. Chenery expected large assets of foreign exchange for the oil-exporting countries in 1980. He obviously thought that the price elasticity of demand for oil was the same in the long run as in the short run. In fact, some of the OPEC countries are already experiencing balance-of-payments troubles (which may partly be due to expenditures rising to meet income).

4. LDCs should be able, of course, to orient themselves on a trend of export earnings. Such behavior would make them immune to fluctuations of any relevant parameter. See H.G. Johnson, *Economic Policies Towards Less Developed Countries* (Washington, D.C., 1967).

5. See, for example, J.E. Meade, "International Commodity Agreements," *Lloyds Bank Review* no. 73 (1964).

6. If speculators expected the production of a primary commodity to be unusually low tomorrow, they would increase prices today. Thus, less of the commodity would be consumed today and more of it would be available tomorrow. The price fluctuation would thus be smaller.

7. See H.G. Johnson, "The Cost of Protection and the Scientific Tariff," *The Journal of Political Economy* 68 (1960): 327-345; S.P. Magee, "The Welfare Effects of Restrictions on U.S. Trade," *Brookings Papers on Economic Activity* 3 (1972): 645-707; H.H. Glismann, "Die gesamtwirtschaftlichen Kosten der Protektion," *Kieler Diskussionsbeitrage* 35 (October 1974); G. Fels and H.H. Glismann, "Adjustment Policy in the German Manufacturing Sector," in Organization for Economic Cooperation and Development, *Adjustment for Trade: Studies on Industrial Adjustment Problems and Policies* (Paris: Development Centre Studies, 1975), p. 68.

8. This differs from the assumption made for cartels. It seems realistic that if production shrinks, marginal costs neither rise nor fall, whereas additional production (well above the competitive equilibrium point) will usually encounter rising marginal costs.

9. See H.G. Johnson, "Cost of Protection and Scientific Tariff."

10. This conflict can only be solved by giving strict priority to one group (which would presumably cause the other group to leave, so that something like

a cartel would develop). A case where this was not done is the common agricultural policy (CAP) of the EC. The treaty of Rome called for (1) increased per capita incomes for farmers and farm workers; (2) adequate prices for consumers; and (3) stabilizing markets and securing supply. In fact not only none of these aims was reached. Despite enormous subsidies, CAP's per capita incomes do not satisfy farmers or farmers' lobbies. Consumers bear high excess costs because prices are far above world market prices (and quality is perpetually sinking). If the deviations of supply and demand indicate market stability, CAP did not stabilize anything at any time. In fact, CAP destabilized both EC markets and world markets.

11. United Nations Conference on Trade and Development, *The Indexation of Prices,* Report by the Secretary General of UNCTAD, TD/B/503 (New York: United Nations, 1975).

12. "General Review and Special Issues," *Proceedings of the United Nations Conference on Trade and Development,* Third Session, Vol. 4, (New York: United Nations, 1972), p. 71; Commonwealth Secretariat, "Towards a New International Economic Order," report by a Commonwealth Experts Group (London, 1975), p. 26.

13. See G. Fels, K.W. Schatz, and F. Wolter, "Der Zusammenhangzwischen Produktionsstruktur und Entwicklungsniveau," *Weltwirtschaftliches Archiv* 106 (1971): 240.

14. See United Nations International Development Organization, "Preliminary Note for the Preparation of a Plan of Action on Industrialization," Prepared by the UNIDO Secretariat (Vienna: United Nations, (October 1974). TD/B/C. 3/27)

15. This estimate is based on an annual average growth rate for real GNP of 4 percent for the LDCs and of 3 percent for the industrialized world, both of which are substantially below the UNIDO figures.

8

Third World Exports of Manufactures
Jaleel Ahmad

This chapter examines some aspects of the developing countries' exports of manufactures in the context of the New International Economic Order. The current debate on the role of manufacturing sectors in the New International Economic Order is already tending toward polarization. On one hand, proponents maintain that for all but the poorest of the developing countries a vigorous development of manufacturing sectors is the base on which a vastly altered set of international economic relationships must be built. To that end, they advocate radical changes in the economic and behavioral parameters underlying the international division of labor (Algiers International Symposium, 1975). On the other hand, opponents tend to resist any change in the status quo, while pointing to the inadequacies of developing countries' internal efforts at reform, rather than giving precise attention to what is being sought (Finger and Kreinin, 1976).

It is ironic that even before policy options underlying the New International Economic Order have been clarified, supporters and opponents are starting off debating the wrong question. The view that a balanced growth of manufacturing sectors in the Third World is intimately linked with their economic development is beyond dispute. That the plight of the developing countries has nothing to do with the current structure of international economic relations is unproven and unprovable. Moreover, exhorting the developing countries to swing into growth patterns without profound changes in the trading structure is like advising a person to bail out of a flying aircraft with a handkerchief. Needless to say, the debate in these terms is sterile and can only be regarded as a distraction from the real issues.

This chapter must start with a few predilections of its own. While it is pointless to attempt quantification based on uncertain parameters, some reasonable growth of developing countries' exports of manufactures to the industrial countries would be highly desirable, whether within or outside of the New International Economic Order. Secondly, there is little doubt that trade relations between rich and poor nations need profound changes. The structure of existing trade and capital flows is increasingly becoming far less important than the domestic transformation of production structures in the developing countries. Consequently, the need for a flexible international economic system capable of accommodating new directions of manufacturing growth is evident. Finally, it is necessary to overcome the existing biases that hamper trade in manufactures among the developing countries themselves. Such reflections are likely to point to changing directions of manufacturing growth, with respect to both its composition and its flow. These suggest somewhat higher probabilities of success than debating old issues of "access" and "dependence."

This chapter presents a three-pronged strategy for dealing with developing countries' exports of manufactures. The strategy may be viewed as a chain with three links of different and variable weights.

The developing countries' desire for a greater participation in world trade of manufactures does not arise from the sheer pleasure of producing industrial goods. Development of manufacturing sectors is simply a proxy for concomitant changes in labor productivity, technological progress, the quality of entrepreneurship, and an environment more conducive to overall development.[a] Such sectors must therefore play a critical role in their structural transformation under any conceivable strategy of development. The call for a New International Economic Order, following the Lima Declaration and a special Seventh Session of the United Nations General Assembly, simply reinforces the need for such changes. Indeed, it is difficult to visualize continuing growth in per capita income without a large and growing industrial sector, whether within or outside of the New International Economic Order.

While progress toward the New International Economic Order implies a simultaneous thrust on a wide range of issues, it is clear that manufacturing sectors occupy a central place in that hierarchy. Any new international division of labor—if it is to have any meaning at all—must actively seek to allocate a larger share of world production of manufactures to the developing countries. This realization lies behind the Lima Declaration, which envisages an increase in the developing countries' share of world industrial output from the present 8 percent to 25 percent by the year 2000.[b] While the Lima Declaration specifies neither concrete initial steps nor the dynamics of moving toward this target, there is little doubt that coordinated international efforts are necessary to enlarge the developing countries' manufacturing sectors.

I can visualize three general approaches (either singly or in concert) to increasing the developing countries' share in world industrial production. The first approach suggests that the growth rate of domestic demand for industrial goods in the developing countries could increase. This increased demand could conceivably be supplied entirely by enlarging domestic capacity, without changing import or export ratios. In other words, the burden of increasing the developing countries' share of industrial production could fall entirely on domestic demand, implying no change in international trading patterns. The second approach would raise the share of industrial production by changing import

---

[a]The important issues bearing on structural change and manufacturing sectors are discussed fully in Ahmad (1977) and Sutcliffe (1971).

[b]Some pertinent data on world trade in manufactures are summarized in table 8-1.

Table 8-1
World Trade in Manufactures
(millions of dollars, f.o.b.)

Exports from	Developed Countries	Developing Countries	Socialist Countries	World
Developed Countries				
1968	87,320	26,090	4,805	118,840
1972	165,990	42,720	8,630	218,420
Developing Countries				
1968	3,795	2,215	293	6,300
1972	9,480	4,390	627	14,530
Socialist Countries				
1968	2,020	2,341	11,000	15,410
1972	3,880	3,321	18,310	25,640
World				
1968	93,120	30,650	16,120	140,550
1972	179,360	50,410	27,570	258,590

Source: United Nations Conference on Trade and Development, Geneva.

ratios where domestic production substitutes for goods previously imported. In this case, while domestic demand need not rise, domestic production rises appreciably to supply a larger proportion of consumption. Finally, the third option requires that the growth rate of exports of manufactures from the developing countries rise substantially, thereby raising the ratio of industrial to total production in developing economies. This approach markedly reduces the burden of accommodation on the growth of domestic demand and of import substitution.

While in practice all three sources of growth are potentially relevant, it is difficult to visualize a vigorous growth of manufacturing capacity solely through increased domestic demand or decreased import ratios. For domestic demand to absorb the projected rise in industrial capacity, per capita incomes will have to rise substantially faster than can be reasonably projected. Also, growth in per capita incomes alone is not sufficient to ensure a rising demand for manufactures of the kind that lie within the current technological capabilities of the developing countries. A change in the distribution of incomes would also be necessary to change the composition of demand toward such products. Similarly, a significant increase in domestic manufacturing capacity unaccompanied by growth of exports will require a drastic fall in import ratios. However, the thin domestic markets of even the larger developing countries, coupled with critical shortages of capital and technology, painfully limit the role of import substitution. The overall import ratio cannot be lowered indefinitely without the substitution process extending into "nontraditional" manufactures. This extension would severely strain the economic capacities of most developing countries. In any event, this would be inefficient because it would happen at the expense of gains from trade through specialization and exchange.

The inherent difficulties of relying on growth of domestic demand and on import substitution can be greatly reduced if the increased share of manufactures is accommodated by a rise in exports of manufactures. This will not only permit manufacturing sectors in developing economies to grow without undue strains, but will also mean a better allocation of resources in the international economy as developing countries begin to acquire and develop their potential comparative advantage in appropriate lines of manufactures. This transition, however, cannot be achieved within the current structure of international trade; it requires a more flexible framework.

So far we have concluded that the growth of manufacturing sectors is vital to the developing countries in any emerging economic order, and that this growth should ideally be based on increased exports. Economic growth in developing countries is currently contingent on their ability to finance imports of capital goods—as well as technology embodied in such goods—from the industrial countries. A large part of developing countries' imports are noncompetitive, that is, no domestic production competes with them. Despite unceasing rhetoric about the role of foreign aid, official development assistance has played a relatively minor role in the overall balance of payments of the Third World. Even before the rise in petroleum prices, the Third World's total exports and commercial capital imports were regularly ten times the size of aid flows (Helleiner 1975, p. 4). In 1973, for instance, export receipts alone accounted for $98.1 billion of the $131.8 billion total foreign exchange available to the developing countries (Helleiner 1975, table 2, p. 4). The capacity to import, therefore, needs to be strengthened through increased exports of manufactures to the industrial countries. If import capacity is impaired, the developing countries' efforts toward economic growth will suffer severe strains. The prospects for substantially reducing the imports of capital goods—either through factor substitution or through changes in product mix—are not entirely overwhelming. Does the New International Economic Order promise any solutions?

Most current conceptions of the international division of labor do not look beyond the most immediate problems of adjustment. They fail to envisage a built-in mechanism for accommodating continuous changes in the division of labor. The prime example of this lack of perspective is the rather loose way in which the developing countries' role in international division of labor is considered. Even when they grudgingly recognize that developing countries should participate in international trade in manufactures, many academic and offical proponents of the new international division of labor visualize or concede only a limited role for the developing countries. This role is invariably a marginal movement from specialization in primary production to specialization in simple processing and labor-intensive manufactures. While the development of processing and labor-intensive manufactures is necessary for development, it is not a sufficient basis for industrialization. The notion of "thus far and no further" implied in such a division of labor is contrary to the needs of a balanced and self-sustaining development. It truncates the process arbitrarily, according to prevailing whims of trade theory or political exigencies of the moment. Division of labor on these lines will "allocate" to the developing countries a handful of slow-growth labor-intensive industries and thus deprive them of utilizing the linkages and external economies which are the essence of development. The new international division of labor will very quickly ossify into the old one.

It is therefore important for the new international economic order to avoid the traditional mistake of freezing a dynamic and cumulative process. The practical implications of a more open process are that the developing countries will initiate newer lines of manufactures as changes in demand, factor use and technology give them comparative advantage. This is not to say that all developing countries can produce and export all lines of manufactures, but that different developing countreis will develop different lines of manufactures within the range of their individual resource endowments, skills, productivities and basic development needs. This cannot occur unless world trading relationships remain capable of affording the developing countries indefinite possibilities for entering newer lines of manufactures. It must avoid relegating to them a handful of manufacturing activities based on static conditions of production, thus aborting the future course of their development.

The painful history of negotiations and the subsequent evolution of access for the exports of developing countries through current GSP schemes is all too well known. However, the problem of access goes much further than the one posed by current trade barriers on traditional manufactures of the developing countries. It will extend to those products in which the developing countries may foster and acquire a comparative advantage. Cumulative consequences of initial industrial activity in the developing countries must take them beyond the "textiles and leather" stage into newer lines of manufactures. In general, it must take them beyond the production and export of customary labor-intensive goods through changes in the growth and composition of demand, greater availability of capital at current rates of saving and accumulation, and the filtering of technological change into wider areas of production. As the degree of articulation among industrial sectors increases through heightened input-output relations, a range of manufacturing activities, many of them with distinct export orientation, are likely to develop simultaneously.

These linkages in domestic transformation are the very heart of the development process. The international division of labor is constantly evolving, and the structure of trading relationships must be redesigned to facilitate this continuous process. This wider aspect of access goes beyond granting preferential treatment to exports of manufactures from the developing countries on an ad hoc and selective basis. New approaches must offer genuine concessions and must be free of the ubiquitous escape clauses which make the current GSP schemes an exercise in fraudulent economic diplomacy. The main function of preferences should be to provide an open framework for developing countries' participation in world trade of manufactures on an indefinite basis. Such an open framework is necessary for long-term movement of resources; the developing countries are commonly saddled with trade barriers in industrial countries as soon as they begin to develop competitive exports.

While certain features of the existing GSP schemes are worth preserving, the New International Economic Order requires more fundamental changes in the rules underlying the institutional framework of world trade. First of all, some form of preferential treatment for developing countries (depending on their individual stage of development) must be given a status comparable to the "most favored nation" (MFN) clause of the GATT. Since they are intended to deal with two different problems, these two do not conflict. Multilateralism as embodied in the MFN clause has ensured a nondiscriminatory expansion of world trade between industrial countries with roughly comparable economic characteristics and equally diversified production structures. For obvious reasons, the MFN provisions are pitifully inadequate to deal with trading problems of the developing countries. Indeed, they are largely responsible for assigning the developing countries a peripheral role in the postwar growth of world trade. It has long been apparent that measures other than the MFN clause would be required to draw the developing countries into the mainstream of world trade. The principle of preferences for developing countries under specified conditions would be complementary to the principle of nondiscrimination in trade—not contradictory as often thought. In fact, MFN for the rich and preference for the poor countries will constitute an optimal combination of policies.

In the same vein, it may be necessary to repeal or modify the automatic "escape" provisions under article XIX of GATT. These seriously threaten to disrupt exports through unilateral imposition of QRs and other nontariff barriers on products of developing countries. The rather arbitrary imposition of QRs, often without regard to actual protection needs of the domestic industry, are more harmful to the developing countries' exports than tariffs. Although tariffs do restrict trade, after a while everyone gets used to tariffs and trade continues, albeit at a lower level. While tariffs often unfavorably affect the terms of trade of the exporters, they restrict volume much less than do QRs. Lastly, the current deliberations under the Tokyo Rounds of multilateral trade negotiations must pay genuine attention to reducing the inequities of tariff escalation, which is particularly harmful to latecomers to the industrial scene. The level of effective protection against the developing countries is much higher than could be justified by legitimate domestic objectives in the industrial countries and undoubtedly shields many uneconomic endeavors.

Another mechanism that needs to be explored is the negotiated market-sharing agreements for Third World exports. This will require institutional changes in market-oriented industrial countries (Hammarskjold Foundation, 1975). Planned expansion of imports from developing countries may require a governmental committment to purchase directly or to assure a certain level of imports by national industries and sectors. This would enable the governments of industrial countries to have an overview of the type of committment they could accept. Such market-sharing arrangements, though cumbersome, could permit the developing countries' exports to play a greater role in sectors where domestic demand is rapidly growing.

Effective means must be found to generate an environment of support for the developing countries before bargaining can take place on actual policy instruments. It is important to distinguish between what must be assumed constant during any particular period and what is truly variable in the policy matrix. Helleiner (1975, p. 14) points out that international development policy must attempt to convert undesirable "constants" into variables. One such conversion is the increased access to the industrialized countries' markets for manufactured exports. Such changes, which are important to the developing countries, involve no serious cost to the developed countries. In fact, the reduction of barriers to importing manufactured products from the developing countries is a non-zero-sum game. Of course, if such international efforts fail to materialize, attention must gradually shift to policy instruments that do not depend on negotiations and can be pursued unilaterally.

The preceding section argued that it would be desirable to increase the developing countries' exports of manufactures to the industrial countries. Regardless of the outcome of current negotiations on this issue, efforts should be made to increase trade in manufactures among the developing countries. Developing countries' exports of manufactures (SITC classes 5 through 8) totaled to $14.5 billion in 1972. Of this, fully two-thirds, that is, $9.5 billion, was destined for the industrial countries, while only $4.4 billion was sold to other developing countries. Exports among the developing countries, while doubling in value between 1968 and 1972, fell from 35 percent of total exports to 30 percent. By contrast, developing cuntries' imports from the developed countries amounted to $43 billion in 1972, roughly ten times imports from other developing countries. Clearly, trade of manufactures among the developing countries is not only a small proportion of their total trade, but has not kept pace with its growth.

As the basic parameters of economic structure in the developing countries begin to change, possibilities of mutually beneficial trade among them emerge. The most important change that warrants optimism on this count is that a few developing countries are gradually emerging as important suppliers of manufactures. Despite many production bottlenecks, these countries have built up a fairly diversified industrial capacity—often less than fully utilized—which could form the basis of intensive trade among themselves.

Mutual gains result when countries with disparate resource endowments or demand patterns trade with each other. In addition, much of the trade in manufactures takes place between countries with broadly similar patterns of demand. On both these counts, developing countries offer promising opportunities for increasing the volume of their mutual trade. The Third World contains heterogenous countries with widely different resource endowments and stages of development, and their individual modes of specialization will complement each other. By the same token, the developing countries have a fairly uniform and overlapping pattern of demand for manufactures. This affords important opportunities for producing and supplying one another's demand. As a practical step in this direction, it would be necessary to develop a typology of production possibilities within subgroups of developing countries, which could then be matched with a typology of demand to delineate the composition and direction of trade among them. Such a matching of supply and demand patterns in manufactures will have an important side effect: it will increase the possibilities of mutual trade in primary commodities. It will also focus greater attention on comparative advantage, particularly in heavy industry.

The question of developing countries' mutual trade in manufactures is closely allied with their current commercial policies. Because a broadly similar range of domestic industries has developed through protection, potential exports of industrial goods among developing countries face formidable trade barriers. To enlarge mutual trade in manufactures, these countries must change their commercial policies toward each other. This change could aim at achieving a preferential and nondiscriminatory treatment of industrial products originating in and traded between the developing countries. One may conceive of the entire set of developing countries as a vast preferential trade area for manufactures of designated variety. This larger set undoubtedly contains smaller subsets of free trade areas and common markets. A regime of preferential trade among the developing countries as a whole can be dovetailed into the existing regional integration framework. For instance, in free trade areas where intraunion trade is liberalized, preferential tariffs applicable to developing countries outside of the area could be lower than "most favored nation" rates. For common markets, these rates could lie anywhere between zero and the height of the common external tariff. These devices will ensure that existing or incipient economic integration movements will not be eroded.

Closer trading ties among the developing countries will reduce their constant need to generate "hard currency" exports. Stewart (1975) argues for active discrimination in favor of trade between the developing countries on "infant industry" grounds, through overcoming biases in the infrastructure—financial institutions, aid, investment and technology—which favor trade between developed and developing countries over to trade between developing countries. Clearly, import substitution at the group level offers an important avenue for expanding industrial production in developing countries.

Our final point concerns the future *direction* of growth of manufacturing sectors in the developing countries. While trying to increase exports of manufactures, it is also necessary to shift the orientation of manufacturing sectors toward producing consumer goods that satisfy the basic "needs" of the largest possible number of people within individual countries. This does not necessarily mean limiting the expansion of manufacturing sectors, as is often implied by writers on the "other development." In fact, to cope with their economic and social problems, in manufacturing sectors the developing countries need to grow more rather than less. Here again the match of production possibilities and consumption patterns referred to in the previous section will be useful in developing cooperation among the developing countries. Unfortunately, very little analytical work has been done in this area. Future research should be directed toward this important problem.

However, income concentration and resulting inequalities in many developing countries are a significant constraint to the continued growth of manufacturing sectors. The rather thin domestic markets of even the larger and more prosperous developing countries appear inadequate to support large-scale manufacturing activities. A highly skewed income distribution in these countries isolates the majority of people from the market for industrial goods. Thus, even though there may be a demand for a broad range of manufactures, the demand for any single product tends to be smaller than the minimum efficient scale of production. If income could be distributed so that the domestic market for basic consumer goods would expand, existing industries could expand and new ones could be set up. The interindustry ramifications of an enlarged consumer goods sector would probably diffuse the process to intermediate and capital goods sectors as well.

Such a change in the orientation of the manufacturing industry implies that domestic production would increasingly be based on needs rather than on suitability for export. This option does not embrace the position of extreme autarky; it merely suggests that producing basic goods for consumption may be more worthwhile than a single-minded pursuit of exports.

The strategy outlined in this paper aims toward increasing the developing countries' participation in international trade in manufactures. I have proposed a three-pronged strategy—two ways of increasing exports and a way to change the direction of growth and reduce the need to export. The three elements of the strategy can be seen as embodying different "weights" according to the intensity with which each must be pursued to realize some basic aims of the New International Economic Order. The first element of the strategy—the increase in exports to the industrial countries—should initially command priority, since only in that case would the emerging order be truly international. If international policies can be worked out to attain this objective, the weights of the other two elements of the strategy—exports within the developing countries and non-export-oriented growth—will be correspondingly lower. However, since the weights are variable, lack of progress on the first element may force progressively greater emphasis on the other two elements. The three options map out a continuum between freer participation in world trade and a position implying a fair measure of autarky. Uncertainty about the relative "weights" precludes working out their dynamics.

I believe these alternatives represent a realistic perception of shifts in developing countries' approaches to these matters. Note Diaz-Alejandro's (1974) characterization of these shifts as embracing unintrusiveness (independence in international links); decomposability (diversification and absence of commercial "packages"); and reversibility (continuous evaluation and renegotiation). Finally, I cannot resist pointing out that proposals for private investments, loans and aid of the kind thrown in at UNCTAD IV are really not alternatives to changes in the structure of international trade. They merely put the problem under the rug for a short while, for the question of full participation in trade is bound to arise again with renewed urgency and probably with an enlarged capacity to export.

References

Ahmad, J. (1977), *Import Substitution, Trade and Development,* Johnson Associates Press (forthcoming).

Algiers International Symposium (1975). "Making Operative the New International Economic Order and the Charter of Economic Rights and Duties of States" (Paris: Center International Pour le Developppment).

Diaz-Alejandro, Carlos F. (1974), "North–South Relations: The Economic Components," Economic Growth Center, Yale University (mimeo).

Finger, J.M. and M.E. Kreinin (1976), "A New International Economic Order? A Critical Survey of the Issues" (mimeo).

Hammarskjold Foundation (1975), "Report on Development and International Cooperation," *Development Dialogue* no. 1/2.

Helleiner, Gerald K. (1975), *A World Divided: The Less Developed Countries in the International Economy* (Cambridge: Cambridge University Press).

Steward, Frances (1975), "The Direction of International Trade: Gains and Losses for the Third World" in *A World Divided: The Less Developed Countries in the International Economy,* G.K. Helleiner, ed., (Cambridge: Cambridge University Press).

Sutcliffe, Robert B. (1971), *Industry and Underdevelopment* (London: Addison-Wesley).

9

Tariff Preferences and
Multinational Firm Exports from
Developing Countries
Murray Tracy[a]

One of the most original new initiatives in international trade policy aimed at stimulating economic development is the concept of preferential treatment for the developing countries. In a strict sense the concept is not new, because the industrial center has historically devoted special attention to the periphery, especially under colonial arrangements. Grants in aid and concessionary development loans are other examples. However, the new initiative takes a nontraditional approach by granting exports from developing countries preferential access to the markets of the industrial center, that is, these preferential arrangements constitute a trade policy rather than a more traditional aid policy.

The idea for this new initiative was formally introduced at the UN Conference on Trade and Development (UNCTAD) when it first convened in Geneva in 1964. The goal of this conference was to establish a new international trade policy that would contribute to raising the material wealth of the developing countries through trade rather than aid. However, the results can hardly be called a great success for the developing countries, as no substantive trade measures emerged. Nevertheless, as a result of this conference the UN General Assembly established UNCTAD as a permanent organ of the General Assembly.

UNCTAD provided an ongoing forum for publicizing the trade problems of the developing countries. In 1968, when the second Conference convened in New Delhi, the principle of generalized tariff preferences was formally accepted. This resolution also established the Special Committee on Preferences to negotiate the implementation of the Generalized System of Preferences (GSP). On November 14, 1969, the developed countries belonging to the Organization for Economic Cooperation and Development (OECD) submitted their preference "offers" to the developing countries through the secretary general of UNCTAD. Further negotiations ensued as these offers were revised and refined. Finally on July 1, 1971, the European Community (EC) of six member states implemented the first preferential tariff "scheme."[1] Soon after, preference schemes were also implemented by Japan (August 1971); Norway (October 1971); Denmark, Finland, Ireland, New Zealand, Sweden, and the United

[a]The research for this paper was sponsored by an IBM Post-Doctoral Fellowship in International Business Studies. Much of the information was derived from direct interviews with executives of multinational corporations headquartered in the United States and Europe; as agreed, their identities remain confidential. Neither IBM nor the corporations interviewed influenced my use of the information. The author alone is responsible for the conclusions presented.

129

Kingdom (January 1972);[2] Switzerland (March 1972) and Austria (April 1972). The developing countries had to wait substantially longer for preferences from the remaining industrial nations of the West, Canada and the United States, who finally implemented their schemes in July 1974 and January 1976, respectively.[3] Under the GSP, imports of manufactured and semimanufactured products from developing countries are granted preferential tariff reductions (generally duty-free), in comparison with the most-favored-nation (MFN) duties charged on imports from other sources. The preferential tariff reductions will stimulate developing countries' exports at the expense of imports from non-preferred sources as well as at the expense of domestic producers.

The adoption of the Generalized System of Preferences established a new international precedent of overt preferential treatment for the developing countries. The developing countries are vigorously pursuing an expanded application of this principle, for example regarding commodities, technology transfer, shipping, multinational corporations, debt forgiveness, and the law of the sea, to name only a few. As such the GSP is considered to be an integral part of the ongoing negotiations for the establishment of a "New International Economic Order" as contained in resolutions of the sixth and seventh Special Session of the UN General Assembly.

However, the GSP is not an uncomplicated system which is certain to benefit the developing countries. The negotiated "Agreed Conclusions" which led to its implementation contain a number of paragraphs in which the developing countries recognize that the developed countries will take special measures to safeguard their domestic producers. Thus the preferential treatment contains a number of loopholes designed to safeguard the trade interests of the developed countries. These loopholes severely reduce the trade benefits likely to accrue to the developing countries under the GSP.

The loopholes in the GSP are embodied in various technical regulations governing GSP trade. Besides constraining trade under the GSP, these regulations contain complicated administrative procedures that frustrate the attempts of suppliers in the developing countries to qualify their exports for GSP treatment. I will argue that these procedures place local producers at a serious disadvantage, but that multinational corporations (MNC) have the experience and expertise to understand and comply with these regulations. Consequently, if anyone is to benefit from the GSP it is likely to be the MNC first, and developing countries second—through employment generation, tax revenues, and other such linkages between the MNC and the host country. And conversely, if the MNC finds little advantage to trade under the GSP, suppliers in the developing countries will find even less.

Trade Benefits Under the GSP

The GSP was never thought to be a panacea for solving all of the complex problems of economic development.[4] Nevertheless, the developed countries considered it an important new step toward helping the developing countries help themselves. Examining the system, however, yields rather discouraging conclusions. As it operates today, the GSP can be criticized because: (1) many important products of export interest to the developing countries have been excluded from one or more of the preference schemes; (2) the measures designed to safeguard the interests of domestic producers often result in denial of GSP treatment to developing countries' exports of products included in the GSP; and (3) the "rules of origin," which guarantee that the benefits of the GSP actually accrue to the exporting developing country, often require production processes which are beyond the capabilities of many developing countries. These criticisms will be discussed in turn.

Product Coverage

As already noted, the primary objective of the GSP is to expand exports of the developing countries by offering them preferential tariffs. Hence, the GSP will only assist in exporting goods subject to duty. Goods already admitted duty-free by the developed countries—especially agricultural commodities and industrial raw materials—by definition fall outside the scope of the GSP or any preferential tariff program.

Based on 1970 trade patterns, nearly three-fifths (58 percent) of the exports of the beneficiary developing countries enter duty-free on an MFN basis. These are largely primary commodities and other products historically exported by the developing countries during the colonial and post-colonial periods. In addition, the term "manufactured and semimanufactured products" (to which the GSP applies) has been interpreted by the developed countries to mean manufactured *industrial* products. Thus, processed agricultural and fishery products have generally been excluded from the GSP; such products account for another 14 percent of beneficiary trade with the developed countries. After excluding duty-free and agricultural goods, we find that the developing countries' exports of manufactured goods potentially eligible for GSP tariff treatment account for only one-fourth of their trade with the developed countries.

Moreover, the developing countries agreed that the developed countries would take special precautions to safeguard their domestic producers of sensitive import-competing products. Most of the preference-giving countries (donors) safeguarded their most sensitive industries by excluding such products a priori from their preference schemes. The EC exluded all industrial raw materials (to accommodate the trade interests of the African States associated with the Community as much as to protect domestic producers); textile imports were granted GSP tariff treatment by the EC only if the exporting developing country complied with the "voluntary" export restraints of the Long Term Cotton Arrangement (LTA) under the auspices of the GATT. (In 1974 the LTA was superceded by the expanded Multifiber Agreement.) The United States has the most extensive list of exluded products, including textiles, shoes, petroleum products (which really don't matter anyway), electronics, glass, and selected steel items. Japan followed the United States' lead by excluding textiles, leather, and petroleum-based products, among others. What remains is shown in table 9-1, which presents a breakdown of the developing countries' exports to the preference-giving countries in 1970. As the breakdown demonstrates, only about 12 percent of developing countries' exports to the developed countries are in fact covered by the GSP.

Nevertheless, it would be too much to conclude that the GSP offers such a small potential. Many factors have contributed to the creation of the current pattern of trade. The structure of tariff rates is one of these factors. Thus, changes in the structure of tariffs can lead to changes in trade patterns. It is not unreasonable to anticipate that the GSP could lead to some reallocation of production favoring the developing countries, and to some expansion of their manufactured exports. The preferential reduction in tariff rates should give the developing countries an incentive to export industrial goods and consequently should stimulate greater investment (domestic and foreign) in the productive capacity of export items. Whether this development will be realized is as yet uncertain; it takes time for these incentives to be translated into action. However, as will be seen shortly, these incentives are thwarted by additional safeguard measures embodied in the GSP schemes, especially those of the United States, the European Community, and Japan, who together account for nine-tenths of the developing countries' exports of manufactures.

Table 9-1
LDC Exports to Countries Providing GSP

Product Groups	Beneficiary Exports	
	Value in $mil.	Share in %[a]
All Products	35,779	100
less duty-free	20,719	58
less dutiable agricultural and fishery items not covered by GSP	5,145	14
less dutiable petroleum items not covered by GSP	3,065	9
less other dutiable industrial items not covered by GSP		
—textiles and footwear	637	2
—industrial raw materials excluded by EC	591	2
—import-sensitive electronic items excluded by U.S.	557	2
—miscellaneous other exclusions	612	2
GSP Product Coverage	4,453	12

[a]The shares do not add to 100 due to rounding.

Safeguard Measures

Besides restricting product coverage, the developed countries imposed a safe-guard system to protect against any unanticipated increase in imports from the developing countries. All GSP schemes include an escape clause whereby the country reserves the unilateral right to withdraw preferential tariff treatment on specific products of preferential imports increase sufficiently to injure domestic producers. In practice, this safeguard has not been a serious problem.

But some donor countries have also specified limitations on the amounts of trade that may receive preferential tariff treatment. The three major schemes (United States, EC and Japan) embody such limitations. The schemes of the EC and Japan contain ceiling type limits to GSP trade, which at first glance appear reasonable. Preferential tariffs apply on imports up to a ceiling; MFN duties are charged on imports in excess of this ceiling. Thus, the ceilings do not limit imports, but determine the tariff rate to be applied. This seems like a justifiable safeguard. Domestic producers are protected only by MFN tariffs, and then only when imports from the developing countries grow too rapidly, that is, when they exceed the ceilings, which are administered product by product. Of course, whether this is restrictive depends on the magnitude of the ceilings; of primary importance is whether the ceilings are larger than the volume of trade that would occur without the GSP. For preferential tariff treatment to contribute to an expansion of trade, it must apply on *expanded* levels of trade. However, the ceilings for many products fall far short of the normal level of trade. And these tend to be products of major export interest to the developing countries. The GSP simply creates an incentive for traders of such products to "race the goods to the border." Successful "racers" will receive a windfall profit equal to the GSP preferential tariff margin—this windfall will presumably be divided in some way between the donor country importer and the developing country exporter. But in any case the monies received do not stimulate an expanded trade flow; the funds the exporter actually receives are more appropriately considered an aid flow than a trade benefit. (The funds received by the importer can be considered a transfer payment paid for by the donor country's consumers.)

Since the ceilings apply to imports from all beneficiaries combined, one particular developing country might generate a significant increase in preferential trade even within the confines of an overall restrictive ceiling. The EC and Japan, however, prevent this, under the rationale of spreading the benefits of the the GSP among the developing countries by reserving a portion of each ceiling for the less competitive. Maximum amount constraints limit preferential treatment under the GSP on imports from individual beneficiaries, with different limits applying on different products. Thus, no single developing country can receive preferential treatment on exports exceeding one-half of the ceiling (in many cases the maximum amount is only 20 or 30 percent). Such a limitation might be reasonable if developing country trade were evenly spread across many developing countries. In practice, however, imports from the beneficiaries are highly concentrated. For any given manufactured product there are generally less than five major beneficiary suppliers; most often there are only one or two. With such an uneven distribution of trade, the maximum amount provision simply cuts off the major supplier, reserving a significant portion of the ceiling for minor suppliers that are unable to take advantage of it. A large part of the ceiling can therefore be expected to remain needlessly underutilized. This is supported by recent evidence.

In addition, for products considered "sensitive," the EC allocates the ceiling among its member states according to a fixed formula which applies for every product. This procedure transforms each European Community ceiling into seven separate country ceilings (Belgium, Luxembourg and the Netherlands have a common allocation). But actual EC imports from developing countries are not distributed among the member states according to the fixed shares for every product. Consequently, developing country exports will exceed some countries' quotas and underutilize others. Preferential imports in excess of a given country's allotment cannot gain preferential treatment in another EC country. This has led to a portion of beneficiary trade's becoming sterilized and losing its preferential status. More recently, the Community has introduced a reserve quota which provides that part of any unused allocation of one member state can be transferred to another.

The ceiling system of the EC and Japan also creates uncertainty for importers who, because of the ceilings, cannot know in advance whether GSP tariffs will apply to their goods. Consequently, importers are likely to be reluctant to contract for goods at prices reflecting preferential tariff rates. More important, this uncertainty is likely to dampen the investment incentive for new productive capacity for GSP products in developing countries. This is not to say that such investment will not take place. Rather, the GSP advantages are likely to be heavily discounted by investors. Thus the GSP is unlikely to provide the stimulus anticipated by the developing countries when they originally negotiated the new system.

The US GSP scheme also embodies a framework for limiting preferential treatment which at first glance seems reasonable. The United States has specified "competitive need" criteria which provide that preferential treatment will not be granted (instead MFN duties will be charged) when normal US imports of a given product from a single beneficiary developing country exceed (1) $25 million, adjusted annually in proportion to the growth in US gross national product, or (2) 50 percent of total imports of the product. Other beneficiary developing countries will continue to enjoy preferential treatment on the product and the affected beneficiary will continue to enjoy preferential treatment on other products. These criteria provide for a withdrawal or phasing out of preferential treatment when it can no longer be justified on the grounds of promoting the development of a particular industry in the developing country concerned. This provision also provides some advantage for the less competitive developing countries by giving them preferential treatment over the major beneficiary suppliers affected by the criteria. On the other hand, where US imports are small and originate primarily in a single developing country, the 50 percent limit will preclude preferential treatment on a modest flow of trade. Unlike the ceiling systems of the EC and Japan, these "competitive need" criteria are an "all or nothing" limit; once either limit is exceeded, preferential treatment ceases and is not renewed at the beginning of the following year.

These safeguard measures of the EC, Japan and the United States severely limit the trade advantages of their GSP schemes. The product coverage of the GSP is reduced by 68 percent for the EC, 89 percent for Japan and 53 percent for the United States. The effective GSP product coverage for all three schemes is 33 percent of the GSP product coverage, or only 4 percent of total developing country exports to these three major donor countries combined (9 percent if duty-free trade is excluded). Given these results, it seems reasonable to challenge the application of such stringent *automatic* safeguard measures and argue instead for a more flexible safeguard based on a casual tie between increased GSP trade and injury to a domestic producer or group of workers. This would treat those cases in which preferential trade causes import adjustment problems for domestic producers of particular products. At the same time it would recognize the severe supply limitations that exist in developing countries and the resulting improbability that the GSP would stimulate a rapid expansion of trade across a broad spectrum of products.

Rules of Origin

An initial aim of the GSP was to stimulate production and employment in the export sectors of beneficiary countries. However, preferential tariff rates might bring abut an unintended result—a deflection of international trade among industrial countries. Instead of one industrial nation exporting goods directly to another and facing MFN tariffs, the exporter might send the goods first to a beneficiary developing country for importation and them immediately reexport them to the industrial nation initially intended, thereby gaining entry at the GSP preferential tariff rate. In this way, the GSP could initiate a system of diverting trade through beneficiary countries, stimulating the creation of trading houses rather than industrial production. To prevent this, rules of origin were established to prevent beneficiaries from simply reexporting goods produced elsewhere without substantial processing.

In addition to adding complexity, the rules of origin contain a number of clauses that reduce the scope of the GSP. Various goods contained in the lists of products which qualify for GSP treatment have been excluded de facto because the minimum transformation requirements are too difficult to meet. For example, transistor radios do not qualify for GSP treatment in the EC if they are made with imported transistors, which few developing countries can produce domestically. Thus, for all practical purposes, the EC does not grant GSP treatment on transistor radios. The United States limits imported materials and components to 35 percent of the domestic processing cost, which excludes such cost items as executive salaries, local transportation, royalties and license fees, and profits. This lowers the base for determining the maximum allowable import content for GSP goods to a figure far below the implied 65 percent; it often falls to 10 percent or 15 percent and would even preclude GSP duties on wholly produced items whenever indirect costs exceed 65 percent.

I know of no scientific estimates of the impact of these rules on GSP trade, but my best guess is that roughly one-fourth of the effective GSP product coverage will be denied GSP tariff treatment because of the origin requirements. One multinational corporation which imports into the EC informed me that one-third of their trade in GSP products fails to comply with the rules of origin. This does not mean, however, that the origin rules should be tremendously liberalized. As mentioned above, the origin problem is a two-sided knife; overly liberal rules reduce the incentives for industrial production in favor of trading house activity, while overly restrictive rules limit the de facto scope of the GSP. The need for compromise between these two extremes is well recognized in the ongoing negotiations on the rules of origin; it is likely that the more obvious inconsistencies between minimum processing requirements and the technical feasibilities of industrial production in developing countries will be eliminated gradually over time.

Given the limitations and restrictions in the existing GSP trading regulations, the trade benefits likely to accrue to the developing countries will be quite meager at best. To reiterate: (1) many products of current export interest to the developing countries have been excluded from the GSP; (2) the major products included in the GSP face ceiling-type limitations which eliminate the incentive for expanded trade flows—the benefit that is derived from the GSP amounts to the windfall tariff revenue excused on those imports which actually receive preferential GSP treatment (and this windfall is divided between the donor country importer and the beneficiary country exporter); and (3) the rules of origin reduce the effective product coverage by eliminating some products from GSP eligibility de facto by establishing minimum processing requirements that are beyond the capabilities of developing country producers. These factors make it extremely difficult for producers in the developing countries to exploit the opportunites that do exist under the GSP. For products of current export interest they must closely monitor the administration of the ceiling limits to which products remain eligible for GSP tariffs as the year progresses and which donor countries are still granting GSP tariffs on products of interest. Furthermore, they must be knowledgeable about alternative production technologies to adjust their production processes to comply with the minimum processing requirements.

Finally, for nontraditional industrial products (which enjoy vastly more liberal GSP treatment) the primary barrier to export expansion is the lack of effective marketing and distribution channels.

However, there is one major exception to the general conclusion that the GSP offers very little for developing country exporters: the MNC with production facilities in developing countries and marketing outlets in the developed countries. The MNC is in a much better position to exploit the GSP than are producers in the developing countries. First, MNCs can easily monitor the ceiling administration from day to day, thereby knowing the likelihood that GSP trade will actually receive preferental tariff treatment; they would know which products exported from which developing countries and imported into which donor country would qualify. Also since the MNC would be both the importer and the exporter, any windfall profit would accrue to the MNC, thereby eliminating this element of uncertainty. They can interpret the minimum processing criteria and adjust the production process to comply with these criteria whenever possible (or change the sources of input materials and components from foreign to local producers). Finally, they have established marketing outlets. These considerations suggest that the MNC might contribute to the ability of the developing countries to expand their exports under the GSP.

The Role of the Multinational Corporation

The MNC has a long history of activities in developing countries. Their early activities mainly concentrated on sources of agricultural commodities and industrial raw materials for export, and in fact their primary activities today are in these sectors. Nevertheless, since World War II there has been an increasing emphasis on manufacturing activities; current growth rates in manufacturing are much higher than in the traditional sectors.

Since the GSP is primarily a program to stimulate manufacturing, I will concentrate my attention on MNC activities in this area. Besides, in the few cases where GSP treatment is accorded primary products, the GSP trade involves products which were traded long before the GSP was introduced. The advantage of the GSP is limited to an expansion in this trade flow resulting from the decrease in tariffs. The fact that the tariff reduction is preferential is immaterial, since there generally are no nonpreferred sources of supply. This should not be taken to mean, however, that GSP treatment is unimportant for all agricultural products. In some cases the MFN duties are quite high and the GSP provides a significant reduction in the landed import price. But the advantages to the developing countries and the incentives to MNCs would be equally great if the tariff reduction were extended on an MFN basis instead of under the GSP.

Before looking at the operations of MNCs in developing countries and their responses to the new tariff advantages under the GSP, I will discuss the MNC decision to establish production facilities in developing countries. My discussions with MNCs revealed very similar stories of the evolution of MNC manufacturing activities in developing countries. The MNC's first entry into a developing country takes the form of satisfying a local market via exports. If the exporting activity is successful and the local market grows sufficiently, local sales offices are set up; this is the first stage of explicit MNC activity in a developing country. As the local market continues to expand, the MNC considers establishing productive facilities, generally in the form of local assembly of imported components. The underlying motivation to relocate production activity may be based on a company philosophy (that is, that whenever possible a local market will be served by local production), it may be based on peculiarities in local customs or consumer tastes that require special modifications in the product design (this is especially true for processed food items), or it may result from governmental pressure through import substitution tariffs or tax incentives. Of course, other motivations may also operate, such as a corporate belief that the market will continue to grow and the MNC wants to be in on the ground floor; such a feeling is common when considering the more advanced developing countries such as Brazil.

Over time the developing country governments normally exert pressure to increase the local content of locally sold products. Such pressures lead to the local production of the most basic, standardized and elementary input components and materials. Often the MNC's local assembly operation simply substitutes inputs produced locally by other firms (domestic or the affiliates of another MNC) for imported inputs rather than investing in capacity to produce such inputs in its own local affiliate. As might be expected, the material and component costs will rise as local (small-scale) producers displace imports. The importance of this tendency cannot be exaggerated, since roughly 40 to 50 percent of the costs of producing manufactured goods are accounted for by materials and components purchased by the manufacturing operation.[5] In the final analysis, manufacturing operations located in developing countries tend to incur substantially higher materials costs than their counterparts in developed countries. As a result, finished manufactured products from developing country plants are generally not price-competitive in world markets.

There are, however, exceptions to this point. When there is a concentration of productive activity in a given industry (for example, electronics in Asia) some MNCs may invest in manufacturing plants with the intent of serving the entire market for a given input component or material. In this case efficient large-scale production is possible, in contrast to the normal suboptimal scales of operation that prevail in most developing countries—scales dictated by the limited local market for the finished good.

The decision to invest in productive capacity located in developing countries is a "go slow" decision that is generally "marginal." The MNC begins assembly operations as an extension of sales activities in a market which is currently being serviced. Simple component manufacturing is added to an assembly plant. Gradually more and more components will be manufactured—and so on. This gradual approach minimizes the risk that the market will not grow as fast as anticipated. The firm definitely wants to guard against locking itself into a larger productive facility and workforce than is needed to satisfy the local demand, since government regulations and pressures would greatly discourage an MNC from laying off workers or otherwise cutting output. It is highly unlikely that a developing country government would permit an MNC to fully shut down productive activities and subsequently satisfy its established market through importing. Once local assembly or production begins, the MNC is virtually committed to maintaining its presence in the developing country as long as it continues selling in that local market.

In developing countries, governmental pressures for the MNC to generate ever-increasing economic benefits for the host country have recently been getting stronger and stronger. The governments are now screening investment applications by MNCs and imposing more rigid conditions on the companies, which further complicates the investment decisions for the corporations. For example, Mexico requires the MNC to have a local partner with at least 51 percent ownership (the MNC often maintains control by entering into a multipartner joint venture where it retains 49 percent ownership and at least 2 percent is owned by a local partner who is sympathetic to profitable and efficient operation—often a bank is the sympathetic local owner). The Andean code requires that 80 percent of the output be exported (this is likely to discourage manufacturing activities other than processing local raw materials such as copper). Mexico prohibits the payment of royalties (which will discourage the MNC from bringing frontier technology to its Mexican affiliate). Brazil limits the repatriation of profits to a fixed percentage of the initial investment financed by foreign capital.

The problems of operating in the developing countries are many. As already mentioned, the local market is often too small to warrant the construction of an optimal scaled plant—and in manufacturing, scale is essential for efficient for low-cost production. In addition, the local infrastructure is often inadequate—undependable transport systems, excessive electricity interruptions, inadequate housing near the plant, and so on. Governmental inefficiency is another problem; for example, occasionally production is interrupted because of delays in obtaining import licenses for crucial input components and materials that are not available locally—this is also true for machinery spare parts. The impact of such import licensing delays is minimized by maintaining large inventories of input materials and spare parts—but, of course, at higher costs. Similar problems occur during plant construction such as excessive time delays—often subcontractors must work at arms length from developed country bases (since local counterparts don't exist). Such problems lead to plant costs which are much higher than in developed countries. Moreover, because of the infrastructure problems, plants located in developing countries often include backup electrical generators (daily power interruptions are not uncommon in some developing countries), self-contained water and sewage systems, etc. This further increases plant costs.

One major advantage in operating in developing countries is that wage rates are relatively low, though they tend to rise quite rapidly. However, labor productivity is also low and requires very substantial supervision at no small cost. These latter factors often result in higher labor costs than in developed countries; but in any event labor accounts for a relatively small share of total costs in most manufacturing activities.[6]

A final problem is that the developing countries' governments continue to monitor MNC activities, and often change the rules of the game. Tax incentives are reduced, as is tariff protection; local content rules are increased, as are export requirements; local ownership requirements are increased while permissible royalty and profit repatriation payments are reduced.

When all is said and done, manufacturing in developing countries is a high-cost activity. Most often the final output is not price-competitive in world markets unless the government has an export subsidy program. Its major justification for MNCs is to satisfy local markets. In fact, the decision to enter a particular developing country is more often based on anticipated local markets; MNCs normally forecast a five- to eight-year payback period. This means that MNCs don't really allocate productive activity according to comparative advantage based on international factor prices. Instead they are induced to produce in various countries by local incentives provided via trade restraints and differential tax treatments.

The conclusion that manufacturing activities result in finished products which are not price-competitive in world markets holds for the bulk of developing country production. There is, however, a major exception. The last decade has witnessed a phenomenal increase in developing countries' exports of products produced primarily for the export market. Most often this trade is influenced by firms of developed countries (that is, by multinational corporations or by developed country importers designing the product, monitoring production for quality control, etc.) seeking lower cost goods for their home markets. The underlying incentive for such trade is generally to lower labor costs. In some cases the move offshore by the developed countries' firms was defensive; for example, several US electronics firms sought Asian sources of supply to counter the increased competition from Japan.

This phenomena has been analyzed recently by Professor Helleiner, who concludes that the most promising potential for continued export growth by the developing countries lies in "vertically integrated industries."[7] This conclusion stems from two factors:

1. Most developing countries have insufficient markets to warrant efficient large-scale production of manufactured products for the local market—from

which export sales have traditionally evolved for the developed countries. Thus efficient production of manufactures initially requires large-scale export markets.

2. The developed countries have shown strong resistence to relocating industrial production according to international comparative advantage. Instead political pressure emerges to protect the existing structure of production—often to the detriment of developing countries' exports; obvious examples include textiles and shoes.[8]

On the other hand, if developing countries' exporters concentrate on large-scale production of a single component of a manufactured product, the industry in the developed country need not fear import displacement. The imported component is inserted into the production process with minimal adjustment in the developed country's production process; employees can simply be transferred to other tasks within the same production plant.

Another example would be to allocate a *new* industry's activities according to international comparative advantage by locating the product development and improvement activities in the United States, with actual large-scale production taking place in developing countries. If mass production is not initially introduced into the United States, there will be no domestic interest group to lobby for protection. An example of such an industry would be small electronic calculators, initially developed and miniaturized in the United States. The early models were domestically produced using small-scale techniques and sold at high prices. Over time the mature models came to be mass-produced offshore while the frontier models were being developed in the United States, produced using small-scale technology and sold at high prices. Technology has been progressing so rapidly that high-cost small-scale labor-intensive production of the frontier models is necessary to maintain the flexibility required to adjust rapidly to an even later frontier model.

Another element which has tied such international industries together is the "offshore assembly" provisions which have been introduced into the tariff schedules of the developed countries (for example, items 806.30 and 807.00 of the Tariff Schedules of the United States). These provide that tariffs charged on US imports of products containing previously-exported US components would be reduced in proportion to the value of the US components contained in the finished article. In essence, tariffs are charged only on the value added offshore, provided US components are used in the production processes.[9] Such provisions contain incentives for a particularly vertically integrated industry—the labor intensive assembly process moves offshore in accordance with international comparative advantage, while the skill- and capital-intensive process of component production remains in the United States. Of course, not all components contained in the final product would be produced in the United States. Over time, the low-value mature components (such as transistors and semiconductors) would increasingly be made offshore, and the high-value, high-technology frontier components would be produced in the United States. It has been estimated that the economic benefits of the offshore assembly provisions come out slightly in favor of the United States; the stimulation of components production (and export) in the United States is slightly larger than the discouragement of US assembly activity (and import).[10]

Nevertheless, US labor opposes these provisions, and they are getting their point across—as evidenced by the removal of electronic articles from the list of products eligible for GSP treatment. The final verdict is not yet in on the fate of the internationally integrated industry and the role of the multinational company. In the meantime, developing countries' prospects for expanded exports of manufactured products look brightest in this area.[11]

MNCs and the GSP

As mentioned earlier, the GSP regulations contain a number of restrictions (ceiling, maximum amount and EC ceiling allocation limits, minimum processing requirements, documentation rules, etc.) that complicate trading under the preferential tariff schemes. These restrictions, together with the more traditional problems of transportation and marketing, are likely to make it quite difficult for local producers in developing countries to benefit much from the GSP. In contrast, MNCs, with international marketing networks and skilled customs lawyers, would be better able to exploit the opportunities created under the GSP. This section will suggest that while this may be true, the MNCs also face difficult problems. But more importantly, the GSP is only of limited interest anyway.

As a first point, it is true that MNCs have established marketing outlets. But they also have established production facilities located in or near the markets they have been serving. Moreover, the production facilities located in the developed countries, are more efficient than counterparts located in developing countries. Finally, social responsibilities (and governmental pressure) would dictate against displacing such production and employment to make way for increased imports from the developing countries. Developing countries' exports might be allowed to increase to satisfy part of an expanding European market, but seldom to displace existing production. An exception to this point is that occasionally GSP exports have been substituted for EC exports to other European countries such as Sweden or Switzerland. In such cases GSP tariff treatment has resulted in trade diversion in favor of developing country exports—one intended consequence of the GSP. Unfortunately, I am unable to quantify such trade and therefore cannot assess its relative importance.

The main institutional features of the GSP which influence its attractiveness to MNCs are the system of ceiling limitations and the rules of origin. These two items will be discussed in turn.

Ceiling Limitations

The EC ceiling system limits GSP imports (1) into the EC from all beneficiary developing countries combined; (2) into the EC from individual beneficiary countries; and (3) into each EC member state from all beneficiary countries combined. Unlike local developing country producers, the MNCs are in a position to monitor GSP imports from day to day and to know when a ceiling-type limit is in effect. Recall that the bulk of EC imports of GSP products is likely to face the reimposition of MFN duties at some time during the year.

In considering these restrictions, the MNC can do nothing if the overall ceiling is filled; MFN duties will be charged on further trade flows. However, if a maximum amount limit is reached, the MNC may switch its source of supply from the major beneficiary supplying country to a minor supplier. Likewise, if one EC member state's allocation is filled, the MNC could clear GSP goods through another member state's port, thereby gaining GSP tariff treatment, and then tranship the goods to the initially intended market under the "free circulation" provisions of the Treaty of Rome. Of course, this would be feasible only if the tariff saving exceeded the additional transport expenses.

In discussing these possibilities with MNCs I found no evidence of their switching the source of supply from one beneficiary to another as a result of a maximum amount limit. However, there were cases where an MNC switched the destination of GSP goods from one EC member state whose ceiling allocation was closed to another having an open allocation.[12] The scope of this activity is quite small, due to the internal transport charges. Typically such transhipment is profitable only when the final destination of the goods is far from the sea and can be reached equally well from several ports located in different member states, for example, southeastern Germany or northeastern France where goods could be cleared through Dutch, Belgian, German, French or Italian ports and transhipped by rail.

Of more concern to the MNCs was the uncertainty involved in not knowing exactly when the ceiling would be filled and MFN tariffs reestablished. The typical incentive was for the MNC to plan well at the beginning of the year and to "race the goods to the border" to get as large a share of the GSP trade as possible. The major GSP trading companies that I talked to confirmed this behavior; they also indicated that roughly one-third of their trade in GSP products failed to gain GSP treatment because of the ceiling system.

Rules of Origin

The rules of origin contain two major elements of concern: (1) minimum processing requirements and (2) documentation to certify that the goods are entitled to GSP tariff treatment. Perhaps MNCs, knowing precisely what is required to meet the minimum processing criteria, can adjust the production process or change the source of inputs from imports to local firms to meet these criteria.

My discussions revealed no attempts by MNCs to alter the production process. However, they changed the source of inputs on occasion, though the scope of such activities is limited. In some cases local producers of input materials or components are unwilling to document that these inputs are of local origin. The MNC interviewees suggest that local producers might want to hide certain activities from taxing authorities. It also could be that the materials are really not produced by the local firm but instead obtained by smuggling. If local producers are unwilling to certify that inputs are locally produced, the exports of GSP products will be refused GSP tariff treatment.

More typically the minimum processing requirements are simply at variance with productive technologies of developing countries. The primary rule underlying the EC minimum processing criteria is that the exported good cannot contain any imported components that would be defined under the same tariff heading as the finished product. This rule is extremely restrictive, since the EC tariff schedule is based on the Brussels Tariff Nomenclature, which defines products according to their input materials. For example, radios come under the same tariff heading as radio antennae. Because of economies of scale and tradition, most of the world supply of radio antennae is produced in Japan; hence radios will not qualify for GSP treatment unless the antennae are not installed until after the radios have been cleared for customs in Europe. The cost of such installation would probably exceed the GSP tariff saving, except for the more expensive radios. Also television sets contain some 1800 parts, many of which cannot be easily produced in developing countries but fall under the same tariff heading as finished television sets. A host of such problems are encountered by MNCs and local producers of manufactured products which are covered by the GSP and exportable from developing countries. I mentioned earlier that roughly one-quarter to one-third of the GSP trade is denied GSP tariff treatment because of the rules of origin.

One way to improve the prospects of meeting the minimum processing requirement is to allow the cumulation of origin among developing countries—that is, to permit GSP treatment for those products containing imported materials or components, provided the imported components originated in another beneficiary developing country. The MNCs indicated that cumulative origin would not be very helpful because of the tremendous problems involved in trade among developing countries—problems such as slow shipping, undependable timing of shipments, inefficiencies in governmental processing of import licensing, etc. In the end, the MNCs would be forced to maintain large inventories of input materials, adding substantially to their expenses for interest and warehousing. A better alternative for the MNCs would be to allow donor country components to be counted as local components; that is, EC imports of GSP products would qualify for GSP tariffs provided all imported inputs falling within the tariff heading were *either* locally produced in the beneficiary exporting country *or* produced and originally exported from the EC. Some of the more militant developing countries oppose such a provision on the grounds that it would make producers in the developing countries dependent upon components from developed countries.

The MNCs do export from developing countries under the GSP. They take advantage of the preferential tariff rates whenever they can. However, they often bypass GSP treatment because its benefits to be gained are not large enough to cover the additional expenses of meeting the rules and regulations. I did come across an example that illustrates the degree of sophistication MNCs use in taking advantage of the GSP when it is profitable; it also points out how relatively insignificant the program is. The company exported manufactured products from developing countries to the EC prior to the introduction of the GSP. During the early part of each year the company uses local input materials so that the product will qualify for GSP tariffs. The exports are then "raced to the EC to get our fair share of the ceiling." The intent is to fill the ceiling as early as possible so that future imports will face normal MFN tariffs. Once the MFN tariffs are reimposed, the company switches the source of its inputs from local producers to EC suppliers. Subsequent imports are cleared through customs under the reduced duty provisions of "offshore assembly" regulations. For the company, GSP exports have the primary objective of filling the ceiling to prevent competitors from getting a competitive edge, rather than benefiting from GSP tariff reductions.

The major conclusion of this paper can be stated as a question. If the sophisticated MNCs find the GSP of minor significance, how likely is it that producers in developing countries will benefit significantly from it? Before answering this question consider that what might be insignificant for a large MNC may be quite important for a small developing country. How much additional profit might an MNC earn from a $1 million increase in exports from developing countries when the alterntive is simply to produce the product elsewhere? In contrast, the consequent increase in employment, tax revenues and foreign exchange earnings may be very important to a country such as Afghanistan, Chad, Haiti, Malawi or Western Samoa. And for the local developing country producers facing limited local markets, exporting is an all-or-nothing proposition—either expand sales and profits via export markets or don't expand them at all.

Notes

1. In fact, Australia introduced the first preferential tariff system in 1965, which was more limited and independent of the UNCTAD negotiations.

2. Subsequently, Denmark, Ireland, and the United Kingdom joined the EC. As of January 1, 1974, these "joiners" began participating in the preference scheme of the EC, and their individual schemes were terminated.

3. The more developed socialist countries of Eastern Europe have also introduced preferential trade measures in favor of the developing countries. However, because of a lack of information on the operation and effects of these measures, preferences granted by the socialist countries will not be discussed.

4. For a more extensive examination of the GSP see Tracy Murray, *Trade Preferences for Developing Countries* (London: Macmillan, 1977). This section also draws heavily on Peter J. Ginman and Tracy Murray, "The Generalized System of Preferences: A Review and Appraisal," in K. Sauvant and H. Hasenpflug, eds., *The New International Economic Order: Confrontation or Cooperation Between North and South?* (Boulder, Col.: Westview Press, 1977).

5. Of course, the percentage varies from product to product and is highly influenced by the degree of vertical integration. However, the range quoted was reported to me by a surpising number of MNCs manufacturing quite different products.

6. Most MNCs indicated that labor discipline was not a major problem at all. Absentee rates were acceptable. Labor union activities are much more of a problem in developed countries; often the developing country's government intervenes to settle labor disputes with a minimal loss of work time.

7. "Manufactured Exports from Less-Developed Countries and Multinational Firms," *Economic Journal,* March 1973.

8. There are examples where international trade has completely displaced US production (for example, black and white television sets), leading to the displacement of thousands of US workers over a relatively short period of time. There is little pressure to reestablish this industry in the United States; however, these examples add substantially to the force of protectionist arguments. Witness the reemergence of the Hartke–Burke Bill, which would impose quotas on US importation of virtually every import item. A more immediate example is the tendency for the US government to negotiate "voluntary export restraints" for products which threaten to displace US production.

9. The provisions of other developed countries are similar in that, say German import duties will be reduced provided German components are used, and so on. There are some minor differences in the provisions of various countries, but their impact is similar. See J.M. Finger, "Tariff Provisions for Offshore Assembly and the Exports of Developing Countries," *Economic Journal,* June 1973.

10. J.M. Finger, "Trade and Domestic Effects of the Offshore Assembly Provisions in the U.S. Tariff," *American Economic Review,* September 1976.

11. The petrochemical area is quite different and involves only a small group of countries. Currently, natural gas in being "burned off" in many OPEC countries. However, this gas is an excellent second-stage raw material for the

petrochemical industry. European manufacturers currently "crack" crude oil to produce the second-stage input, which is obviously more expensive than using a material which is currently being discarded. Economists would say the OPEC countries have a "zero opportunity cost" input. There is little doubt about the ability of the OPEC countries to enter this industry and produce petrochemicals that are internationally competitive. But even here, technology dictates that the output is likely to be limited to mature petrochemicals as opposed to frontier items.

12. Such cases are less important today, since the EC recently introduced a reserve quota to reallocate ceilings from member states whose ceiling allocation remains unfilled to other member states whose ceiling allocation is exhausted—typically from France and Italy to Germany and the Netherlands.

10 Developing Countries' Debt Relief and Development Assistance
Neal P. Cohen

The plight of the Third World's burgeoning debt crisis achieved formal international recognition in September 1975, when a resolution was adopted by the United Nations stating that the UN Conference on Trade and Development would convene to reassess the status of debtor, creditor, and donor nations with an eye toward alleviating the serious situation of the neediest countries.[1]

In February 1976 in Manila the Third World refined this statement with specific pleas for expanded and improved short-term financing facilities to mitigate their balance-of-payments problems. At this same conference, the debtor countries called for relief in the form of waivers or postponement of interest payments, amortization, or both, and in some cases, even cancellation of principal.

Subsequent meetings in Nairobi in June, and Paris in July of 1976 provided the forum for Third World demands for debt relief, particularly for land-locked developing countries and island developing countries.[2] Put simply, the LDCs are demanding some form of complete or partial debt cancellation, forgiveness of debt service payments, and renegotiation of the terms of outstanding loans. They have also called for the establishment of guidlines for dealing with future debt problems.

This study argues that the demands for debt relief are misplaced. Very few LDCs who would be affected by cancellations or moratoria are in danger of imminent default. Furthermore, debt relief as a tool for international aid has serious flaws and is relatively inconsequential. Perhaps the increasing emphasis on debt relief is attributable primarily to a failure to make progress elsewhere in increasing financial flows to LDCs.

Only Sweden and the Netherlands have reached the UN target of 0.7 percent of GNP transferred as net official development assistance (ODA). Many other Development Assistance Countries (DAC) countries are actually decreasing the percentage transferred. In the period from 1965–1967, DAC transferred 0.42 percent, and in 1975 only 0.36 percent. Italy, Japan, the United Kingdom and the United States have all decreased their percentage contribution. The major increases in net flows to LDCs have been private sector nonconcessional flows.[3]

Higher import costs, due to the increases in oil prices and worldwide inflation, coupled with recession-induced decreased demand for Third World exports have forced many LDCs to resort to increased use of debt instruments to meet balance-of-payments shortfalls. The World Bank estimates that there was a 20 percent increase in the amount of official debt of a group of 86 LDCs in 1975.[4]

Morgan Guaranty Trust estimated an increase of about 24 percent in official and officially guaranteed debt in 1975.[5] The United States Treasury estimated that private bank credit extended by US banks will increase 11 percent in 1976.[6] They also noted:

... bankers are expressing a preference to reduce maturities of LDC loans, re-investing proceeds of maturing loans at short-term. . . .The widening of the LIBOR spread on loans to LDCs which has been hiked to higher than 2½% by front-end and commitment feeds charged by lending banks, reflects a more cautious attitude toward sovereign-risk or government guaranteed loans. . . .A constraining factor on LDC loans, besides national credit worthiness, is country lending limits.

Thus at the same time that many LDCs need to contract more debt, or roll over existing debt, the terms are tightening. Many countries are approaching the limits of borrowing.

The servicing of debt is becoming another impediment to development for some countires. The use of the debt service ratio as a measure of debt servicing problems[7] is still a reasonably good indicator of the magnitude of the problem despite certain limitations. A few countries now have debt service ratios of over 20 percent and the International Monetary Fund (IMF) notes that in 1975 the total debt service ratio rose from 26.1 percent to 29.5 percent for a selected group of important debtor countries. Public debt alone increased from 18.3 percent to 20.5 percent.

This upswing was especially important, since it came after a secular decline in the debt service ratio. In his speech of June 11, 1965, the Indian representative to the Conference on International Economic Cooperation said:

Debt relief must be viewed in the context of development and in particular as an important element of the concessional transfer of resources to the developing countries.

With some of our historic aid donors the present level of aid flows are actually less than the repayments and servicing of past debt. If debt relief is not available to us from these countries it necessarily means that there would be a net transfer of capital resources on official account from India to these important historic donor countries.

He could have gone further and noted that a number of low-income countries are making net transfers of money to selected developed countries. The problem is caused by a shift in the pattern of new aid disbursements. Former recipients of relatively high levels of aid and loans find that as their access to new assistance is curtailed, their repayments continue.

Debt relief is necessary when a country has insufficient foreign reserves to pay for needed imports (however defined) and also to repay loans. There are a number of possible reasons that a country might lack these reserves. One is that the "cost of external borrowing exceeds the benefits to the debtor's economy."[8] Here the country cannot generate enough foreign currency at the right times to repay the loan. The benefits derived from the loan may be long-term, while the repayment schedule is short-term. The economic return of a project may not have been accurately assessed. A country may be unable to roll over its debt, that is, to repay debt by incurring new debt, which is a fairly standard procedure used by many governments. If there is a crisis of confidence and the government cannot secure new loans, then it may have to default. Finally, short-term reasons such as a poor harvest, export shortfalls, or bunching of repayments may explain insufficient foreign reserves.

A more useful way to classify the causes of debt servicing problems is to divide the reasons into two groups: those that the government can control and those it cannot. We can then subdivide the second group into three categories. Those reasons which the affected government cannot control, due to lack of domestic control tools, international vagaries which one government cannot significantly influence, predominantly noneconomic occurances such as war, and natural events such as drought, locusts, and floods.

The government could take remedial action: (1) to improve economic analysis of projects; (2) to assure a level of investment in programs that would provide benefits sufficient to repay or service loans; and (3) to control domestic shortages and inflation.

Under those causes essentially out of domestic government control are:

1. the incurrance of foreign debt, the use of foreign exchange, or amount of goods imported.
2. international factors such as change in the price or volume of exports or imports, change in product demand due to recession or substitution, change in the quantity of ODA or new loans; and
3. noneconomic causes.

Some causes of rescheduling are given in table 10-1. A Chi-squared test established with 95 percent confidence that we can reject the hypothesis that the reasons for rescheduling have not changed significantly. This is demonstrated in table 10-2. Of marked significance is the decreased importance of short-term indebtedness and excessive investment programs as reasons for rescheduling. The government could, to some extent, control both of these variables. Excessive investment partly resulted from initial feelings in the 1950s and 1960s that the development effort would be possible if only sufficient capital were mobilized. These countries contracted large amounts of debt without adequate economic analysis, as they generally assumed that the economic return would easily be greater than the cost of capital.

Of increasing importance are the aftereffects of a preceding crisis, the recent deterioration of the terms of trade, and other erratic factors. These factors are

Table 10-1
Likely Main Causes of Debt Crises

Cases	Excessive Short-Term Indebtedness I	Budget Deficit and Inflation II	Insufficient Exports, etc. III	Excessive Investment Programs IV	Deterioration of the Terms of Trade and Other Erratic Factors V	Flight and/or Insufficient Net Inflow of Private Capital VI	After-Effects of a Preceding Crisis VII
Argentina							
1956	X	X	X		X		
1962	X	X	X		X		X
1965	X	X	X				X
Brazil							
1961	X	X		X	X		
1964		X		X			X
Chile							
1965	X	X		X			
1972	X	X			X	X	
1974		X					X
Egypt							
1966	X	X				X	
1968–69					X		
Ghana							
1966–68	X	X	X			X	
1970			X				X
1974		X	X		X	X	X
India							
1968			X	X			
1973			X				
1974		X			X		X
Indonesia							
1966		X	X			X	
1967							X
1968							X
1970							X
Khmer Rep.							
1972 I		X	X		X		
1972 II			X		X		X
Liberia							
1963	X		X	X			
Mali							
1966	X	X	X				

Table 10-1 Continued

Cases	Excessive Short-Term Indebtedness I	Budget Deficit and Inflation II	Insufficient Exports, etc. III	Excessive Investment Programs IV	Deterioration of the Terms of Trade and Other Erratic Factors V	Flight and/or Insufficient Net Inflow of Private Capital VI	After-Effects of a Preceding Crisis VII
Pakistan							
1972			X		X		X
1973					X		X
1974			X		X		X
Peru							
1968	X			X			
Turkey							
1959	X	X		X	X		
1965	X			X			X
Uruguay							
1965–68	X	X	X			X	
Yugoslavia							
1965–68	X			X			
Zaire							
1976	X	X			X		

Source: Organization of Economic Cooperation and Development, DAC/FA (71) 4 Page 20: Update with reference to IMF–Multilateral Debt Renegotiations–Experience of Fund Members, 1971–74. Zaire: County Reports (OASIA and IMF).

largely outside the control of the debtor country. Creditor clubs view rescheduling as means of monitoring country behavior and are requiring it frequently rather than just once.

A similar test demonstrates that rescheduling has taken place for differenct reasons in Latin America than in Asia or Africa. Latin American countries have emphasized the term structure of debt as the cause of the problem; Asians and Africans have greater problems with the volume of export growth. From a slightly different standpoint, Latin American rescheduling came about predominantly because of internally controlled factors. African countries have had to reschedule primarily because of domestic demand mismanagement and insufficient export growth. We can contrast this to Asian causes where external factors dominate, such as external demand, prices, and terms of trade.

Table 10-2
Reasons for Debt Rescheduling
(percent)

	I^a	II	III	IV	V	VI	VII
1956–1962	100	100	50	50	100	0	25
1963–1969	63	50	44	44	6	25	31
1970–1976	15	46	54	0	69	15	62

[a]See Table 10-1.

The international Monetary Fund notes that most reschedulings since 1970 have been multilateral and that international organizations are playing a larger role. International organizations have increased their proportion of new loans. Whereas in the mid-1960s expenditures by multilateral institutions were 5 percent of net ODA, they are currently just under 10 percent. Other characteristics we note are that more debt is being rescheduled. Figure 10-1 shows a generally rising trend in a three-year moving average of debt rescheduled. While the average number of countries requesting reschedulings in any given year has dropped from 3.3 in the 1960s to 3.0 in the 1970s, the individual requests represent larger amounts. Finally, we see from table 10-3 that rescheduling has changed its geographic distribution. From almost exclusive incidence in Latin America, we find that 68 percent of debt reschedulings now take place in Africa and Asia, two areas that did not have any reschedulings between 1956 and 1962. India and Pakistan account for 35 percent of the reschedulings since 1970.

The first set of problems with generalized debt relief concerns the attitudes of the industrially advanced countries. The United States and West Germany face legal constraints on any generalized debt relief. Most other DAC countries include debt repayments in their ODA budget. If less is repaid then new ODA is reduced.

We shall limit further discussion of generalized debt relief to the most seriously affected (MSAs) and least developed countries (LLDCs). Those countries needing special assistance over the short and medium term due to the 1973 oil price rise and the subsequent inflation and recession, were classified by the UN as most seriously affected (MSAs). They are distinguished by low per capita income (up to $400 per capita, but ususally less than $200 per capita), sharp deterioration in their current account balances, and modest growth prospects. Usually their current account deficit had to be at least 5 percent of their current imports. The original list consisted of thirty-three countries. Nine were added in 1975 and two in 1976. No country has been removed from the list.

The UN designated another group of less developed countries qualified for special assistance. These least developed countries (LLDCs) have: Gross Domestic Product (GDP) per capita of less than $100, manufacturing comprising under

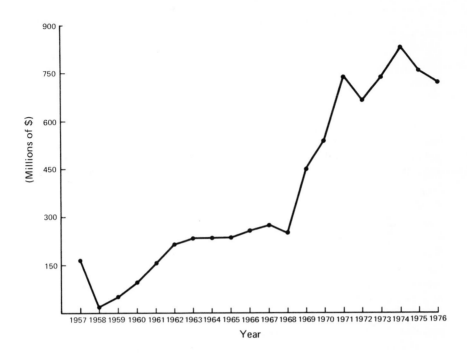

Figure 10-1. Estimated Value of Multilateral Debt Reschedulings, Allocated by Length of Consolidation Period (in millions of dollars). Three-year centered moving average.

10 percent of GDP, and literacy below 20 percent of the adult population. Only five LLDCs are not also MSAs. Over half the African countries are either MSAs or LLDCs, but almost 60 percent of the people living in MSA/LLDCs live in India. Only four Latin American countries are MSA/LLDCs, and one, Guyana, no longer ought to be listed because its per capita income is over $400 which would leave no South American country on the list of MSAs or LLDCs.

The MSA/LLDCs range from thirteen countries with per capita incomes of less than $100, five of which experienced reductions in per capita income between 1965 and 1973, to countries close to the $400 per capita limit and also

Table 10-3
Geographic Distribution of Debt Reschedulings
(percent)

	1956-1962	*1963-1969*	*1970-1976*
Africa	0	22	18
Asia	0	17	50
Latin America	80	39	14
Europe	0	9.	9
Mid-East	20	13	9

having high growth rates, for example, Cape Verde at $340 and 6 percent growth and Ivory Coast with per capita income of $380 and growth of 3 percent. The exposure to debt also varies, from the Ivory Coast's estimated 1974 debt service per capita of $19.64 down to Rwanda's $0.13 debt service per capita. Summary statistics are deceptive; the impact on development is impossible to generalize.

If current receipts of ODA measure need for debt relief, then there is a correlation of 0.491 with debt service due; if per capita income measures need, then the correlation is a positive 0.737. If current account balance measures need, then the correlation is a negative 0.467. Finally, if the growth rate of per capita GNP measures need, we find a positive 0.104 correlation. Thus for at least two measures of need for debt relief, the correlation has the wrong sign; in no case is the correlation very strong. Econometric work has shown[9] that economic variables are frequently insignificant in explaining ODA.

The MSA/LLDCs that gain most from generalized debt relief are the relatively richer, more populated, faster growing countries. Small, poor, slow-growth economies are helped very little.

Generalized debt relief does not provide adequate assistance to those who need it most. Debt relief tends neither to reward those countries undertaking policies to control their balance-of-payments difficulties nor to discourage the continuance of unsound policies. Finally, the real effect of such debt relief may be that some LDCs will have to pay higher interest rates because of a perceived reduction in the creditworthiness of LDCs as a group. Table 10-4 presents data on MSA/LLDC borrowing in the Eurocurrency markets. The big borrowers are countries that are more likely to gain from debt relief. If the private market should view debt relief as decreasing creditworthiness, many of the MSA/LLDC borrowers may be net losers.

One major defense of debt relief is that it assists the development effort. It is preferred because of its untied quality and quick disbursement, and because it frees hard currency.

Debt relief is not acceptable to the donor countries because debt service reflects past priorities in official development assistance, not present ones. A

Table 10-4
MSA/LLDC Borrowings in the Eurocurrency Markets
1972-1975
(millions)

Egypt	$230.0
Guyana	50.5
Haiti	10.0
India	10.0
Ivory Coast	208.0
Kenya	19.5
Malawi	5.3
Pakistan	7.5
Senegal	65.0
Cameroon	10.0

donor country which has shifted its priorities might be loath to give increased assistance via debt relief to a country. Would Sweden be willing to increase her present aid to the Sudan by over 30 percent in order to accomodate debt relief? Would Australia be willing to do likewise for Bangladesh? Or the USA for Cameroon, Ghana, Ivory Coast, Malagasy, Somalia, Afghanistan, Sri Lanka, India, Pakistan, and Haiti? Table 10-5 provides useful information for answering these question.

In many cases, policy "tilts" have left one country owing another a large amount of money and receiving very little ODA to help repay such indebtedness. In fact in 1975 there were negative net flows in many MSA/LLDC cases, as seen in table 10-6. To a large extent the net flow of resources from MSA/LLDCs to Italy reflects Italy's shift from foreign assistance to solving domestic problems.

The relationship between the DAC countries and the MSA/LLDCs is represented in table 10-7. If we had figured the debt service as a proportion of total ODA and not just that scheduled for MSA/LLDCs, the ratio would have been only 15.2 percent (for West Germany), except for Italy where it would have been 24.6 percent. The United States and West Germany are the clear leaders in debt outstanding, 74 percent of the total for DAC. Debt relief would not cause a major financial dislocation if it were limited to official and officially guaranteed debt for one year. Whether ODA would be increased to cover the relief in those countries where debt service is a part of the aid budget is a separate question.

While debt relief would not be a great burden on DAC, it would not be of much real assistance to the MSA/LLDCs. Table 10-8 shows that in only one case is the increase in GDP over 1 percent. The assumptions here are exceptionally generous; more realistic assumptions would render even less significant results than those shown. If current political leanings in DAC are such that foreign assistance is to be at certain levels obtainable through a combination of

Table 10–5
Creditors Who Will Have to Increase ODA by Over 30% to Accommodate MSA/LLDC Debt Relief[a]
1974
(percent)

Recipient	Australia	Austria	Canada	Denmark	France	Germany (W)	Italy	Japan	Sweden	Switzerland	UK	USA
Botswana												
Burundi												
Cameroon							X				X	X
Chad						X						
Ethiopia												
Ghana							X				X	X
Ivory Coast							X					X
Kenya							X				X	
Lesotho												
Malagasy Rep.							X					X
Malawi												
Mali												
Mauritania												
Niger												
Rwanda												
Senegal						X	X					
Sierra Leone						X	X				X	
Somalia												X
Sudan							X		X		X	
Tanzania							X				X	
Uganda				X							X	
Upper Volta												
El Salvador						X						
Honduras												
Guyana												
Afghanistan							X				X	X
Sri Lanka					X		X				X	X
India		X			X	X	X	X		X	X	X
Nepal												
Pakistan			X				X	X				X
Bangladesh	X											
Haiti					X							X

Sources: IBRD, *World Debt Tables*. Organization for Economic Cooperation and Development, *Data on Disbursements and Commitments in 1974,* Paris 1976.

[a]Official public government-to-government debt service as a percentage of gross ODA (both figures 1974).

Table 10-6
MSA/LLDCs with Net Negative Flows to DAC Countries, 1974

Flow From	To	Amount (millions)
Egypt	Italy	$12.32
Cameroon	Italy	0.39
Guinea	France	1.64
Guinea	Switzerland	0.04
Kenya	Italy	0.22
Malagasy	Italy	0.31
Sierra Leone	United Kingdom	0.35
Sudan	Italy	0.82
Tanzania	Italy	1.52
Uganda	United Kingdom	1.39
Sri Lanka	Italy	0.27
India	Italy	0.70

Source: Organization for Economic Cooperation and Development, *Data on Disbursements and Commitments in 1974: Geographical Distribution of Financial Flows to Developing Countries* (Paris, 1976).

Table 10-7
Financial Relationship of DAC Debt Donors with MSA/LLDCs, 1976

DAC Country	Debt Owed to DAC Country by MSA/LLDC ($ Millions)	Scheduled Debt Service Due from MSA/LLDCs ($ Millions)	Ratio of Debt Service to Net Bilateral ODA (MSA/LLDC Only)
Belgium	54.075	3.788	6.7%
Canada	887.940	37.732	11.9%
Denmark	135.948	4.065	7.6%
France	773.454	103.683	30.9%
W. Germany	2626.948	256.200	57.7%
Italy	250.187	45.169	37.6%
Japan	1049.540	129.377	58.7%
Netherlands	297.665	15.787	14.7%
Sweden	219.284	4.810	5.1%
Switzerland	35.094	7.115	39.4%
UK	2005.601	124.655	48.6%
USA	6172.933	326.216	39.5%

Source: International Bank for Reconstruction and Development, *World Debt Tables,* and OECD, *Financial Flows.*

grants and new loans *plus* debt relief, then debt relief reduces the other components and a redistribution of the benefits of the assistance results, as shown in the last column of table 10-9.

Under these more realistic assumptions, very few of the LLDC/MSAs stand to gain. Those countries involved in debt, who are, incidentally, the richest of these poor countries, are the ones who gain the most.

Table 10–8
Effect of MSA/LLDC Debt Relief on GDP and Government Investment

Country	Percentage Increase in GDP	Percentage Increase in Government Investment
Asia		
Afghanistan	0.49	17.60
Bangladesh	0.08	1.50
India	0.36	12.77
Nepal	0.03	1.39
Pakistan	1.58	39.11
Sri Lanka	0.74	14.04
Africa		
Botswana	0.98	13.75
Burundi	0.03	1.59
Cameroon	0.43	18.99
C.A.R.	0.02	0.95
Chad	0.60	14.65
Benin	0.11	1.38
Ethiopia	0.24	9.77
Ghana	0.22	10.55
Ivory Coast	0.56	18.75
Kenya	0.44	16.99
Lesotho	0.08	1.76
Malagasy	0.31	22.23
Malawi	0.64	16.80
Mali	0.48	11.47
Mauritania	0.59	21.11
Niger	0.25	10.00
Rwanda	0.02	1.63
Senegal	0.47	11.98
Sierra Leone	0.31	15.77
Somalia	0.26	9.42
Sudan	0.18	9.65
Tanzania	0.67	8.18
Uganda	0.38	7.96
Upper Volta	0.34	57.74
Latin America		
El Salvador	0.20	1.47
Haiti	0.34	9.73
Guyana	0.16	1.81

Source: 1973 GDP GI data, *UN Statistical Abstracts,* World Bank Estimates '77 Official Gov't.-to-Gov't. Debt Service. Assumes all debt relief is available (no defaults), all goes into government capital budget, and all has MKOR of at least 2.0.

Table 10-9
Distributional Impact of MSA/LLDC Net ODA and Debt Relief

	Net ODA from DAC ($ millions) 1974 (1)	As Percent of Total Net ODA of MSA/LLDC (2)	Debt Service Due in 1976 ($ millions) (3)	As Percent of Total Net Debt Service of MSA/LLDC (4)	Ratio of Debt Service to Net ODA (4/2) (5)
Gainers					
Guinea	5.1	0.20	21.300	1.94	9.73
El Salvador	7.7	0.30	14.700	1.34	4.45
Pakistan	265.2	10.35	208.726	25.54	2.47
Afghanistan	16.2	0.63	14.769	1.34	2.12
Uganda	6.8	0.27	6.164	0.56	2.11
India	602.2	23.51	498.646	45.36	1.93
Guyana	8.6	0.34	7.042	0.64	1.91
Sierra Leone	4.5	0.18	3.279	0.30	1.70
Haiti	9.4	0.37	5.277	0.48	1.31
Ivory Coast	51.6	2.01	26.311	2.39	1.19
Ghana	25.7	1.00	12.904	1.17	1.17
C.A.R.	18.5	0.72	8.224	0.75	1.04
Losers					
Sudan	33.2	1.30	13.841	1.26	0.97
Sri Lanka	58.2	2.27	23.834	2.17	0.95
Egypt	105.9	4.13	42.672	3.88	0.94
Honduras	14.5	0.57	4.900	0.45	0.79
W. Samoa	4.3	0.17	1.200	0.11	0.65
Cameroon	48.0	1.87	12.855	1.17	0.62
Malagasy	31.0	1.21	8.002	0.73	0.60
Malawi	30.5	1.19	6.806	0.62	0.52
Somalia	7.3	0.29	1.515	0.14	0.48
Kenya	99.4	3.88	19.559	1.78	0.46
Senegal	62.8	2.45	10.409	0.95	0.39
Burma	60.0	2.34	9.008	0.82	0.35
Mauritania	25.5	1.00	3.749	0.34	0.34
Chad	37.9	1.48	4.027	0.37	0.25
Ethiopia	79.8	3.12	8.403	0.76	0.25
Mali	60.2	2.35	3.974	0.36	0.15
Tanzania	140.2	5.47	9.172	0.83	0.15
Niger	82.6	3.22	5.221	0.47	0.15
Upper Volta	50.2	1.96	3.039	0.28	0.14
Benin	18.5	0.72	0.812	0.07	0.10
P.D.R. Yemen	5.0	0.20	0.200	0.02	0.09
Nepal	20.5	0.80	0.656	0.06	0.07
Botswana	29.9	1.17	0.838	0.08	0.07
Yemen Arab Rep.	27.4	1.07	0.634	0.06	0.05
Lesotho	12.6	0.49	0.260	0.02	0.05
Burundi	18.7	0.73	0.226	0.02	0.03
Bangladesh	344.2	13.44	3.947	0.36	0.03
Rwanda	31.6	1.23	0.124	0.01	0.01

Thus very few of the LLDC/MSAs would gain from a redistribution of aid from new loans and new ODA towards debt relief. Furthermore, if debt relief supplements ODA and does not replace any, the potiential effect on growth is minor. If debt relief is extended to non-MSA/LLDCs, the benefits would begin to be skewed away from the MSA/LLDCs. However, if debt relief only goes to the MSA/LLDCs but some of the reduction in new ODA comes from the other low-income countries, there will be a net benefit for the MSA/LLDC group.

With the cautions discussed earlier about using the past as a guide to the present or the future we can look at the underlying economic conditions that led to past reschedulings and use various econometric tools to attempt to establish a relationship. There have been many studies of reschedulings in the 1950s and 1960s. These were primarily single-variable explanations of the need for rescheduling.[10] There have been five major econometric models of reschedulings that utilize a number of different explanators and also are more sophisticated in their technique.[11] Some of these do not sufficiently define the variables to allow us to use them for forecasting purposes (that is, there are a number of possible definitions of the debt service ratio, and the balance-of-payments situation is also subject to many different interpretations). Using the data provided by Peterson and Mobius, reschedulings can be forecasted.[11] These forecasts are presented in table 10–10. (Those countries that actually rescheduled are bracketed.) Out of fourteen forecasts, five are correct. The Pakistan rescheduling in 1974 was a four-year exercise. Furthermore, they failed to forecast Ghana (1974) and Zaire (1976). Nor would their method have predicted the private bank reschedulings in 1976 for Argentina, Peru, and Brazil.

Using the method and data definitions of Frank and Cline[12] results in the forecasts presented in table 10–11. They err for Chile (1975) and Zaire (1976). Peru underwent a private bank rescheduling in 1976, so that forecast is probably correct.

Grinols' study did not show any forecasted reschedulings in 1976.

We were unable to utilize the other studies with sufficient accuracy to warrant reporting them here. But the major point is that, based on the economic

Table 10–10
Peterson-Mobius Forecasts

1974	1975	1976
(Chile)	(Chile)	Chile
Indonesia	Indonesia	Indonesia[a]
India	(India)	(India)
(Pakistan)	Pakistan	Pakistan
Egypt		
Sudan		

[a]Completing their data yields this result.

Table 10-11
Frank and Cline Forecasts

1975	1976	1977
Colombia	Chile	Bangladesh
(India)	(India)	Chile
Mexico	Mexico	Mexico
Pakistan	Pakistan	Pakistan
Peru	Peru	Peru
Sudan	Sudan	Sudan
Uruguay	Uruguay	

variables underlying past reschedulings, there has been no massive increase in the number of countries rescheduling nor is there any forecast of a marked increase in reschedulings.

Given the unsettled nature of international economics, more reschedulings might have been expected. The private bank sector, however, had funds available to loan to low-income countries. Without them we might have noticed more formal reschedulings. Many of the private banks are beginning to believe that they entered the field of low-income country debt without proper analysis. If the private bank sector is overextended, there will be some increased likelihood of default if that source of debt is reduced.

Based on the past, there is no reason to forecast a large number of imminent default reschedulings in the coming years. (Bangladesh, Pakistan, India, and Chile will still need reschedulings to complete past work and to handle anticipated foreign exchange shortfalls.) Burma may need to be rescheduled in 1977.

As a group, LLDC/MSAs cannot afford debt relief. Very few would gain anything substantial. Many of those who gained would eventually lose benefits if the private market reduced their credit standing and thus did not loan as much money to them. For the most part the MSA/LLDCs are more involved in grants than in debt, and thus debt relief is not an efficient policy objective.

Increased flow of money to the LDCs is one demand of the New International Order. Debt relief is only one aspect of that demand. Given the possible lack of immediacy about debt relief, and its possible redistributive impact within the MSA/LLDCs, other ODA matters—such as improving the terms and quality of aid and directing more aid to those most in need—are issues more worthy of the effort currently being expended on debt relief.

Notes

1. *Manila Declaration and Programme of Action*, 77/MM(III)49 February 7, 1976.

2. See *Fourth Session of United Nations Conference on Trade and Development,* 5-31 May. (New York: United Nations, 1976). See also special background UNCTAD papers for more detail.

3. *IMF Survey,* July 19, 1976, page 216.

4. New York *Times,* September 23, 1976, page 65.

5. Morgan Guaranty, *World Financial Markets,* January 21, 1976.

6. "Treasury Says Greater Selectivity is Likely to Slow Growth of US Banks' Lending Abroad," *American Banker,* August 3, 1976.

7. See, for instance, IMF, "Alternative Forms of External Debt Limitations," June 26, 1975, or Raymond Mikesell, "The Capacity to Service Foreign Investment" in *U.S. Private and Government Investment Abroad,* 1962.

8. Organization for Economic Cooperation and Development: *Debt Problems of Developing Countries,* Paris 1974, page 11.

9. M. Kim: "U.S. Foreign Aid to Low Income Countries" unpublished paper, St. Louis University.

10. See, for example: John Alter, "The Servicing of Foreign Capital Inflows by Underdeveloped Countries" in H.S. Ellis, ed., *Economic Development of Latin America,* St. Martin's Press, New York 1969; Dragoslav Avramovic, *Debt Servicing Capacity and Post War Growth in International Indebtedness,* Johns Hopkins Press, Baltimore, 1958; Dragoslav Avramovic, et. al., *Economic Growth and External Debt,* Johns Hopkins Press, Baltimore 1964; P. Finch, "Investment Service of Underdeveloped Countries" *IMF Staff Papers,* II; R.V. Gulhati, "The Need for Foreign Resources, Absorptive Capacity and Debt Servicing Capacity," in John Adler, *Capital Movements and Economic Development,* St. Martin's Press, New York 1967. Raymond Mikesell, "The Capacity to Service Foreign Investment" in Raymond Mikesell, ed., *U.S. Private and Government Investment Abroad,* University of Oregon Press, Eugene, 1962; Raymond Mikesell, *The Economics of Foreign Aid,* Aldine, Chicago 1968.

11. P. Dhonte, "Describing External Debt Situations: A Roll Over Approach," *IMF Staff Papers* (1975); G. Feder and R.E. Just, "A Study of Debt Servicing Capacity Applying Logit Analysis," California Agricultural Experiment Station, March 1976. Charles R. Frank Jr. and William R. Cline, "Measurement of Debt Servicing Capacity: An Application of Discriminant Analysis," *Journal of International Economics* 1 (1971). N. Peterson and K. Mobius, "Debt Problems of Developing Countries: A Pragmatic Approach to an Early Warning System," Germany Institute for Economic Research, Berlin, February 1975; F. Grinols, "International Debt Reschedulings and Discrimination Using Financial Variables," MIT, 1975. A detailed discussion of the first four of these studies is contained in Neal P. Cohen, "Econometric Debt Early Warning Systems," unpublished paper.

12. Frank and Cline, ibid.

11

The Multinational Corporation: Hate Object or Public Servant
Charles T. Goodsell

The "New International Economic Order" could easily fail to include a prominent role for the multinational corporation (MNC). This is particularly true for MNCs based in the United States, which have encountered widespread suspicion, resentment, and outright hostility. Actions by nation states and international organizations to limit, control, and excise foreign investments of this kind may eventually eclipse the MNC. Of course, American business investments are unwelcome in (or have already been forced out of) several countries in Latin America and Africa, among others.

Without taking a position on whether the MNC is generally "good" or "bad" as a world institution (perhaps the question is unanswerable in global terms), I shall argue in the following pages that the long-term viability of multinational business will depend on its development of an appropriate political strategy. In economic matters, corporate managers are accustomed to thinking in terms of systemic and long-term strategies. In political decisions, by contrast, corporate executives tend to think tactically—whom to approach to secure a certain contract, how to buy off legislators about to vote a threatening tax bill, or how to get favorable media coverage on a particular event. Management must substitute for this short-term, piecemeal approach to political action a distant time horizon and steady sense of direction.

What should this strategy be? This chapter argues that the multinational corporation should deliberately assume a sizable and activist noneconomic function in countries where it operates, offering public service to groups and populations in host societies. Although secondary to the traditional economic function of the corporation—production of goods and services—this public service function would be extensive, openly performed, and carefully managed. It would support projects designed to serve the health, educational, and cultural needs of less-privileged persons. The function would complement the economic activity of the firm. Even though its motiviation would be frank self interest for the corporation, this function would nevertheless render significantly beneficial service to the host society. The strategy would contemplate a mutuality of benefits for the MNC and its host: the local society receives tangible additions to socioeconomic programs mounted by its own government, while the company earns a political climate more conducive to its long-term survival.

In presenting this proposal I shall first elaborate on the political adversity faced by the MNC today, arguing that the multinational firm, especially if based in the United States, is almost inevitably a "hate object" in Third World countries. Second, I will explore the problems and potentialities of developing a "public servant" strategy. My position is that the top management of MNCs has a momentous choice to make: to allow the image of hate object to become increasingly (and hence irreversibly) established, or to adopt an extensive, dramatic, and meaningful public service role.

Why a Hate Object

It is understatement to remark that the multinational corporation is not politically likeable in most countries of the world. In fact, the MNC has in recent years become something of an international bete noire, comparable to fascism, communism or colonialism earlier in this century. In contrast to these other hate objects, the MNC is essentially an economic rather than political phenomenon, and hence is especially unprepared to survive a political maelstrom.

The defenders of the MNC marshal economic arguments on its behalf: it provides needed capital and technology, contributes to a country's balance of payments, creates jobs and income, and so forth. Often its opponents respond with economic counterarguments: imbalanced or distorted development, excessive repatriation of profits, hidden transfer prices, and so on. But these are basically points made by the specialists and intellectuals who understand them; underlying the MNC's bad image—particularly in the Third World—is a series of less intellectual and deeper fears and resentments.

The multinational strikes fear in many hearts because it is huge, efficient, and foreign. Because it is the most elaborate manifestation of capitalism since the colonial trading companies, it is anathema to the political left. The fact that most MNCs are headquartered in the United States raises the hacles of all those who, for one reason or another, are anti-American. At one level of perception, this giant, external and incompatible intruder seems to represent real dangers: political interference, secret control of public policy, inescapable dependency, and erosion of the society's most fundamental values. At another level, the MNC symbolizes those with more power and wealth; as such it is a convenient receptacle for the inevitable frustrations and disappointments within a struggling society.

Several forces of contemporary history have converged to cause this resentment to grow. Although the MNC is not conceptually new, its widespread emergence is relatively recent. Its growth in numbers and reach has alarmed many; certainly attention given to the MNC in the natonal and international communications media has exploded, which is perhaps more important than the reality itself. At the same time, Third World countries are becoming ever more sensitive to foreign, capitalist intrusion as an aftermath of the retreat of colonialism, the intensification of nationalist assertiveness in many countries, and the acceptance of governmental policies bent on radical redistribution of income.

In one of the few instances where relevant public opinion survey data are available on MNC popularity over time, public sentiment in Lima, Peru, in favor of expropriating US or foreign business rose from 36 percent in 1958 to 39 percent in 1961 to 47 percent in 1962 and to 75 percent in 1966.[1] Similar progressions have undoubtedly occurred in many capital cities around the world.

It is usually forgotten that the MNC, operating in numerous cultures as it does, faces an unusually difficult problem in maintaining acceptance. The organization must adapt to each cultural environment in which it finds itself; yet doing so requires contrasting and sometimes opposing behaviors, since societal value systems differ. The nearly comprehensive nature of world communications assures that MNC conduct revealed in one country is known in every other. For example, when a corporate affiliate in a Middle Eastern or Latin American society pays what would be called "bribes" in America, it is conforming to the business norms of that society (although some MNCs make such payments more aggressively than others). This is not seen as unusual or particularly "wicked" in that host society, but is considered irresponsible and immoral in the United States. Similarly, laying off employees from a plant which is losing money is considered a responsible and even essential business act by American standards of economic efficiency; but in an LDC this is viewed as an unforgivably anti-social action. In both situations the MNC sustains a political black eye. When an enterprise operates in as many as one hundred societies, it is likely to originate unfavorable publicity somewhere. By its very global reach, the MNC is more vulnerable politically than any purely domestic corporation could be.

A "Public Servant" Strategy

To counter its political difficulties the multinational enterprise might adopt any of several strategies. It could "circle the wagons" and hope for the best. It could play a "hard-nosed" game and exploit host economies for all they're worth until time runs out. Or, it could simply "play businessman" and pretend that politics is none of its concern.

Each of these strategies has grave shortcomings and cannot or should not be followed. The strategy I propose in contrast to these unacceptable alternatives takes the offensive rather than relying on defensive measures, and assumes that time does not necessarily have to run out.

It is proposed that MNCs begin to see themselves—and invite others to perceive them—as "public servants" of the host society, in addition to practitioners of the economic production process. This service function would supplement rather than replace the economic function; I am not suggesting that entrepreneurial activity or profits be foregone. Indeed, it is the very income-producing capacity of the corporation which can underwrite significant public service activity.

MNC affiliates, preferably in joint action, should publicly declare that hence forth in a particular society they shall set aside a stated proportion of their income for public service programs. These programs would involve the transfer of sizable corporate resources—financial, human, and material. They would be carefully designed to contribute tangibly to identified social needs of the host country. Public service projects would be formulated not by management alone but in an interactive process with societal leaders. Implementation of the programs would be—with a few exceptions—directly in the hands of societal groups and community organizations. Evaluation, feedback, and accountability mechanisms would be incorporated so that project participants, external observers, and MNC managers themselves would know what went on, its results, and its impact. A charity orientation wold be avoided by presenting the programs as a self-imposed obligation rather than a gift. The corporations would, in effect, be paying their dues as especially fortunate members of the host society. This posture and its articulation would be open, public, and not shrouded as to motive; in fact, steps would be taken to cast it in routine, unemotional terms.

The hoped-for advantage to the business enterprise is long-term political viability. To directors and stockholders, management would justify a significant public service function as reducing costs or risks or both over time, by reducing the probability of harrassment, punitive taxation, cancellation of contracts, expropriation, and so on.

Although in a crude way this strategy would involve an exchange of desirable policy for good behavior, its mechanisms could in reality be subtle and far-reaching. First, the proposed public service function would involve several levels of penetrating interaction between the MNC and host society, none or little of which existed previously. Managers would frequently consult with community and group leaders of all kinds, including those from the "underside" of the population—the very poor, fiesty activists, forgotten minorities, and the like. From this interchange, better understanding would emerge on both sides. Secondly, the mounting of truly beneficial projects—rather than mere media events—would transmit the clearest signal possible that the MNCs enlightened self-interest can coincide significantly with that of the host society. The corporation would be seen as capable of a direct contribution to the alleviation of suffering and distress in the society. The foreign enterprise would be seen as more than a mere component of the economic engine whose benefits eventually and indirectly trickle down. In short, its public servant role would show that the MNC affiliate is not as "foreign" as one might think, and that its size and efficiency can be tangible assets to the host society.

Constraints and Potentialities

Clearly, such a public service function must operate within constraints. It must not become so large and ambitious that it overshadows the host government's own public welfare activities. The corporations would carefully avoid taking any overall responsibility for socioeconomic development. To do so would be to impose a new form of "economic imperialism." Instead, MNC projects would be integrated into national development plans (or at least not counter to them) and would be responsive to host government leadership and policies in all respects. Compared to the undertakings of governmental agencies (including foreign and international), corporate programs would be relatively small in size and scope. The MNC as public servant would merely add to public service already being rendered.

Other constraints relate to the intent or perceived intent of projects. Even the *appearance* of political intrusion must be avoided. Assistance must not be given to "friends" of the company and withheld from political opponents or those who refuse to cooperate with management in some way. For example, a firm could not support a public work project of a town council with the implicit string attached that local officials in turn take actions favorable to management. Similarly, it would be unwise to grant scholarships for a pro-private enterprise business school and not for a left-wing liberal arts college.

Also, great care must be taken not to intrude culturally. Projects should support the host society's cultural milieu, not that of foreign mangement. Contributions to American and European schools and hospitals—intended to serve local communities of foreigners—should not be counted as part of the public service effort. Importation of foreign performers, translation of foreign books into the national language, or subsidy of English language instruction should be avoided. Furthermore, assistance should not be granted to programs that clearly run counter to the host society's values—for example, a sex education project, seemingly admirable in American eyes, would be quite unacceptable in many cultures.

Those responsible for MNC-sponsored public service programs would have to keep in mind that bitter resentment rather than increased acceptance can easily be the final outcome of gift giving. Studies of donee psychology have shown that recipients of assistance tend to turn against their beneficiaries if they believe donors have ulterior motives, are condescending, or are themselves not worthy of respect.[2] The corporations must avoid a patronizing attitude, state openly their reasons for the programs, reveal the magnitude of their giving, and maintain a continuous dialogue with recipient organizations. To win friends, firms will have to treat beneficiaries as equal partners in a larger enterprise.

Noting these limitations, the MNC is more capable of performing a public service function than many might think. First, the more enlightened side of the American business community has a long history of philanthropy, although such giving is seriously deficient in many ways. "Social responsibility" is even something of a fad among numerous companies. What I am proposing builds on an existing idea.

Second, the international corporate affiliate possesses resources very useful for public service. In addition to working funds, expertise, and equipment, the

MNC can supply entrepreneurial capability. Although the good businessman is normally not conceived as such, he more fully possesses some qualities of a successful change agent than the typical public bureaucrat—receptivity to innovation and willingness to accept risk.

Finally, the MNC manager has the advantage of wide and deep contacts within his host society. Unlike the foundation executive, foreign diplomat, or even visiting American scholar, the corporate executive deals not only with local private and governmental elites but with labor leaders, local small businessmen, middle-level bureaucrats, representatives of the mass media, and sometimes thousands of working-class employees. These relationships provide the potential for an understanding of the society that is comparatively thorough for a foreigner, assuming the manager remains in the country for an extended time.

Current Corporate Philanthropy Abroad

Corporate giving is traditional in the United States but deficient in several ways. This is particularly true of charitable and philanthropic activities overseas.

First, the philanthropy of US affiliates abroad is meager and uneven in size. Recent reports on this subject by the Conference Board are revealing.[3] According to a survey of donations in sixteen countries, almost 80 percent of reporting companies give less than $25,000 per year. This is about the salary of one junior executive. Although a few isolated firms have mounted programs costing hundreds of thousands of dollars annually, median donation budgets are often less than $5,000. The biggest programs are offered by big companies; but contrary to what some might expect, small firms are proportionately more generous. The domestic charitable contributions of US firms in 1972 were 2.4 percent of pretax net income for companies with less than 250 employees and only .68 percent for those with 25,000 and more.[4] This is not an unusual pattern.

Another point is that donation activities are usually undertaken in an unsystematic, casual manner. Apart from the corporate foundations, the donations function is handled by nonline executives who perform numerous other tasks. Actions on gift requests are made by contributions committees who see their work as peripheral to management's interest. Only a small minority of companies have written guidelines or policies in this area.

Donations also tend to be given in the safest, most painless way. A high percentage of grants goes to umbrella organizations such as the local version of the United Fund. In most Third World countries the traditional charities are conservative and tied to a patronizing upper-class establishment. Many causes popular with MNCs involve relatively privileged beneficiaries, such as the Boy Scouts, YMCA, and men's service clubs. In general the affiliates tend to provide the same assistance (adjusted for inflation) to the same organizations every year. Also companies watch each other's charitable actions carefully, not wanting to stand out as niggardly or to waste money by giving above the norm. A kind of iterative feedback cycle results, which stabilizes amounts of support at a common level.

A final deficiency is a matter of style. Gifts are given as charity contributions rather than participating in meeting the society's needs. Applicants for assistance are checked for worthiness or their relationship to a possible quid pro quo. They are then given an outright gift, normally of money, with little or no subsequent involvement. Usually no attention is given to long-term changes in the capability of the recipient, such as reduction of self-esteem or increased self-sufficiency. The consequence of this approach is often bitterness that the handout was not larger; it effects no lasting improvement in people's lives.

But, corporate philanthropy overseas need not be limited, casual, conservative and patronizing, as proven by examples of constructive public service projects which have actually been carried out. In Mexico the Ford Motor Company facilitated the establishment of rural extension services to small farmers previously beyond the reach of such programs. Ford provided an outfitted truck, with gasoline and maintenance, for each of more than a score of mobile extension units. The Ministry of Agriculture then supplied and paid agronomists to ride in them. Also in Mexico, Ford contributed matching funds for the construction of six-room schools in remote rural areas. Local Ford dealers were assigned the task of spearheading the fund drive to raise the necessary match. The Mexican Ministry of Education staffed and operated the many schools built in this way.[5]

Before it was forced out of Peru in 1968, the International Petroleum Company became involved with a community development project which was a textbook model of success. The project was at Cabo Blanco, a tiny fishing village on the northern coast. In the early 1960s the residents asked IPC social workers for a gift to build a new church. Demurring, the company suggested instead that the fishermen rebuild the village itself, which consisted of wooden shacks without plumbing, surrounded by freely running livestock. IPC promised help if the community would form community committees, make plans, and tax themselves. The company agreed to sell the committee construction materials at cost; it also furnished desalinated water at cost, with the understanding that it would be resold to residents at a modest markup and the margin would go into the development project. The villagers then proceeded to carry out their plan: the animals were penned, the shacks were gradually replaced by cinderblock houses, and eventually a school and a church were constructed. When IPC departed Peru it left behind a socially and physically reconstituted Cabo Blanco, accomplished by the villagers themselves. Unfortunately for Standard Oil, its reputation for past political and social sins against Peru completely obscured this unusual instance of good works. If such behavior had characterized the corporation's posture toward Peruvian society all along, the outcome would probably have been entirely different.[6]

Developing a Public Service Function

The proposal made in this chapter calls for a bold change in established practice and attitudes, which obviously will be very difficult to implement. In fact, a realistic view suggests that the MNC will adopt a clearly defined and extensive public service function only if initiatives are taken from several sides.

Governments of less developed countries (LDCs) should consider demanding a sizable public service role as a requirement for operating within their borders. In bargaining over the terms of new investments, public service projects could be a topic for negotiation. Foreign investment codes drawn up by international organizations and regional pacts should include explicit guidelines on the subject.

Pressures on the MNC can also be mounted elsewhere. The large foundations could take a lead by formulating and operating demonstration public service projects and by offering to participate financially in programs. The private philanthropic associations could also stimulate interest by promoting the idea and exploring methods of implementation; the National Council on Philanthropy is already quietly working with MNCs in this area. Business organizations such as the Conference Board, Committee for Economic Development, and Council of the Americas could exert influence. Also they could perform relevant research and guidance functions.

Finally, the United States government should not be reluctant to promote behavior by American corporations that will serve their own long-run interests. The State Department's Office of Private Cooperation is already modestly encouraging public service abroad; there is no reason why this effort should not become more intensive and aggressive. Probably the most effective State Department leadership will be at the embassy level, however. Ambassadors in appropriate LDCs should sternly warn American corporate affiliates (and local American chambers of commerce) that if significant *social* investments are not made in host societies now, it will not be possible to collect on *business* investments later.[7]

Yet no one will be able to convince MNC managers to adopt a new order of public service commitment if they cannot convince themselves. The corporate sector itself will obviously have to supply the principal impetus to forming this new role. Top management will have to recognize that a public servant function is not only realisitc but essential for continued survival. Indeed, MNC executives owe it to their shareholders to develop such a strategy.

Let me now turn to a series of concrete steps that might be taken in developing a public service function. First, United States-based affiliates in a given country or region should collectively and publicly declare a quantitative standard of support for public service activities. Such a standard might best be expressed as a percentage of net income before taxes. A five percent standard, for example, would generate unprecedented levels of resources for corporate public service abroad, even though it would not be outlandish for domestic US giving.[8] Expressing the standard in this form would: (1) give the commitment a tangible symbolic expression; (2) facilitate joint action by companies; (3) make contributions proportionate to what a firm "takes" from the society, thus giving program levels an inherent legitimacy; (4) make donations proportionate to income, with the big enterprises paying their full share; and (5) relieve managements from dollar commitments which may later become intolerable if revenues decline.

Second, MNC managers should deliberately involve external organizations in the planning of corporate public service programs, projects, and budgets. Those firms who have declared a public service standard should periodically sponsor a joint planning conference, inviting leaders of prospective recipient organizations, affiliate general managers or their immediate subordinates, officials or interested third parties such as business groups and foundations, and US and national government officials as observers.

The purpose of these meetings would be to engage in open dialogue on the future content of public service programs. Ideas would be received, examined and debated. No doubt discussion would also extend to experience under current or past programs. The meetings would be kept informal, without speeches, testimony, resolutions, or votes. They would not be intended to make decisions, but to furnish ideas and reactions, to uncover service gaps and hidden resentments, and to provide an opportunity for program coordination and general cross-fertilization between the private, public, and nonprofit sectors. Perhaps most importantly, the conferences would provide yet another visible signal that MNCs are serious about their public service role and about the need to shift from unilateral charity to mutual consultation.

Next, I suggest a new format for donation. Handing over a check evokes the image of the patron and the patronized. Making the recipient sign an IOU or postaudit authorization suggests a lack of trust. A device compatible with mutual respect and self-esteem would be a bilateral contract, signed by officials of the corporation and the organization assisted. The donor's signature would commit the MNC to a specified level and type of assistance as well as a payment shcedule and prospects for renewal. The contract would commit the recipient organization to a set of objectives for the project, the expected time period for achieving them, and arrangements for evaluation of impacts. The texts of these contracts would then be made available to interested persons, including the press.

With the philanthropic act thus depersonalized, the donee is elevated from the position of beggar and the donor dethroned from the status of lord. Any hidden requirements for reciprocal favors—often suspected as accompanying traditional charity—would be either eliminated or very difficult to enforce. If either side retreated from its commitments, the other would be free to declare itself relieved of further obligation. The gift would be similar to a normal business transaction.

A final proposal relates to conducting appropriate research. An American business association or similar organization should prepare a corporate contribution manual for overseas affiliates. Manuals now exist for domestic but not foreign use. The manual would encourage public service activity of the appropriate scope, extent, and philosophy. Guidlines would be suggested for setting a declared standard, holding joint planning conferences, an utilizing the public service contract device. The volume would also supply valuable background information to MNC managers: relevant legal requirements for donations in various countries, an inventory of possible project ideas collected from corporate and foundation experience around the world, and a discussion of techniques for assessing projects. The manual would also be useful to recipient groups, to stimulate thinking on what might be done with MNC participation.

Conclusion

Almost inevitably doomed to being hated in many quarters, the multinational corporation must begin to take radical steps in the political sphere if it expects to remain viable in the economic sphere. The proposal advanced here does not guarantee long-term survival of the MNC, of course, but it deserves an experimental trial at the very least.

The proposal will not dovetail with management's traditional preoccupation with reduction of costs and enhancement of profits. It also runs counter to management's usual disdain for contribution programs. But, it can be argued, successful business practices, even narrowly defined, now justify a political strategy of this kind rather than othrodox political tactics such as short-term pressures, bribery, and public relations campaigns. The proposal has the further advantage of being essentially initiated and controlled by MNCs themselves. It is better than an externally imposed solution.

At the same time, such a strategy by MNCs will lead to the implementation of many health, education, cultural, manpower, community development, and other such inherently worthwhile projects. The poorer societies of the world will not be importantly altered or developed in the aggregate sense, but the lot of many thousands of individual persons will be improved.

Notes

1. See Charles T. Goodsell, *American Corporations and Peruvian Politics* (Cambridge: Harvard University Press, 1974), p. 114.

2. Kenneth J. and Mary M. Gergen, "The Psychological Evaluation of International Aid," draft manuscript, 1976.

3. See James R. Basche's series of six studies under the general title *U.S. Business Support for International Public Service Activities* (New York: The Conference Board, 1973–75). Summary data are found in the Conference Board's newsletter, *Worldbusiness Perspectives* no. 23, October 1974.

4. John H. Watson, *Biennial Survey of Company Contributions* (New York: The Conference Board, 1973).

5. International Management and Development Institute, *Top Management Report on Government–Business Cooperation in the Field of International Public Affairs* (Washington, D.C., 1975), p. 21.

6. See Goodsell, *American Corporations and Peruvian Politics*, especially p. 183.

7. I have proposed, as a "Self-Preservation Model," this approach for general protection of corporate interests abroad. See my "Diplomatic Protection of U.S. Business in Peru," in Daniel A. Sharp, ed., *U.S. Foreign Policy and Peru* (Austin: University of Texas Press, 1972), pp. 237-257.

8. Corporate donations in the United States as a percent of pretax net income are usually around 1 percent in the aggregate. However, some industries have gone as high as 3 to 4 percent and a 5 percent standard has sometimes been suggested for domestic use. Using data from the *Survey of Current Business* for 1974 (Vol. 56, May 1976, Table 12) I calculated that a 5 percent standard would have generated $615 million for use in LDCs alone. With the tendency for understatement in Commerce Department figures on foreign investment, this figure would probably be closer to $1 billion.

12

UN Proposals for a Code of Conduct for Multinational Enterprises and the New International Order

Werner J. Feld

Introduction

Although investment in the Third World is less than one-third of total direct foreign investment by multinational enterprises (MNEs), the problems and questions arising from MNE activities in less developed countries (LDCs) are both much more intensive and broader than those encountered in advanced countries. Two main reasons account for this disparity: (1) the differences in scale between the operations of huge MNEs and the relatively small size and primitive nature of many LDC economies; and (2) the often extraordinary difference in power between MNEs and host governments. The problems are compounded by two peripheral, though very significant, issues: the achievement of economic growth and development in the Third World through the New International Economic Order adopted by the UN General Assembly in 1974, and the changing perceptions about the value of private enterprise. These issues have made MNE problem areas in the Third World—such as balance of payments, trade, employment, taxation, transfer of technology and skills, and political, social, and cultural effects of MNE activities—flash points of struggle between the LDCs and economically advanced countries.

A major question in the MNE-LDC relationships is the distribution of benefits and drawbacks for the parties involved; since perceptions of these depend very much on where participants or observers "sit," they disagree about what is a benefit or draw back for whom. Of course, "where you sit" also influences your behavior, and therefore conflict has crept into many of the MNE-Third World relationships. While many Third World countries would like to tap the extraordinary resources of multinational corporations to improve the economic welfare of their people, leaders of LDCs have a number of anxieties that make their relationship with MNEs very tenuous. For example, the question of responsiveness of multinational enterprises to the need for expanded employment has been raised agian and agian. Other questions relate to the reluctance of MNEs to carry out research and development activities in poor countries, and how these countries can acquire skills for research and raise technological levels within their borders. A third major issue is the difference in objectives of nation states and MNEs.

The overwhelming economic power of MNEs has made it difficult for many Third World governments to come up with effective terms for either the establishment of a new subsidiary by an MNE or the continuation of its operation.

177

Although national governments can pass and enforce laws limiting the operations of MNEs, they frequently hesitate to exercise these powers because of the real or perceived costs entailed. Consequently, negotiations between Third World governments and MNEs are frequently awkward and tend to overplay the anxieties of the governments, so that MNE do not enter, or curtail their existing operations. Therefore, whatever help multinational enterprises could provide for the purposes of development is lost because of misunderstandings and tensions.

In the face of these dilemmas, LDC governments have turned increasingly to the United Nations for help. Since the late 1960s the United Nations Conference on Trade and Development (UNCTAD) and the International Labour Office (ILO) began to address themselves to these problems through studies on the impact of MNEs on development, the transfer of technology by MNEs, and problems of social policy.[1] In 1975 the UN secretary general established the Commission on Transnational Corporations (CTN) composed of representatives of forty-eight UN member states,[2] and an administrative support unit, the UN Centre on Transnational Corporations (CTC), to which was attached an Information and Research Centre (IRC). The functions of the IRC are:

1. To provide substantive and administrative services to the Commission on Transnational Corporations;
2. To collect, analyze and disseminate information and to conduct research and inquiries as directed by the Commission; and
3. To organize and coordinate technical programs, especially for host developing countries, in matters related to multinational corporations.

Since the CTC's activities relate to those of other United Nations bodies a coordinating committee has been set up, composed of the heads (or their representatives) of the following units, organs and agencies: The Department of Economic and Social Affaris, the Office of Legal Affairs, the United Nations Industrial Development Organization, and the International Labour Office. Where the need arises, other agencies in the United Nations system will be invited to participate in the meetings. The executive director of the CTC is a member ex officio of the coordinating committee.

The First Commission Meeting

The Commission on Transnational Corporations held its first session at the UN Headquarters from March 17 to 28, 1975. It was convened in conformity with Economic and Social Commission (ECOSOC) Resolution 1913 of December 1974 (Fifty-seventh Session) which requested the commission to submit a detailed work program with due regard for the guidelines on MNEs contained in

General Assembly Resolutions 3201 and 3204 (Sixth Special Session) of May 1974, and Resolution 3281 (Twenty-ninth Session) of December 5, 1974.[3] Eleven meetings were held, in which all members of the commission were represented except Zambia. In addition representatives of UNCTAD, UNIDO, ILO, FAO, UNESCO, and the IMF attended.

Interestingly, other intergovernmental and nongovernmental organizations sent representatives to this first session of the commission. Among the former were the European Communities, the Organization for Economic Cooperation and Development (OECD), the Organization of African Unity (OAU), and the Organization of American States (OAS). Among the latter were the Chamber of Commerce of the United States, the International Chamber of Commerce (ICC), the International Confederation of Free Trade Unions (ICFTU) and the World Federation of Trade Unions (WFTU). Clearly, the interests of all these organizations were likely to be touched by the deliberations and decisions of the commission and the concern their participation suggested was legitimate.

The officers elected by the Commission members by acclamation for this session reflected the influence of the Third World on this UN body. The chairman was a delegate from India and two vice-chairmen were drawn from the Argentinian and Ugandan delegations. Another vice-chairman came from Bulgaria and the rapporteur was an Australian.

Both the Group of Seventy-seven (Third World countries) and a group of Western delegations (France, West German, Italy, the United Kingdom, and the United States) submitted lengthy lists of concerns that deserved particular attention in the work program of the commission and the IRC. Significantly, the Group of Seventy-seven's list focused on the operation and activities of MNEs, expressing many of the fears discussed earier, while the Western group concentrated more on the relations between MNEs and governments, including discriminatory treatment of MNE subsidiaries, expropriations, and the type of investment climate prevailing in various LDCs. The Soviet bloc countries also submitted a short list of issues, which referred only to the negative impact of MNEs on labor conditions, balance-of-payments matters, and the raw materials situation.[4]

An air of confrontation pervaded some of the meetings of the delegates.[5] Considering the disparate economic and political philosophies espoused by the various delegations, this should not have surprised anybody. As in other forums during the last few years, the developing countries participating in this meeting presented a united front in pressing for a work program whose views on MNE–government relations were in line with the New International Economic Order. This meant that the preeminent priority of the commission would be a code of conduct for MNEs, which would compel them to conform to the policy objectives of countries in which they operate, and contribute to their advancement.

The commission mapped out for itself and the IRC a preliminary program of projects in several broad and overlapping categories, including:

1. preliminary work on the foundations of a code of conduct;
2. establishment of a comprehensive information system;
3. research on the political, economic, and social effects of the MNEs;
4. organization and coordination, at the request of UN member governments, of technical cooperation programs concerning MNEs; and
5. work leading to a proper definition of MNEs.[6]

The Second Commision Session

The commission's second session took place in Lima, Peru, from March 1 through 12, 1976. Its atmosphere was relatively nonconfrontational, and it produced a long-term work program that appears reasonable. Of course, actual progress toward the goals of the first session has been small, because the first task in 1975 and early 1976 was to set up the organizational and administrative machinery for the CTC and the IRC. Nevertheless, some useful initial survey work on the vast MNE literature had been accomplished by the time of the second session of the commission; this offered analytical insights into the problems to be faced and solved by the CTC.

The election of officers for the second session basically maintained the pattern of geographic distribution. The chairman was from Peru, the three vice presidents were from Bulgaria, Algeria, and the Netherlands, and the rapporteur was a native of Thailand. Various UN specialized agencies and a number of intergovernmental organizations—the European Communities, the OECD, and the OAS—were represented. Several nongovernmental organizations—for example, the ICC and some international labor federations—also sent representatives.

The results of the deliberations were mainly programmatic and procedural, following closely the concepts adopted in the first session. The highest priority was the elaboration of a code of conduct, although it was recognized that this task was closely related to the establishment of a comprehensive information service, research on the various effects of MNEs, and the definition for MNEs that would be accepted. At the same time, the commission did not overlook the need for technical cooperation programs to strengthen the negotiating capabilities of Third World countries, and the desirability and feasibility of separate agreements on specific subjects. Work was also to be continued on a proper definition of the term "transnational corporation."

To formulate the code, the commission decided to establish an intergovernmental working group, in which at least four members from each regional grouping would participate. Obviously, the IRC would play a pivotal role in this endeavor; in addition ECOSOC was to request the UN Regional Commissions to assist. Regional meetings of LDCs would be scheduled to identify concerns relevant to the code. Consultants familiar with MNE operations and practices will be selected from business, organized labor, public interest groups, and academia, on the basis of balanced geographic and functional representation. The working group's task must be related to UNCTAD's ongoing efforts to develop rules on the transfer of technology and on restrictive business practices, and ILO's work on employment issues. Finally, the working group must also consider the studies conducted and actions taken by other forums, such as the OECD and European Communities.

The members of the commission hoped that an outline of the proposed code could be submitted to its third session beginning April 25, 1977 in New York. Because of the IRC's many tasks and its role in elaborating the code of conduct,[7] and the commission's small staff, the working group may be unable to complete the task. An annotated outline of the code will probably not be ready until the middle of 1978.

The Code: Voluntary or Mandatory?

Some delegations thought that the code should be mandatory, while others opted for a voluntary code. Of course, the enforcement problem needs to be considered; a number of delegations therefore felt that the consideration of this matter was premature.

Those wanting a mandatory code thought that a simple declaration of principles would not remedy what they consider undesirable practices and would not ensure that MNEs would make a positive contribution to establishment of the New Economic International Order and the Charter of Economic Rights and Duties of States. However, others said that a mandatory code required international enforcement machinery, which would require consent of all nation states—a very time-consuming process with little prospect for eventual success. A voluntary code could be hammered out much faster and would be preferable, given the diversity of national legislation and policy objectives. Once the commission accepted the code and the member states and MNEs recognized it, a mandatory concept might evolve as a matter of legitimacy and effectiveness. No agreement could be reached on this issue, but the commission was urged nevertheless to draft the code, reflecting a declaration of political will in this endeavor.[8]

The Substance of the Code

The Third World and the Western countries are far apart in certain areas, but compromises appear possible in others. The Commission's Latin American and Caribbean delegations submitted a rather detailed paper as a basis for preliminary work for a code of conduct. (In contrast, a broad note on areas of concern was submitted by some of the Western delegations, including the United States.[9]

According to this paper, MNEs should be subject to the laws and regulations of the host country; in case of litigation, they should be subject to the exclusive jurisdiction of the courts of the country in which they operate. Private agreements on court jurisdictions or settlement of disputes by arbitration—permissible under international law and considered highly desirable by Western advanced countries—would be impossible.

The paper argues that MNEs should be obligated to conduct their operations so that the host country receives *net* financial resources. This would be a continuing obligation following the initial transfer of funds and would be measured by the impact of MNE operations on the host country's balance-of-payments. These provisions reflect the apprehension host countries feel about excessive repatriation of capital, profits, royalties, and other payments for transferred technology, and about undue restrictions on imports from and exports to MNE affiliates, including international market allocation. Obviously, these provisions seriously limit the freedom of MNE managements and may not be acceptable as stated. This is also true of another point in the paper, which would require MNEs to contribute positively to the host country's national policies, objectives and priorities for development. This would not only constrain MNE subsidiaries in the countries concerned, but would also require managements to adapt their corporate strategies.

Another provision in the paper subjects the MNE "to the exercise by the host country of its permanent sovereignty over all its wealth, natural resources and economic activities." This opens the door to any kind of nationalization and expropriation measure. MNE subsidiaries are also enjoined to operate in a way that ensures that nationals of the host country can manage and operate the enterprise at all levels, an obvious prerequisite for successful nationalization or expropriation by the host country's government.

Finally, the disclosure requirements about the MNE as a whole are escalated. Disaggregated data are sought that will allow "the most exact determination possible of the contribution to the national development" of the host country by the subsidiary. While advanced home countries may agree with a higher level of disclosure, they are likely to defend very strongly legitimate confidentiality of trade secrets and management strategies that do not violate any laws and have been traditionally regarded as fully acceptable. Of course, the proper dividing line may defy precise definition.

Other parts of the Latin American paper are less controversial and agreement with the Western members of the commission on specific points should not be too difficult. The injunction that MNEs should not interfere in the internal affairs of the states where they operate nor disturb relations between host and other governments may *generally* be well received by Western countries, but may also raise a variety of questions in the event of slow or inadequate indemnity when facilities of a foreign MNE are nationalized. Western advanced MNE home countries are unlikely to give up their traditional rights under international law to protect their nationals in the event of perceived illegal action. Differing legal views will have to be reconciled and the solutions clearly spelled out in the code. The same applies to the request that MNEs should not serve as instruments of the foreign policy of another state or extend into the host country the juridical order of another state (generally the MNE home country). Antitrust and certain tax laws are the main problems here. Another concern of the Third World—in restrictive business practices—is also recognized as a basic evil by the Western advanced countries; they agree practices such as tied sales or administered import or export prices of goods moving between subsidiaries of an MNE without regard to cost and normal profit are undesirable, but the precise parameters need to be defined.

The second session of the commission made few serious attempts to reach agreement on the substance of the code. Perhaps it was felt that this would interfere with or prejudice the intergovernmental working group, which should be allowed to consider afresh the various positions and concerns of the opposing parties. Moreover, experts from different universities and nongovernmental organizations need to be heard and their views evaluated before the group can begin working on an annotated code outline, which in turn must be coordinated with related programs in UNCTAD and the OECD. At its third session in New York in 1977, the commission will review the progress of the intergovernmental working group, including the annotated outline of the code, and provide guidance for the fourth session's finalizing of the draft code in 1978. However, the annotated code outline is not likely to be completed before the fourth session.

Corrupt Practices of MNEs

In December 1975 UN General Assembly Resolution 3514 asked the commission to determine measures against corrupt practices by MNEs and other corporations and their intermediaries. During the second session of the commission many delegations called for immediate action to end such practices. It was also argued that all governments should take necessary measures, including legislative action, to prohibit and penalize such illegal acts within their jurisdictions and that uniform legislation in several countries could produce uniform legal rules. In particular MNE home countries should require the disclosure of all payments related to production and sales activities in foreign countries, regardless of whether they have subsidiaries in these countries.

The United States delegation proposed negotiating a multilateral international agreement to deal with all corrupt practices, based on the following principles:

1. It would apply to international trade and investment transactions with governments.

2. It would apply equally to those who offer or make improper payments and to those who request or accept them;

3. Importing governments would agree to (1) establish clear guidelines concerning the use of agents in connection with government procurement and other covered transactions, and (2) establish appropriate criminal penalties for defined corrupt practices by enterprises and officials in their territory;

4. All governments would cooperate and exchange information to help eradicate corrupt practices;

5. Uniform provisions would be defined for disclosure by enterprises, agents and officials of political contributions, gifts and payments made in connection with covered transactions.

The Commission decided to forward this proposal to ECOSOC and recommended that it be considered on a priority basis, with appropriate action to be taken by the 1976 fall session of ECOSOC.

While everybody is against corruption, it would be naive to expect quick agreement on the multilateral agreement proposed by the United States, no matter how much priority ECOSOC and the General Assembly give it. Bribery, kickbacks, and large gratuities concealed as "commissions" have been part of commerce for centuries, standards of public morality vary among countries, and officials who have benefited from these practices are likely to find many bureaucratic means to delay or obviate the negotiation of such an agreement by their government.[10]

The Transfer of Technology Code

UNCTAD's efforts to develop a code of conduct on the transfer of technology have progressed further than the general code for MNEs. Draft outlines of the former were formulated early in 1975 by Brazil for the Group of Seventy-seven and by Japan for Group B, the Western industrialized countries. Their documents were circulated for the UNCTAD Trade and Development Board meeting in May 1975, and expanded and revised in November 1975.[11]

The framework of UNCTAD's efforts can best be seen by quoting from Item 12 of the Provisional Agenda for the Fourth Session of UNCTAD in Nairobi in May 1976.[12]

(A) new phase is beginning in the developing countries—a phase marked by a radical shift of vision and the search for new policies. The peripheral policies of the past, involving minor modification to existing forms of relationships, are being replaced by a search for fresh patterns drawing upon economic, social and cultural resources indigenous to the territories of the Third World. The strengthening of national technological capabilities is assuming a central place in development plans and policies. Attempts are therefore being made progressively to loosen those ties with developed countries which hamper the attainment of this objective, and to move toward greater co-operation amongst developing countries themselves.[12]

UNCTAD's concern with the need to altering the international legal environment and practices in the area of technology transfer to meet the interests and perceived needs of the Third World dates back to the first UNCTAD conference in 1964. However, despite some major studies undertaken by the UNCTAD Secretariat and the formulation of action programs for the governments of LDCs, including regional and interregional cooperation and action by advanced countries, little was done between 1972 and 1975 to implement these plans. In May 1975 the secretary general of UNCTAD convened an Intergovernmental Group of Experts on the Code of Conduct on Transfer of Technology, which considered two separate draft outlines. To push this endeavor along, resolution 3362 adopted during the seventh Special Session of the General Assembly stated:

All States should cooperate in evolving an international code of conduct for the transfer of technology, corresponding, in particular, to the special needs of the developing countries. Work on such a code should therefore be continued within the United Nations Conference on Trade and Development and concluded in time for decisions to be reached at the fourth session of the Conference, including a decision on the legal character of such a code with the objective of the adoption of a code of conduct prior to the end of 1977. . . .

UNCTAD has also begun to try to restructure industrial property systems and specifically to revise the Paris Convention for the Protection of Industrial Property of 1883. These efforts were guided by the following considerations:[13]

1. the importation of the patented product is not as a general rule a substitute for the working of the patent in the developing country granting it;

2. more adequate provisions are required to avoid abuses of patent rights and to increase the probability of patents being worked in the developing country granting them;

3. the introduction of forms of protection of inventions other than traditional patents (e.g., inventor's certificates, industrial development patents, and technology transfer patents) should be examined;

4. the need for technological assistance to developing countries in the field of industrial property, and in particular for expanded access to and utilization of patent documentation by developing countries must be recognized, in order to facilitate the transfer, absorption, adaptation and creation of suitable technology;

5. an in-depth review of the provisions on trade marks should be carried out;

6. there should be new and imaginative studies of possibilities of giving preferential treatment to all developing countries.

To make the code on technology transfer and review of the patent laws meaningful for most LDCs, UNCTAD has also recognized the need for requisite institutional machinery. Technical personnel must be trained and perhaps exchanged, regional joint research centers may be useful, and information centers must be set up that can also handle the dissemination and exchange of technologies originating in developing countries. But again, these ideas must be translated into reality. Rapid industrialization may seem a very meritorious goal to LDC governments, but without a proper infrastructure it may be nothing but a pleasant vista of the future.

The Group of Seventy-seven Outline

The draft of the code presented by the Group of Seventy-seven minces no words about its intentions, especially in its preamble. Technology is seen as "a part of universal human heritage to which all countries have the 'right' of access in order to improve the living standards of their people. All countries have therefore the 'duty' to promote the transfer of technology, whether proprietary or otherwise, on favorable terms," in accordance with the national policies, plans, and priorities of the developing countries. Indeed, an adequate transfer should become an "effective instrument for the elimination of economic inequality among countries and for the establishment of a new and more just international economic order." For this reason, the code should be "universally applicable" and internationally legally binding.[14]

Of course, preambles tend to be hyperbolic and in the body of the proposed code the tone is less strident. It emphasizes the obvious right of home and host countries to regulate the transfer of technology through national legislation. Such legislation must assure protection of domestic recipient enterprises and prevent the displacement of national enterprises by foreign collaboration arrangements. Payments for technology are to be treated as profit whenever they are made to parent companies or other subsidiaries of an MNE, or when the supplier and recipient companies "form an economic unit or have community of interests."

A long chapter of the proposed draft outline deals with restrictive business practices in the transfer of technology. About forty specific restrictions are named that may adversely affect the technology recipient. Some of these are reasonable, such as the prohibition of horizontal cartel activities, MNEs and home country governments should be able to support them; others are likely to be rejected as unduly limiting the freedom of contractual agreements between suppliers and recipients. Another chapter requires numerous guarantees from enterprises supplying technology. Apart from assurances that the technology will perform as stipulated, the guarantees include adequate training of nationals to use technology already available in their countries.

In addition to the draft proposal's strong bias in favor of technology recipients, special preferential treatment is stipulated for enterprises in developing countries. This includes fiscal and other special incentives for technology suppliers in the developed countries to provide the most favorable conditions to the Third World countries for technology transfer and use, and the promise by the supplier countries not to restrict imports of products from developing countries that have been manufactured by means of the newly-acquired technologies. Assistance is also to be given by the governments of developed supplier countries for the establishment of national, regional, and international institutions that can help the Third World in its quest for greater technological capabilities.

To settle disputes arising from technology transfer agreements, the laws of the technology recipient are to apply. Only if these laws specifically permit it can the parties concerned submit such disputes to arbitration.

The Western Group (B) Proposals

A wide conceptual gap separated the Group of Seventy-seven's draft outline from the initial proposal of the industrially advanced countries, which insisted on voluntary compliance by MNEs and governments, maximum freedom, and the sanctity of contractual agreements. This proposal was clearly biased in favor of MNEs and the "proper" investment climate, although it acknowledged the basic needs of Third World countries for appropriate technology and recognized the legitimacy of some of their demands. The problem of restrictive business practices is dealt with in one line, and the responsibilities of technology-supplying enterprises and their governments are couched in qualifying terms such as "to the extent practicable", "feasible", "appropriate", and "reasonable".

The revised draft outline on technology transfer submitted by the Western industrialized countries in November 1975 is much more comprehensive and positive, and narrows appreciably the gap between the Third World and the Western industrialized camps. Of course, their insistence that the code be voluntary remains, and they continue to stress respect for individual agreements under international law. But perhaps reflecting changed US foreign policy and the apparent, though qualified, responsiveness of the Third World leadership to American policy suggestions, the revised proposal clearly states that the development of indigenous technological capabilities in the Third World should be promoted and that restrictive business practices which adversely affect the transfer of technology should be avoided. Moreover, the proposal assigns specific responsibilities to technology source and recipient enterprises and governments. As a result, accommodations have been made to some of the demands made on MNEs in the Group of Seventy-seven's draft outline, although the concessions on restrictive business practices fall far short of the concepts of some members of the Group of Seventy-seven, which cover any abuse by technology suppliers that might limit accessibility to technological know-how or otherwise place hardships on recipient countries.[15] Nevertheless, the eight restrictive business practices now listed in the Western Group's proposal incude:[16]

a) Restrictions in patent or know-how licences which unreasonably prevent the export of unpatented products or components, or which unreasonably restrict export to countries where the product made pursuant to the licenced technology is not patented;

b) Provisions having the effect of causing tied sales, i.e. which oblige or impel the licensee to accept unwanted and unneeded licenses, or purchase unwanted and unneeded goods or services from the licensor or his designated source;

c) Restrictions preventing the exploitation of a licensed process or product after the date of expiry of a patent under which the licence is granted, or requiring royalties to be paid for the use of these patents as such after that date;

d) Requiring the licensee to assign or grant back to the licensor exclusively all improvements discovered in working the subject matter of the licence, when the effect of this practice is to abuse a dominant position of the licensor.

Of course, the revised proposal of the Western Group emphasizes the confidentiality and proprietary nature of trade secrets and know-how acquired in connection with the transfer of technology. It opposes the view that the law of the recipient state should determine which legal rules should be applied to settle disputes arising from the transfer of technology, and wants the parties to pertinent agreements to choose freely the applicable law, including arbitration.

Despite the narrowing of the disparities between the draft outlines by the end of 1975 considerable differences continued to exist prior to the Nairobi meeting of UNCTAD. Howard V. Perlmutter and Taghi Saghafi-nejad worked up a concise and penetrating comparison between the positions of the two groups on the code which, is found in slightly modified form in table 12–1. Although this table is generally self-explanatory, a few comments will serve to summarize the preceding discussion. For the Group of Seventy-seven, access to technology is regarded as a right and technology itself as a public good, while the Western advanced countries insist that technology falls essentially into the category of private property, with all the implications that flow from that notion.

An important difference is the demand of the Group of Seventy-seven that the code be legally binding. We can see here an analogy to the civil rights movement in the United States, which fought hard and successfully to ensure that its demands were backed up by appropriate changes in the law, either through Supreme Court decisions or federal legislation. Third World leaders seem to feel that once the "law" is on their side, the battle for unfettered access will be won. Whether reality will bear this out is not certain. It involves training personnel by recipient countries to screen and use technology, which is a long-term process.

Table 12-1
Comparison of the Group of Seventy-seven and Western Advanced Group Positions on Codes of Conduct for Transfer of Technology

Issue	Group of Seventy-seven	Western Advanced Group	Synthesis
Nature of Technology (*T*)	*T* is part of universal human heritage; all countries have the right of access to it.	*T* is developed using primarily private resources.	Fundamental ideological and philosophical difference, but Western Group stops short of calling *T* completely private.
Transfer of Technology (*TT*)	Should become an effective instrument for eliminating inequality among countries, promotes New Int. Econ. Order.	Should be encouraged, all parties should abide by equitable general rules, and should be aware of conditions; each *TT* is unique.	*TT* as a vehicle for development, vs. uniqueness and equitable general rules.
Code's Legal Status	An international legally binding code.	A nonbinding code of general and voluntary nature.	Main obstacle was to be resolved in UNCTAD IV, May 1976 (Nairobi)
Length of Draft Code	May 1975: 16 pp.; Nov. 1975: 19 pp. due only to addition of "preamble." All else same.	May 1975: 4½ pp.; Nov. 1975: 9 pp. due to (a) addition of "preamble," (b) other major changes.	Changes in Western Group imply a move *toward* Seventy-seven's position.
Restrictive Business Practices (RBP)	Consists of forty items.	May 1975: only touched upon Nov. 1975: a whole section with eight separate items.	Definitions different. When RBPs mentioned by Western Group position falls short of Seventy-seven's position and definitions.
Duties	Primarily fall on supplying firms. Little mention of duties of recipient countries.	Four parties identified, each to carry part of responsibility.	States are sovereign to Seventy-seven and just one of four parties to Western Group.
Dispute Settlement	Through laws and courts of recipient country, if these nonexistent, then according to each contractual agreement.	Parties to a *TT* agreement to be permitted to freely choose and specify in contract.	West Group wants int. law to dominate in arbit. Seventy-seven won't jeopardize sovereignty.

Source: Howard V. Perlmutter and Taghi Saghafi-nejad, "Process or Product? A Social Architectural Perspective of Codes of Conduct to Technical Transfer and Development," prepared for presentation at the International Studies Association 1976 Convention, Toronto, Canada, February 18, 1976, p. 17.

Technological dependence may not be eliminated except over periods counted more in years than in decades, especially since the economic posture of LDCs shows wide variance, with many small countries having only very limited markets and very poor personnel resources.

Interesting differences can also be found in the last three issues in table 12–1. The Group of Seventy-seven makes little mention of the duties of recipient countries, emphasizing the sovereignty of LDCs dealing with MNEs. Thus, for these countries the legal obligations apply mostly to the technology-supplying firms, and the code reduces their control over the transfer process. This orientation is also visible in the settlement of disputes, which is to be carried out through the laws of the recipient countries. On the other hand, the Western group wants international law to predominate, allowing arbitration if and as specified in transfer agreements.

Despite these differences the West and in particular the United States may gradually embrace more of the LDC position. In September 1975 Secretary of State Henry Kissinger, addressing the seventh Special Session of the UN General Assembly, stated:[17]

The United States is prepared to meet the proper concerns of governments in whose territories transnational enterprises operate. We affirm that enterprises must act in full accordance with the sovereignty of host governments and take full account of their public policy. Countries are entitled to regulate the operations of transnational enterprises within their borders, but countries wishing the benefits of these enterprises should foster the conditions that attract and maintain their productive operation.

The United States therefore believes that the time has come for the international community to articulate standards of conduct for both enterprises and governments.

Similar changes can also be discerned in restrictive business practices issue. Again Kissinger seems to open the door, however slightly, to LDCs concerns when he says:[18]

Laws against restrictive business practices must be developed, better coordinated among countries, and enforced. The United States has long been vigilant against such abuses in domestic trade, mergers, or licensing of technology. We stand by the same principles internationally. We condemn restrictive practices in setting prices or restraining supplies, whether by private or state-owned transnational enterprises or by the collusion of national governments.

The 1976 UNCTAD Conference in Nairobi

It would have been unrealistic to hope that as unwieldy a conference as an UNCTAD quadrennial general meeting could bridge the gaps existing between the Third World's approach to the transfer of technology and that of the Western advanced countries. Nevertheless, progress toward the elaborating a code of conduct was made, although this progress was more procedural than substantive.

The major decision was to establish within UNCTAD an intergovernmental group of experts to work up a draft of the code by the middle of 1977. This group of experts will be free to formulate draft provisions ranging from mandatory to voluntary "without prejudice to the final decision on the legal character of the code of conduct."[19] That decision is reserved to a special UN Conference to be convened by the General Assembly and held by the end of 1977. This conference will also negotiate the final draft of the code of conduct on the transfer of technology and make the decisions necessary for its adoption.

The Nairobi meeting also addressed itself to creating the necessary infrastructure for the development, transfer, and use of technology in the Third World. To this end it adopted a long list of recommendations, some of which parallelled the measures suggested in the revised draft outline for the code submitted by the Western advanced countries. The recommendations for the developing countries include formulating a technology plan as part of their national development plans, establishing a national center for the development and transfer of technology, and optimum utilization of qualified manpower resources. Major emphasis is placed on cooperation among Third World countries through preferential technology arrangements among themselves and the creation of subregional, regional, and interregional centers that could serve as essential links with the national centers. For the developed countries, there is also a long list of recommended actions that are likely to contribute to the successful transfer and use of technology by Third World countries and to the expansion of their capacities to develop technology on their own, including the establishment of a United Nations University.[20]

Much of what UNCTAD IV recommended in Nairobi with respect to technology transfer had become American foreign policy before the conference. In his speech at the opening session of the conference, Secretary of State Henry Kissinger declared:[21]

First, to adapt technology to the needs of developing countries, the United States supports the establishment of a network of research and development institutions at the local, regional, and international level. We need to strengthen global research capacities for development and to expand intergovernmental cooperation. . . .

The second element of our program is to improve the amount and quality of technological information available to developing countries and to improve their selection of technology relevant to their needs. . . .For its part the United States will inventory its national technology information resources and make available . . . consultants and other services to improve access to our National Library of Medicine, the Division of Scientific Information of the National Science Foundaton, the National Agricultural Library, and the Smithsonian Information Service. . . .

Third, to nurture new generations of technologists and technology managers, the United States proposes a priority effort to train individuals who can develop, identify, and apply technology suited to the needs of developing countries. . . .

The fourth element of our approach is to make the process of transferring existing technology more effective and equitable. . . .

The United States also supported the creation of an UNCTAD Advisory service to strengthen the ability of Third World countries to identify, select, and effectively negotiate for the technology most appropriate to their requirements. The Nairobi Conference decided to set up such an organization from the regular budget of UNCTAD.[22] Another project adopted by the Conference and supported by the United States was the convening of a UN Conference on Science and Technology for Development in 1979.[23] Finally, it was decided that UNCTAD should continue to play an important role in reappraising the international patent system and particularly in revising the Paris Convention for the Protection of Industrial Property as it affects the transfer of technology to the developing countries.[24] However, the US proposal for a multibillion dollar International Resources Bank that could assist the Third World in obtaining needed technology was rejected by the Conference. The likely reason for the rejection was the private-investor orientation of the proposed bank, under which the funds of the bank would be used by private corporations for natural resources development and at the same time aid in the improvement of technological, managerial, and marketing capabilities in the host country. Again, the bias against private enterprise and concomitant fear of outside domination, so frequently found in Third World motivation, appeared to carry the day.

What the future holds for the elaboration of codes of conduct is difficult to predict. It certainly will depend on resolving the question of whether the code will be voluntary or mandatory. Beyond that, compromises on substantive issues are likely to reflect the nature of the North–South relationship. The more harmonious that relationship in the years to come, the more likely is agreement on a code of conduct. For this reason, the governments of the Third World countries should keep in mind that interest in the future growth of MNEs and in the proliferation of subsidiaries and affiliates may be slackening for several reasons:

1. The accumulation of private capital in the Western industrialized countries has slowed down. This trend is likely to continue in the foreseeable future. Investment funds may well be rationed and high-risk investments are likely to have low priorities—even for natural resource developments—when they are envisioned in LDCs with hostile investment climates. For example, Exxon halted exploration in Malaysia in 1975 and abandoned plans to install oil production platforms in offshore Malaysian waters. Clearly, the philosophy of "growth at any cost" which used to be espoused by many MNE managements has given way to a careful calculation of costs, risks, and profits.

2. The wage incentive for American and some European MNEs to set up production facilities in foreign countries is slowly disappearing. In mid-1975 average hourly wages in Sweden, Belgium, Germany, and the Netherlands were higher than in the United States. While developing countries such as Mexico or Taiwan have considerably lower wages than North America and Western Europe, wages have risen there also and are likely to rise further, particularly if unionization makes progress.

3. An important motivation for MNEs to invest in foreign plants has been a variety of trade restrictions which make it impossible for goods imported from third countries to compete successfully in national markets. However, tariff and non-tariff barriers have been lowered in successive multilateral trade negotiations. The next multinational tariff negotiations may see certain tariffs eliminated completely.

4. Some of the home country governments, prodded by domestic political forces, may begin to tax profits generated in host countries even if they are already taxed abroad on the same level as in home countries. The United States Congress has begun chipping away at the alleged tax advantage of American MNEs and may go further so that the cost of foreign investment will increase. Such double taxation could well reduce the appeal of international production and marketing activities. Proper tax harmonization among parent and host countries may be necessary to restore interest in setting up additional MNE subsidiaries in new countries.

Thus, the future of MNE operations throughout the world is somewhat clouded by more careful management considerations, and the assumption that the MNE global network will continue to intensify should be accepted only with some reservations.

Notes

1. See UN Department of Economic and Social Affairs, *Multinational Corporations in World Development* (New York: Praeger Publishers, 1974), and International Labour Office, *Multinational Enterprises and Social Policy* (Studies and Reports New Series no. 79, 1973).

2. The 1976 membership list is as follows: Algeria, Argentina, Australia, Bangladesh, Barbados, Brazil, Bulgaria, Canada, Colombia, Democratic Yemen, Ecuador, France, Gabon, German Democratic Republic, Federal Republic of Germany, Guinea, India, Indonesia, Iran, Iraq, Italy, Ivory Coast, Jamaica, Japan, Kenya, Kuwait, Mexico, Netherlands, Nigeria, Pakistan, Peru, Philippines, Senegal, Sierra Leone, Spain, Sweden, Thailand, Trinidad and Tobago, Tunisia, Uganda, USSR, Ukrainian Soviet Socialist Republic, United Kingdom, United States, Venezuela, Yugoslavia, Zaire, Zambia.

3. The sixth Special Session promulgated the Declaration and Action Programs for establishing a New International Economic Order and the twenty-ninth General Session resolution dealt with the Charter of Economic Rights and Duties of States.

4. For details see Commission on Transnational Corporations, *Report on the First Session, 17-28 March 1975* (United Nations, New York, 1975), Document E/5655 E/C, 10/6, Annexes 1-3.

5. Ibid., pp. 7-13.

6. Department of State Memorandum of June 1, 1975, on *Current Status of International Activities of TNEs.*

7. In-depth studies are to be made on all aspects of the following specific subjects: (1) The impact of activities of transnational corporations on the balance of payments of developing countries and others; (2) the service sector, including banking, insurance, shipping and tourism; (3) the implications of investment by transnational corporations for employment in both home and host countries; (4) the extent to which investment and production by transnational corporations affect investment and production by domestic enterprises, who are their competitors, suppliers or customers; (5) extractive, food and beverages and pharmaceutical industries (case studies); (6) obstacles to strengthening the negotiating capacity of governments in their relations with transnational corporations; (7) measures adopted by governments nationally and regionally to strengthen their negotiating capacity in their relations with transnational corporations, and lessons to be learned therefrom; (8) measures adopted by host countries to strengthen the competitive position of national enterprises vis-à-vis transnational corporations; (9) the activities of transnational corporations in southern Africa and the extent of their collaboration with the illegal regimes in that area, taking fully into account work done by the relevant bodies of the United Nations, which should be made available to the commission at its next session. In addition the IRC should carry on continuing studies on the corrupt practices of MNEs and a continuing review of research on MNEs and their activities.

8. For details see Commission on Transnational Corporations, *Report on the Second Session* (1-12 March 1976), Document E/5782, E/C.10/16, pp. 10-16.

9. Ibid., Annex IV, pp. 26-34 and 23-25.

10. See *Wall Street Journal,* November 14 and 17, 1975, "Fiasco in Italy," and "Grease of Grit?" p. 1 in respective issues. Whether the enactment of strict U.S. disclosure laws on foreign bribes paid by American corporations as proposed by President Ford will be an effective means to halt corruption overseas, is open to serious question.

11. See documents TD/B/C.6/AC.1/L.1/Rev. 1, 16 May 1975, and TD/B/C.6/AC.1/L.6, 28 November 1975 (for Brazilian Draft) and TD/B/C.6/AC.1/L.2, 5 May 1975, and TD/B/C.6/AC.1/L.5, 24 November 1975 for the Japanese proposals.

12. Document TD/190, December 31, 1975, p. 1.

13. Document TD/L.112, May 27, 1976.

14. Document TD/B/C.6/AC.1/L.6, pp. 1-4.

15. For details see UNCTAD, Trade and Development Board, *Report of the Second Ad Hoc Group of Experts on Restrictive Business Practices, October 20-24, 1975,* Document TD/b/C.2/AC.5/R.1, 10 November 1975 and TD/B/C, 6/AC.1/L.1/Rev. 1, 16 May 1975, p. 9.

16. TD/B/C.6/AC.1/L.5, 24 November 1975, pp. 7–8.

17. Department of State, Bureau of Public Affairs, *Results of the Seventh Special Session of the U.N. General Assembly, September 1–16, 1975* (Publication #8831), p. 6.

18. Ibid.

19. TD/L.128, 29 May 1976.

20. For details see UNCTAD document TD/L.111, 27 May 1976.

21. Department of State, Bureau of Public Affairs, *UNCTAD IV: Expanding Cooperation for Global Development* (May 6, 1976), pp. 9, 10, 11.

22. UNCTAD Document TD/L.111, p. 7.

23. Ibid.

24. UNCTAD Document TD/L112, p. 3.

List of Contributors

Jaleel Ahmad is professor of economics at Concordia University in Montreal.

Neal P. Cohen is assistant professor of economics and international business at St. Louis University.

Wilfred L. David is professor of economics and management at Fisk University, currently on leave at Howard University.

Werner J. Feld is professor of political science at the University of New Orleans.

Maurice Girgis is professor of economics at Ball State University in Muncie, Indiana.

Charles T. Goodsell is professor of political science at Southern Illinois University.

Karel Holbik is chief of the section for development of financial institutions, Division of Public Administration and Finance at the United Nations in New York.

Richard F. Kosobud is professor of economics at the University of Illinois at Chicago Circle.

Tracy Murray is associate professor of international business in the Graduate School of Business Administration at New York University.

Attiat F. Ott is professor of economics at Clark University.

Bernd Stecher is a fellow at the Kiel Institute of World Economics, Kiel University in Kiel, West Germany.

About the Editor

William G. Tyler is associate professor of economics at the University of Florida, where he has been affiliated since 1969. He did his undergraduate work in economics at Dickinson College and his graduate study at the Fletcher School of Law and Diplomacy, where he received the Ph.D. in 1969. From 1966 to 1969 he was a visiting professor of economics at the Brazilain School of Public Administration at the Getulio Vargas Foundation; and from 1972 to 1974 he was a senior fellow at the Kiel Institute of World Economics at Kiel University. In 1977 Dr. Tyler was a visiting professor at Uppsala University in Sweden. Major consulting affiliations have been with the Brazilian Institute of Economics, AID, and the World Bank. His most recent book is *Manufactured Export Expansion and Industrialization in Brazil,* published in 1976. In addition, his numerous contributions to professional journals have covered a wide range of topics in economic development and international economics.